# Inside Sudan

# Inside Sudan

*Political Islam, Conflict,
and Catastrophe*

REVISED AND UPDATED

## Don Petterson

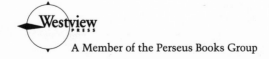

A Member of the Perseus Books Group

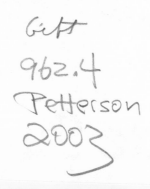
*The Department of State has reviewed the manuscript of this book to ensure that its contents do not compromise national security. This review should not be construed as concurrence with the text. Characterizations and opinions are those of the author and do not necessarily represent official positions of the United States Government.*

Paperback edition published in 2003 in the United States of America by Westview Press, a Member of the Perseus Books Group, 5500 Central Avenue, Boulder, Colorado 80301–2877, and in the United Kingdom by Westview Press, 12 Hid's Copse Road, Cumnor Hill, Oxford OX2 9JJ.

Find us on the world wide web at www.westviewpress.com

Westview Press books are available at special discounts for bulk purchases in the United States by corporations, institutions, and other organizations. For more information, please contact the Special Markets Department at the Perseus Books Group, 11 Cambridge Center, Cambridge, Massachusetts 02142, or call (617) 252-5298 or (800) 255-1514, or e-mail j.mccrary@perseusbooks.com.

A Cataloging-in-Publication data record for this book is available from the Library of Congress.

ISBN 0-8133-4111-6 (pbk.)

The paper used in this publication meets the requirements of the American National Standard for Permanence of Paper for Printed Library Materials Z39.48–1984.

10    9    8    7    6    5    4    3    2    1

*For Julie*

# Contents

*Preface*                                                                ix
*Map*                                                                    xii

1   Assignment Sudan: First the Ending. . .                               1

2   . . . Then the Beginning                                              3

3   Sudan                                                                 7

4   Welcome                                                              19

5   The Troubles Begin                                                   25

6   The Displaced                                                        37

7   Hanging In                                                           43

8   Into Southern Sudan                                                  63

9   From Bad to Worse                                                    85

10  Making Adjustments                                                   97

11  Terrorism                                                           113

12  Tragedy in Southern Sudan Deepens                                   119

13  A Spring of Little Promise                                          137

14  No Peace in Our Time                                                151

15  The Reasons Why                                                     167

16  More Events in Khartoum and Elsewhere                               175

17    Working with the United Nations         187

18    New Year, Same Old Problems         195

19    Farewell         203

20    Afterward         219

*Notes*         249
*Index*         257

# Preface

The most impressive sight in Khartoum is the Nile. At flood in the summer, the Blue Nile (Bahr al-Azrak), swollen by rains in Ethiopia and dropping 6,000 feet from Lake Tana, comes pouring past Khartoum and collides with the White Nile (Bahr al-Abyad) at the north-western reaches of the city. The force of the Blue Nile is so powerful that it impedes the flow of the White Nile and backs it up for miles as the two rivers commingle and flow north to the Mediterranean.

Since I was a boy, I have been fascinated by rivers because of their beauty and their place in human history—what they have done to and for the people near them and what the people alongside them have done to themselves. In my three years in Sudan, when I was in Khartoum, hardly a day went by when I did not either drive by the Nile, run on a street alongside it, or stand at its edge. Time and again I saw it from the air when I arrived at or departed from the city. Occasionally an airplane carrying me somewhere southward from Khartoum was in sight of it for mile after mile.

Often the sight of the Nile evoked thoughts about events it had witnessed over the centuries, events whose telling sometimes has been colored by the passions they inspired. The story of today's Sudan, a country governed by Islamists, at war with itself and at odds with many other countries, is not one that lends itself to detachment.

What I have written in the pages that follow is largely, but not completely, dispassionate; my likes and dislikes show through from time to time. I believe, though, that those feelings have not distorted the accuracy of my personal notes, communications to Washington from Khartoum, or letters I wrote—source materials for this book.

After the American ambassador and his deputy were assassinated in Khartoum in 1973, Sudan became an emotional word in the American Foreign Service. In 1991, when it appeared I might be assigned there, many in the service regarded Sudan as a place to be avoided. The possible physical dangers posed by terrorist organizations in Khartoum, along with a harsh climate and other factors, discouraged some people from serving there. Prospective ambassadors might well have been put off by the "mission impossible" label that had been attached to the American ambassador's job in Sudan. In the early 1990s, at least one senior Foreign Service officer turned down an offer of an ambassadorial assignment to Sudan.

I was fully aware of the drawbacks attached to Sudan, but I did not hesitate for long when, in 1991, I was asked if I wished to be considered to replace James Cheek as ambassador in Khartoum. From past experience, I knew that the most interesting and challenging jobs are often in the most difficult places. And while trying not to be naive or Pollyannish about it, I still believed, after over thirty years in the Foreign Service, that I could make a difference in relations between the U.S. government and the government of the country in which I served. Even after I had been in Sudan a while and realized that my chances of improving relations were meager at best, I never completely abandoned this notion. For the most part, though, I applied it not to overall U.S.-Sudanese relations but to other, possibly more achievable, objectives, such as improving the effectiveness of the international humanitarian aid program in Sudan.

This book is intended in part to help explain U.S. policy toward Sudan since the Islamist government came to power there by force of arms in 1989. It focuses on the various factors shaping that policy— among them, human rights violations, Sudan's civil war and humanitarian assistance needs, and the Sudanese government's harboring of terrorists. It also looks at the impact that the events of September 11, 2001 and the U.S. war on terrorism has had on the Sudan policy. And it examines the evolving U. S. role in negotiations to end the war in Sudan. Moreover, since most of the narrative covers the time that I was ambassador to Sudan, the book offers a firsthand account of the difficulty and concomitant fascination of representing the United States in a country whose aims are greatly at variance to those of the U.S. government.

I hope, in addition, to help correct misconceptions about who Foreign Service officers (FSOs) are and what their life abroad is like. Foreign Service assignments vary greatly from post to post and within each embassy or consulate. Although my experience in Sudan is not a model, it is representative of the kinds of circumstances and difficulties Foreign Service personnel face in many of our posts abroad.

When I was commissioned an FSO of the Department of State in 1960, many inside and outside the U.S. government who were aware of the existence of the Foreign Service subscribed to the inaccurate notion that most FSOs were elitists who had attended Ivy League schools. In addition, some of the mud from the McCarthy era, which had barely ended, still stuck to the State Department and the Foreign Service. "Effete" and "cookie pushers" were two of the kinder epithets that were used to characterize FSOs.

In the early part of this century, the Ivy League label had a basis in fact. However, the merger of the diplomatic and consular services in 1924, the passage of the Foreign Service Act of 1946, and the momentous societal changes in the United States following World War II had drastically altered the makeup of the service by 1960. The influence of the eastern establishment was still strong then but was rapidly declining. In the succeeding four decades, Foreign Service personnel became steadily more representative of U.S. society, with greater diversity of geographical origin and marked increases in the percentages of women and minorities in the ranks of FSOs.

In that time FSOs have been assassinated, killed or injured in bombings, held hostage, taken prisoner in Vietnam, and otherwise placed in danger. Many have faced severe hardships at certain Third World posts. Despite all this, the mistaken belief that the service is heavily populated by irresolute Ivy League elitists has not died.

Finally, I have tried to shed some light on the nature of the Islamist government in Sudan, the interminable civil war in southern Sudan, and the suffering of the Sudanese people. I have avoided criticizing political Islam. Nevertheless my portrayal of the personalities, policies, and actions of the Islamist government of Sudan reveals a repressive system that survives by force. I believe that, at the very least, the Sudanese experience gives credence to the thesis that any government based on religious fundamentalism and intent on propagating its religious beliefs will by its nature be tyrannical, intolerant of dissent, and prepared to use any means, including violence against its own people, to maintain itself in power.

Don Petterson
*January 2003*

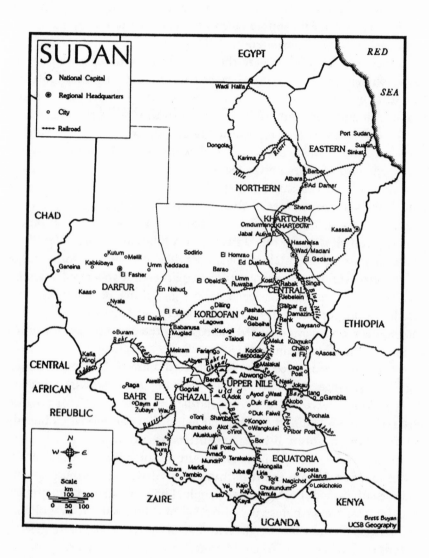

# 1

# Assignment Sudan:
# First the Ending. . .

It was a little after two in the morning when we left the house in Khartoum for the last time. After closing the front door, I paused for a moment on the verandah to gaze at the tall trees in the front yard silhouetted against the dark sky. The American flag atop its flagpole was motionless in the still air, brightly lit by the security lights along the second floor of the house.

As always, my armored van was waiting, parked just off the front porch and close to the heavy metal gate of the high wall that surrounds the house and grounds. My wife, Julie, our sixteen-year-old son, Brian, and I greeted the driver and the American in charge of the security detail and got into the van. The gate was opened, and the van drove out into the street, which was deserted except for the gate guard, a few armed policemen, and the follow-car with my Sudanese bodyguards. In five minutes, we were at the nearby airport. Shortly afterward we left the VIP lounge and made our way to the waiting Lufthansa aircraft.

Years earlier when I was in the Navy, whenever my ship came into a port at night I was entranced by how darkness punctuated by electric lights had transformed what often was an uninspiring scene in the light of day. I was reminded of this as we flew out of Khartoum that night. The city beneath us looked like a magnificent tapestry of clusters of lights with a swath of black—the Nile—running through them. Exposed by the fierce sun during daylight, the harshness of the arid countryside and the general drabness of the city's dusty streets and buildings give Khartoum a much different, unlovely visage from above.

My stay in Sudan's capital city had been somewhat analogous to the two different pictures from the sky above it. Viewed in the full light of the strong political differences between the governments of the United States and Sudan, my three-year tenure as the American ambassador had been a rough assignment. But outside the harsh light of those differences, my time in Khartoum, especially when my wife and son were with me, had many instances of delight and fascination and was warmed by our friendships with Sudanese, Americans, and persons of other nationalities.

It was fitting, I suppose, that Julie and I should be leaving Africa at night. We had arrived on the continent for the first time thirty-two years earlier in the darkness of night at Nairobi. There we boarded a DC–3 and flew on to Zanzibar, landing on the island in even greater darkness on a runway lighted only by kerosene lamps. We had no way of knowing then that six months later we and our two little girls would have a brush with death in the violence of a bloody revolution or that Julie and they would be evacuated from the island because of that violence.

Similarly, when we arrived in Khartoum in the summer of 1992, we had no inkling of the course of events that would severely disrupt our lives for many months. What we did know was that we were happy to be back in Africa, where Julie and I had spent most of our married life, and where Brian, the youngest of our four children, had been born and had lived eight of his thirteen years.

# 2

# . . . Then the Beginning

Rarely would any Foreign Service officer not be elated by an offer of an ambassadorship. In the Foreign Service, the cachet of being an ambassador is more or less the same as attaining flag rank in the military. Only a small percentage of career FSOs become ambassadors, and these days those who do, more often than not do not get a second opportunity to be in charge of their own embassy. As a result, many FSOs would sell at least a part of their soul to get the telephone call or telegram asking if they would like to be put on a list of candidates for Ambassador to Anywhere.

So why did I hesitate when, in the summer of 1991, the State Department's Bureau of African Affairs called me in Zimbabwe, where I was chargé d'affaires of the American embassy, offering to put me on the list of candidates for Sudan? A number of considerations made Khartoum a less than attractive post, but these did not account for my hesitance.

I knew the weather in Khartoum could be brutal, with maximum temperatures sometimes soaring above 115 degrees Fahrenheit. Medical facilities were substandard. Dust storms were frequent during part of the year. Electrical outages occurred often. Cultural amenities were few and far between. The Islamist government exercised tight censorship on the print media—some Western news publications were banned. It usually took hours and sometimes even days to make an international phone call. Satellite-transmitted television was not available to Americans in Sudan in 1992.

However, inconveniences, scarcity of amenities, and bad weather were not unique to Sudan and did not worry Julie or me; they had not bothered us in our other African posts. We believed, and our belief was confirmed after we got there, that there was much that would be enriching or romantic about an assignment to Khartoum. Its setting at the confluence of the White Nile and Blue Nile and the physical vestiges of the colonial era and of the 1881–1885 Mahdist uprising are wonderful to see. From Khartoum one can drive out into the desert and north to the fascinating ruins of the 3,000-year-old Nubian civilization. One can go for a boat ride on the Nile or walk or run along its banks in the early morning hours before the intense heat tightens its grip on the city.

Sudan is a fascinating mixture of Africa and the Arab world. Its people inhabit a land that varies from hot, often windswept deserts in the north to lush savanna and forests in the south. The Sudanese are warm and hospitable people, for the most part approachable and friendly to Americans.

For some Westerners, there is a sense of adventure in being in a Third World country and sharing with like-minded people the excitement of living and working in a place where at times life may not be easy but is seldom boring. American Foreign Service staffers who serve in the more difficult posts often have a sense of belonging and exhibit much higher morale than do their colleagues stationed in large embassies in places like London, Rome, or Paris.

But one thing gave us pause about the offer from the African Bureau, a factor that within the American Foreign Service accounted for a widely held belief, justified or not, that Khartoum was one of the least desirable of assignments: The city was a gathering place for Islamic terrorists, whose hatred for Americans is second only to their hatred for Israelis. Although all the Sudanese governments of the past quarter-century had asserted that they would allow no terrorist organizations to commit acts of violence against foreigners in Sudan, terrorists had targeted Westerners in Khartoum and on occasion had killed or injured Americans or other Westerners.

In 1973, the American ambassador to Sudan, Cleo Noel, his deputy, George Curtis Moore, and the Belgian chargé d'affaires, Guy Eid, were seized by Palestinian terrorists and assassinated. In the late 1970s, discovery of a plot to bomb the American Club averted what could have been a heavy loss of lives. In 1988, Palestinian terrorists threw grenades into the restaurant of the Acropole Hotel, killing a British couple, their children, and a British teacher. (In 1991, just before the Gulf War started, in a demonstration of hostility to the West, the Sudanese government released the five men who had been convicted and sentenced to death for the Acropole murders.) In 1986, an American embassy communicator was seriously wounded when an unknown assailant, believed to have been a terrorist, shot him in the head. No question about it, Khartoum was a place of potential danger for U.S. diplomats, and naturally the ambassador was the most enticing target of all.

After the phone call from Washington, when Julie and I discussed the potential assignment later that day, we considered the negatives and weighed them against our needs and preferences. Neither of us was ready to abandon our foreign service life. We had met in 1961 at the embassy in Mexico City, my first assignment, when she came in for a tourist visa and I was the vice consul who interviewed her. Seven months later, we were married. After we left Mexico in 1962, we set out on an African odyssey that over the next thirty years took us to posts in Zanzibar, Nigeria, Sierra Leone, South Africa, Somalia, Tanzania, and Zimbabwe. Susan, our eldest child, who was born in Mexico, was a year old when we arrived in Zanzibar in 1963; Julianne and John were born during the two and a half years we were there; and Brian came on the scene in 1979 during our posting to Somalia.

Living in Africa had become the norm for us and was the norm for the children throughout their childhood and adolescence. For Julie and me, our service abroad had enriched our lives with extraordinary experiences and many lasting friendships. Sudan held out the prospect of tasting yet another different culture and getting to know a new set of interesting people.

I did not like the idea of what I knew would be strict security procedures governing my movements in Khartoum. At neither of my two previous ambassadorial posts nor during the year I was in charge of the embassy in Zimbabwe did I have bodyguards or need to ride in an armored car. But American ambassadors in a good number of countries have to accept the restrictions imposed by security precautions to counter possible terrorist attacks. If other ambassadors could put up with the restrictions, why couldn't I? I knew, in addition, that although U.S. diplomatic officials had been targeted, their families had not.

Finally, there was the appeal of dealing with the problem of Sudan. The American ambassador in Khartoum has one of the most difficult, and therefore absorbing, jobs in the Foreign Service. The issues arising from political Islam[1] in Sudan, the terrorist presence in Khartoum, the endless civil war in southern Sudan, international aid for millions of people displaced by the war, manifold human rights violations, and the tension between the governments of the United States and Sudan were complex, engrossing, and of interest to some policymakers in the State Department and the White House. From a professional standpoint, I was sure any other job that might be open to me would not be nearly as stimulating.

After looking at all the pros and cons, Julie and I decided to tell the African Bureau to put my name on the list for Sudan, provided there was a good school in Khartoum for Brian. Once we learned that this was the case, I communicated our decision through Jeff Davidow, a deputy assistant secretary of state in the African Bureau. This set in motion the long process, whose outcome is uncertain, of presidential nomination and Senate confirmation.

About a year later—after we had finished our tour in Zimbabwe, the secretary of state's ambassadorial selection committee had blessed my nomination, the White House had given its assent, I had studied Arabic for six months, security and financial background checks had been completed, the Senate had confirmed the appointment, and I had been sworn in—Julie, Brian, and I boarded a flight at Washington's Dulles International Airport and left for Khartoum.

# 3

# Sudan

The Sudan that awaited us was a troubled land, riven by a bitter civil war and beset by crippling economic problems. This was nothing new for the Sudanese; they had been traveling a rocky road ever since Sudan's independence in 1956. The estimated 30 million inhabitants of Africa's largest country (about a million square miles, equal in size to the United States east of the Mississippi) had been, for the most part, misruled and their country's economic potential squandered by successive governments that seesawed between parliamentary democracies and military dictatorships. Sudan's agricultural potential, which included a vast acreage of highly fertile land along and between the White Nile and the Blue Nile, had never been realized, largely because of mismanagement by the various Sudanese governments.

There are more than 450 ethnic groups throughout Sudan and according to the Sudan Institute of Languages, 132 languages are spoken there. Almost all the people of the North are Muslims, and Arabic is the first language of the majority of them. Most of the southern people hold traditional beliefs or are Christians, although Islam has made important inroads there as well.

• • •

The name "Sudan" comes from the Arabic *bilad as-Sudan*, "land of the blacks." It originally applied to the broad belt of sub-Saharan

7

Africa that stretches from the Red Sea to the Atlantic, but now it applies just to the territory of the present-day republic. Contacts between Egyptians and the African people scattered along the banks of the Nile in the upper part of today's northern Sudan, the area that came to be known as Nubia, took place as far back as the Stone Age. Egypt did not establish a presence in Nubia, however, until after the end of the fourth millennium, when kings of the first dynasty conquered upper Nubia. The ensuing interrelationship between Egypt and Nubia was complex, with each influencing the other's art, culture, and religion. Because of its greater military power, Egypt was generally the more dominant of the two. But in times of Egyptian weakness, the Nubians developed their own distinct civilization, which was deeply influenced by African peoples farther to the south.

Nubian-Egyptian cross-fertilization was most pronounced when large numbers of Nubian mercenaries were used against Asian Hyksos invaders of Egypt during a time, 1630–1540 B.C., when Egypt's control of Nubia had been declining. Following the defeat of the Hyksos, Egyptians penetrated farther south in what was to be their most enduring occupation of Nubia. One of Egypt's administrative areas in Nubia was Cush. In the eleventh century B.C., Cush, whose kings were descendants of Egyptianized Nubian chiefs, became virtually free of Egyptian control. In the eighth century B.C., Cush conquered first southern then all of Egypt. Cush's power was short-lived, as the Assyrians invaded Egypt in 671 B.C. and defeated the Cushites. Pushed back to Nubia, Cush ruled the middle Nile for another thousand years. It gradually declined until A.D. 350, when an invading force from the Ethiopian highlands thoroughly defeated it.

Christian missionaries came to northern Sudan in the sixth century. Christianity became well established but eventually gave way to Islam. This did not happen, though, for hundreds of years. The military success in Nubia of Arab invaders, who had conquered Egypt in the seventh century, was marred by such heavy casualties that they agreed to a peace and withdrew their military force. The Arabs and Nubians reached an understanding that Muslims would not settle in Nubia and Nubians would not reside in Egypt. This modus vivendi ended in the late fourteenth and early fifteenth centuries, when Mameluke sultans in Egypt sent military expeditions into Nubia. Weakened militarily by these incursions, the inhabitants were unable to withstand subsequent

Arab encroachments, which led to Arab in-migrations. The Arabs intermarried with Nubians and brought Islam to them. Arab and Nubian customs favored Islam, and in time Islam, further enhanced by the work of Muslim missionaries, supplanted Christianity.

In the nineteenth century, Egypt was a province of the Ottoman Empire. In 1820, Ottoman Egypt's governor, Muhammad Ali, began a war of conquest against Sudan. As the decades passed, a tenuous administrative presence of Turks and Egyptians extended far southward, as far as today's Ugandan border. The slave trade and the administrative incompetence that accompanied the war led to unrest. In 1881, Muhammad Ahmad bin Abdallah, a boatbuilder's son who claimed to be a descendant of the Prophet Muhammad, proclaimed himself the Mahdi (Messiah). He raised an army and in 1882 annihilated the Egyptian army units sent against him. The Mahdi captured Khartoum in 1885, and in the process his forces killed General Charles George ("Chinese") Gordon, a British icon who several years earlier had been governor general of Sudan. Gordon had returned to Sudan about a year before his death to carry out an evacuation of Khartoum, but he obviously stayed too long.

In 1896 conditions were ripe for a British military campaign in Sudan. The British public's desire for revenge for Gordon was high, the British government feared that the French were preparing to move into Sudan, and there was misplaced anxiety that Khalifa Abdullah, the Mahdi's successor, might attack Egypt and the Suez Canal. In the summer of 1898 a British force led by General Horatio Herbert Kitchener reached Khartoum. At Karari, near Omdurman, it fought and decisively defeated the Mahdist army led by Khalifa Abdullah, who was killed in another battle nearly a year later.

After the battle at Karari, an Anglo-Egyptian condominium over Sudan was established. It was proclaimed in 1899. Although Egypt theoretically had equal status with Britain, in actuality it was the British alone who administered Sudan until it became independent in 1956. Sudan is often portrayed as a bridge between the Arab world and black Africa. But during the British colonial era interaction between the Arabized North and African South was restricted by colonial policy. In the North the British shielded the Arabs' Islamic values, helped foster modernization, and laid down an educational system that created an educated Sudanese elite.

The peoples of southern Sudan, who are mainly Nilotics, had been largely isolated from the outside world. They developed many dozens of societies on ethnolinguistic lines, some very large, others quite small. Enslavement of southerners by northerners and other forms of oppression had implanted in southerners' consciousness an abiding suspicion of northerners. Resistance to British rule was fiercer and more prolonged in the South than in the North. Pacification continued for decades. The British devoted few resources to the South, and the area was truly underdeveloped. The little that was achieved in developing the economy and providing education, health, and other services was largely a result of the work of Christian missionaries and a small number of colonial officials.

Southern Sudan was kept separate from the North. Arabic education, Arab-influenced dress, use of the Arabic language, and settlement by Arabs were forbidden in the South. The different attitudes of the colonial authorities toward northern and southern Sudanese, the different administrative systems that were imposed, the Christian education given to southerners and the dominance of Islam in the north, and the sharp inequalities in educational, commercial, and professional fields giving northerners a marked advantage over southerners—all these contributed to the mutual distrust and animosity that underlay the outbreak of civil war between the North and South.

A conference was held in Juba in June 1947 to determine southerners' views on whether and how they would participate in a legislative assembly in the progression to Sudan's independence. What they heard at the conference persuaded southern delegates that South and North should be kept together in a unitary state. The Southerners were given to believe that the colonial government would protect southerners from possible northern domination. By 1955, however, a succession of events convinced southerners that the North was bent on dominating them. For example, it was announced that 800 posts held by colonial officials would become occupied by Sudanese but that only eight of the 800 would go to southerners.

In August, fearing Arabs would take over leadership of the military when British officers left after independence, a regiment of southern Sudanese soldiers mutinied. After spreading throughout Equatoria, the mutiny ended. However, soon after independence southerners perceived that the northern Sudanese intended to Islamize and Arabize the South, and hostilities resumed. Except for a ten-year hiatus in 1972–1982, they have continued ever since.

The fluctuation between civilian and military rule began in 1958, two years after independence. Sudan's second prime minister, frustrated by incessant political turmoil and labor strikes, tried to save himself politically by asking the military temporarily to take over governing the country. But the military officers who assumed control did not relinquish it for six years, when they were dislodged by a popular uprising. A return to parliamentary rule a year later soon brought back political and economic chaos.

In 1969 a group of officers led by Colonel Gaafar Muhammad Numeiry seized power. Numeiry consolidated his grip on the military government and remained in power until he was ousted by a coup d'état in 1985. After a year of transition, general elections led to "a series of coalition governments all characterized by political stagnation, economic decline, and a further deterioration in the security situation in the face of the rebellion."[1] In June 1989 the government of Prime Minister Sadiq al-Mahdi was overthrown by army elements led by General Omar Hassan Ahmed al-Bashir.

In the years before Bashir seized power, economic growth was severely impaired by the devastating civil war waged in southern Sudan because a large part of the North's resources was channeled into the war effort. Everything argued in favor of ending the war after its resumption in 1983. However, political and religious differences between the warring sides were formidable, and personal antagonisms and ambitions were strong. The war went on. In 1989 it seemed that the rebels and Sadiq al-Mahdi's government were about to begin to negotiate in good faith to achieve a peaceful settlement. The National Islamic Front (NIF), headed by Hasan al-Turabi, strongly opposed the negotiating path being taken by the government. Information that became available in later years leaves little doubt that the NIF had a hand in the coup d'état of that June that toppled the government. In any event, the new rulers of Sudan were NIF leaders allied with army officers, like Bashir, who supported the philosophy and agenda of the NIF. The new government did not continue the effort to negotiate an end to the war.

•   •   •

U.S. policy toward Sudan varied over the years following independence. Early on, Khartoum was wary of the United States and of
Egypt and the Soviet Union as well. Because Sudan would not take
the U.S. side in its Cold War struggle with the USSR, Washington was
cool toward Khartoum. The military regime led by General Ibrahim
Abboud, which seized power in 1958, presented the United States
with additional reasons to be uneasy. For example, Abboud formed
closer ties with Gamal Abdel Nasser's Egyptian government, expelled
300 foreign missionaries in 1964, and continued to carry on the war
in the South.

In 1967 Sudan joined other Arab countries in breaking diplomatic
relations with the United States during the Arab-Israeli war. At first,
relations between the two countries did not get any better after Numeiry took power, helped by the Sudanese Communist Party. He supported the pan-Arabism so dear to Nasser and, like Egypt, formed
close ties with the Soviet Union, receiving arms from it. Then, in
1971, Numeiry, believing the Soviets were involved in a Communist-
led coup attempt against him, broke with the Communists and
aligned Sudan with the West.

In 1972 Sudan resumed diplomatic ties with the United States. In
1974, with the Cold War in full flower and Sudan considered by Washington to be of strategic importance to U.S. national interests, and
with the advent of a pro-Soviet military regime in Ethiopia, the Ford
administration was eager for closer ties with Khartoum. As time went
on, Numeiry stressed to Washington the role that Sudan was playing
as a bastion against communism. By 1982 Sudan was getting more
U.S. aid than any other country in sub-Saharan Africa: $160 million in
annual economic assistance and $100 million in military aid.

Washington's friendship with Numeiry began to unravel over his
handling of the war in the South and his increasingly erratic and ever
more dictatorial behavior after he became a born-again Muslim. On a
visit to Washington in 1983, he denounced Israel. In 1985 the United
States suspended its aid to Sudan.

After Numeiry's overthrow and a year of rule by a transitional military government, Sadiq al-Mahdi's government took office. The
United States was pleased that Sudan once more had an elected government but soon became disenchanted with Sadiq. It looked with

disfavor on aspects of his foreign policies, which included maintaining a close relationship with Libya, and also on some of his domestic policies.[2] Washington faulted Sadiq for failing to end the war in the South.

The Americans, like the Egyptians, were initially not unhappy when the 1989 coup occurred. In his book *Intervening in Africa*, former assistant secretary of state for African affairs Herman J. Cohen writes that "An audible sigh of relief rippled through the Africanist community in the US government, welcoming the departure of Sadiq's hopelessly inept regime." This view was reinforced when Cohen had talks with Egyptian officials in Cairo in August of that year. He was told that the coup would be "good for Sudan, for Egypt, and for Western interests." Cohen moved on to Khartoum, where he had a satisfactory talk with General Bashir, but where he also heard some disquieting things about the new regime's human rights practices.[3] By mid-1991, the Egyptians had changed their view about the Bashir government and turned against Khartoum.

Despite its disquiet about the events taking place in Sudan, in late 1989 and the first half of 1990 the Bush administration opted for dialogue with Bashir in hopes of facilitating the delivery of humanitarian aid. In addition, Assistant Secretary Cohen led an American undertaking in March 1990 and again in May to get the government and SPLA on a path toward peace. He proposed to Bashir that the government's forces in the South be reduced by 50 percent and to Garang that his troops withdraw fifteen kilometers from the towns they were besieging. The rejection of this plan by both sides was frustrating but was seen by the Americans as only the opening exchange of a long negotiation. However, Sudan's support of Iraq's invasion of Kuwait put an end to the American initiative.[4]

From the beginning, the U.S. government had no quarrel with the Islamic orientation of the Bashir government. However, because U.S. law obliges a suspension of economic and military aid to any country if its democratically elected government is forcibly deposed, all aid to Sudan, except for humanitarian assistance, was suspended. A presidential waiver of the law might have been invoked if those in power in Sudan had demonstrated they intended to restore democracy and did not intend to rule through force and intimidation. This, though, they did not do. To the contrary, the human rights violations the government committed in consolidating its control and neutralizing any possible threat of a countercoup were such that Sudan's relations with the United States and other Western countries steadily worsened.

Other aspects of the Bashir regime's behavior added to further Western, American in particular, complaints. Both sides to Sudan's civil war were accused of repeatedly making it difficult for donor countries, the United Nations, and private voluntary agencies to provide assistance to the hundreds of thousands of Sudanese who were displaced or otherwise victimized by the war in southern Sudan. In siding with Iraq when it invaded Kuwait and during the Gulf War, the Sudanese government further provoked the West. In the bargain, it also infuriated Saudi Arabia and Kuwait, countries that had been major benefactors of Sudan, and further tarnished its relations with Egypt.

And then there was terrorism, an issue of particular importance to the United States. Sudan was accused of harboring Islamic terrorist organizations. In 1991 Washington warned Khartoum of grave consequences if terrorist activity could be traced to Sudan.

While voicing no concern about the terrorism issue, other Western countries deplored the continuation of the war and spoke out against human rights violations. In addition to Egypt, some Arab countries, like Tunisia, Algeria, and Saudi Arabia, were increasingly hostile to Sudan, fearing the spread of political Islam.

One issue became a focal point for Western condemnation: In early 1992 the outside world became aware that Sudanese authorities were ordering the removal from Khartoum and relocation of hundreds of thousands of people, mainly displaced southerners who had migrated to the city. There were sound reasons for relocating at least some of the migrants, who lived in ramshackle huts in slums around Khartoum. Yet instead of doing it humanely, the government bulldozed homes and took their occupants far from the center of town to camps in the desert having wholly inadequate shelter, sources of water, health facilities, and sanitation. Resistance to the removals was met with force, and some people were shot and killed. Although Western governments and the United Nations spoke out against the forcible removals, they continued.

The leaders of Sudan's government vehemently denied all the accusations leveled against them. They said the reports of human rights violations emanated from their opponents. Western embassies and human rights organizations, they claimed, swallowed these reports uncritically. They insisted accusations that Sudan was abetting terrorism were totally unfounded, pointing out that no substantiating evidence had been put forward.

Washington rejected the Sudanese denials and insisted that relations could not improve unless Sudan stopped supporting terrorist organizations and, in addition, began to take steps to restore democracy, cease gross violations of human rights, and make a good faith effort to end Sudan's interminable civil war.

• • •

During my tenure as ambassador to Sudan, U.S.–Sudanese relations worsened and for several years after I departed in 1995 they deteriorated even further. In 1993 a putative security threat had led to a reduction of the embassy's American staff and evacuation of dependents. In February 1996 all the remaining embassy officials left Sudan. In August 1998 the Clinton administration launched a cruise missile attack against a pharmaceutical factory in Khartoum that the administration said was being used to manufacture an ingredient of nerve gas.

All this notwithstanding, time and again the Sudanese government let Washington know that it wanted better relations. Sudanese officials expressed vexation that Washington did not give the Bashir government credit in May 1996 when, in response to American, Egyptian, and Saudi pressures, it informed Osama bin Laden he would have to leave Sudan, where he had lived for several years. The Clinton administration continued its arms-length relationship with Khartoum, however, arguing that the Sudanese had to do much more to end their support of terrorism.

Impelled by their desire for the advantages of better relations with the United States, by 2000 the Sudanese had satisfied Washington that the Bashir government was at long last moving in the right direction on the terrorism issue. But although there was an increase in interaction between Khartoum and Washington, real progress in improving bilateral relations remained elusive. The Clinton administration believed the Sudanese were still not fully forthcoming on the terrorism question. In addition, the administration saw little if any improvement in the Sudanese government's human rights performance. This view was reinforced by American public opinion, which beginning in the late 1990s took on an increasingly negative cast toward Sudan because of the growing prominence of two issues: slavery in Sudan and the belief by American Christians that the Sudanese government was engaged in an Islamic jihad against southern Sudanese Christians.

With the election of George W. Bush as the forty-third president of the United States came a shift in U.S. policy toward Sudan. Agitation for harsher sanctions against Sudan was increasing from various circles, including one of Bush's core constituencies, the religious right. Despite this, the new administration decided to concentrate on the effort to end the war. Opting for a more active role in the peace process necessarily involved a sustained dialogue with the Bashir government. On September 6, 2001 President Bush appointed former Senator John Danforth special envoy for Sudan.

The terrorist attack that, five days after Danforth's appointment, destroyed New York City's Twin Towers, badly damaged the Pentagon, and took the lives of three thousand people in the three buildings and in the aircraft used by the terrorists as weapons of mass destruction had a profound effect on American foreign policy. How lasting that effect will be remains to be seen, but at least in the short run 9/11 altered U.S. relations with certain countries, Sudan included.

In prosecuting the war on terror, President Bush declared, "Either you are with us, or you are with the terrorists." This resonated in Sudan, whose government had for years provided refuge to terrorist organizations.

The Sudanese were quick to demonstrate to the Americans that Sudan wanted to be counted as an ally in the antiterrorism effort. President Bashir announced that Sudan had severed all its ties with Osama bin Laden and would cooperate with the United States in identifying those responsible for the attacks. Placing some value on the Sudanese cooperation, the administration prevailed on congressional leaders to hold off passage of pending legislation (the Sudan Peace Act) that included punitive steps against Khartoum that would be applied in certain conditions (see chapter 20). In 2002 American diplomats were back at work in the embassy in Khartoum.

Throughout that year and on into 2003, the United States assumed a major role in the international endeavor to end Sudan's civil war. Working together, American, British, and Norwegian officials and an extremely able Kenyan negotiator brought about a cease-fire, which held for the most part, and some essential steps toward a peace agreement.

• • •

The future twists and turns in U.S.-Sudanese relations could not have been foreseen in 1992, when I began my assignment. One thing was clear at that time, however: the differences between Washington and Khartoum were so deep that they would not lend themselves to a quick fix.

Relations between Sudan and the United States were so poor in 1992 that people who knew what was going on in Sudan told me they didn't know whether to congratulate me on my appointment or to offer condolences. A country mired in a civil war, a government controlled by Islamists who appeared to be hostile to the United States, and diplomatic relations between the United States and Sudan dismal—this was the backdrop to my arrival in August 1992.

# 4

# Welcome

Our KLM flight from Amsterdam landed at Khartoum's airport at about 11 P.M., August 13, 1992. Waiting there to greet us were the Sudanese chief of protocol and several people from the embassy. After a few minutes, we were driven to the ambassador's residence, where we arrived about 11:30, a half-hour after the onset of the curfew then in effect in Khartoum.

In our first week in Khartoum, we had two dust storms (*haboobs*) and a heavy rain—unusually heavy for Khartoum. The *haboobs* themselves do not do any lasting damage, but they are a sight to behold. A few days after we had arrived, I was working in my office when my secretary said a *haboob* was coming and I should look out the window behind my desk. I opened the curtains (for security reasons, the curtains on that window were always closed), and there about a mile away was a red-brown cloud sweeping in over the city from the south. In just minutes, the cloud enveloped the embassy. Visibility was cut to less than fifty yards. The acrid smell of the dust was palpable. After an hour, the storm was over, leaving a reddish patina on streets and structures and a fine coating inside even relatively well-sealed houses.

Two days later, another *haboob* blew in, this one accompanied by the heavy downpour. About three inches of rain fell in less than an hour. Many houses were damaged, but the greatest harm was done to the camps of displaced people outside the city. United States Agency

for International Development (USAID) and embassy officers tried
their best, as did UN humanitarian aid officials, to assess the plight of
the people in the makeshift camps. The dirt roads leading to the area
were flooded, though, making it hard for relief officials to get there
and evaluate the situation. Even more of a problem was the government's policy of restricting relief workers' access to the camps.

Until I presented my credentials, I had to defer making official calls
on Sudanese government officials. I used most of my time before the
credentials ceremony to take charge at the embassy, become acquainted with embassy personnel, get briefed by them, and fill them
in on Washington's thinking about Sudan. I also met with heads of
diplomatic missions who were not bound by protocol and wanted to
see me even though I was not yet officially accredited.

On August 25, I presented my credentials. The chief of protocol and
a military aide picked me up in an immaculately maintained beige
1954 Rolls Royce and took me to Friendship Hall, a large, ornate
building designed and constructed by the Chinese, where the ceremony took place. Before I went inside, a band played the American
and Sudanese national anthems, and I received a salute from the honor
guard (about forty turbaned Sudanese soldiers) and passed them in review. Then I was escorted, along with those members of my staff who
accompanied me, into the building to meet President Bashir.

With my aides beside me and his advisers with him, I shook his
hand, spoke briefly to him in Arabic, gave my formal remarks, and
handed him my letter of credence and the letter of recall of my predecessor. He read his formal reply to my speech, then congratulated me
for having assumed my office. He and I, with the foreign minister, adjourned to one part of the room for a conversation.

The talk with the Sudanese president, if it had followed form, was
to have lasted about fifteen minutes. Instead, we conversed for a full
hour. Bashir is of medium height and medium coloring on the light-
brown-to-coal-black scale of indigenous Sudanese. He carried more
weight than he needed, yet he looked fit. On this occasion he wore an
olive-green military uniform with the insignia of a major general.
Most of the times I saw him subsequently he was dressed in the white
jellabiya, or gown, commonly worn by northern Sudanese men. Then,
and almost always when I talked with him, he was pleasant and atten-

tive but inflexible when he expressed his disagreements with U.S. foreign policies.

Bashir was born in 1944 near Shendi, about 150 miles down the Nile from Khartoum. His family belonged to the Ja'aliya, a prominent riverine tribe. A career soldier, he graduated from the Sudan Military College when he was twenty-two, saw military service in the Suez Canal area during the Yom Kippur War, and fought in the civil war in southern Sudan. He was a well-regarded brigadier general at the time of the coup that brought him to power.

Bashir is a typical Sudanese, in that he is open, friendly, and good-humored. And like many Sudanese, he is a devout Muslim. Yet unlike the majority of his compatriots, he is a committed Islamist who for some years before the coup was associated with Hasan al-Turabi's National Islamic Front. In all likelihood, Turabi became his guide.

A Sudanese official whom I talked to later that day made much of the unusual length of my conversation with the president. It was, he said, a very good omen. The prominence the Sudanese press and television gave to the credentials ceremony was also taken as an indication of the government's hope that relations with Washington would improve. However, an upturn in relations would require more than the arrival of a new ambassador and evidence of goodwill toward him. As I told President Bashir, relations were poor and would not get any better unless his government improved its human rights record, which was deplorable. In addition, it needed to ease restrictions on access to the hundreds of thousands of Sudanese displaced by the war in the South and in desperate need of food, shelter, and medicines. And Sudan had to stop harboring terrorists.

Reporting to Washington,[1] I said, in a lead paragraph summarizing the contents of my telegram: "The lengthier time Bashir devoted to our conversation is another sign that the GOS [government of Sudan] wants to improve its relations with the U.S. Be that as it may, our discussion did not break any new ground or indicate that the Sudanese really understand the depth of our differences. Nor did it indicate they are prepared to do anything to meet our concerns about human rights, access to displaced people in dire need of help, the campaign against international NGOs [nongovernmental organizations],[2] terrorism, etc."

• • •

It took very little time for Julie, Brian, and me to settle in at the residence. We were not cramped in our new home. It was a large house
with a wide terrace on two sides overlooking a spacious garden of
lawn, bougainvillea and other shrubs and flowers, and a dozen or so
trees, including several tall, slender palms. Built in the 1950s, it had
been taken over by the government during the Numeiry years. It became a cultural center of the Soviet embassy, then (no doubt after a
careful check for electronic bugs) was leased by the American embassy
in the 1980s.

Downstairs, the high-ceilinged interior of the house contained a
large (thirty-foot by thirty-six-foot) living room, a dining room with
a table that could comfortably accommodate twenty people, two
guest bedrooms, four bathrooms, and a kitchen. Upstairs, we had a
study–family room, a master bedroom and bath, a bedroom and bath
for Brian, and a kitchenette.

In the Arab fashion, the house was surrounded by a wall, which isolated us from the street and the other buildings in the neighborhood. It
was not precisely a residential neighborhood—not many homes.
Down the street was a security police post. The University of Khartoum was nearby. The north wall of our property separated it from the
large house and grounds of a Sudanese family. Because our place was
under surveillance by the security police and Sudanese knew they
could get into trouble with their government if they came to see us,
we saw little of our neighbors during our stay in Khartoum.

Like all parts of Khartoum, ours was tinged an orange-brown by the
fine, dustlike sand that comes in off the desert, swirls around when
the wind blows, and smothers the city when *haboob*s arrive. Although
the looks of Khartoum might not inspire poets, the city has character.
This was not always so. It had been a fishing village until 1824, when
the Turks moved their headquarters there from across the river in
Omdurman. For some years afterward, apparently it lacked not just
character, but almost any other positive aspect. Early travelers to
Khartoum used words like "miserable," "vile," "squalid," and
"filthy" to describe it.[3] But when the author Alan Moorehead visited
Khartoum in about 1960, he was able to say: "It is a delightful river
town with great avenues of banyan trees growing on the Blue Nile
bank, and it contains one of the finest universities in Africa."[4]

Unfortunately, the succeeding years were not kind to the city. Owing to bad management, the advent of economic hard times, and an insufficiency of resources and human energy, it had deteriorated a great deal by 1992. Many of even the better-looking structures were in various states of dilapidation. There was considerable litter in the streets, in vacant lots, and in places where construction was begun but never finished. However, even though much of the cityscape consisted of unadorned boxy structures lacking in charm or personality, some old colonial buildings were impressive, and the skyline was embellished by the minarets of Khartoum's mosques. And in the urban sprawl of Khartoum, Khartoum North, and Omdurman, there were some pleasant parks, tree-lined streets, and the bridges and banks of the majestic Nile rivers.

The city gets an average of only eight inches of rain a year, yet because of the rivers, Khartoum and next-door Omdurman were greener than I had expected. Irrigation produces expanses of vegetation that soften the generally arid landscape. The countryside in the immediate vicinity of the city and for miles around is quite flat, most of it sere and treeless except for thorn bushes.

• • •

Much of the dialogue I had with Sudanese officials as I made calls on cabinet ministers and others consisted of their stating their case (the United States was misinformed about what truly was happening in Sudan) and my repeating Washington's and the embassy's perceptions and concerns. All this was done politely, and the tone of the talks was cordial. I was sure, however, that as time went on and I continued to voice U.S. concerns and criticisms about the situation in Sudan, my honeymoon with the Sudanese government would be over.

Before that happened, I used the era of goodwill to take the Sudanese up on their assurances that they wanted me to travel around the country. I set my own itinerary rather than going just to the places that they wanted me to see. In the last two weeks of September, I made three trips to displaced persons' camps in the "transition zone"—the area more or less between northern and southern Sudan.

Diplomats' travel in Sudan was a vexatious issue. It was bad enough to have to get the government's permission to go to the transition zone and face sometimes lengthy delays and unexplained refusals by the security police. In addition, permission was required for any trip whatsoever outside Khartoum, even only a few miles from the city limits.

In a mid-September meeting at the presidential palace with Ghazi Salah Eddin Atabani, a minister of state in the presidency, I told him that travel restrictions on diplomats were a Cold War anachronism. Why, in particular, did the government control and monitor diplomats' trips in northern Sudan? Ghazi said he would work to end the restrictions. A month later, he told me that he had personally facilitated my three trips into the transition zone and that he had taken the lead in the government to eliminate the restrictions on diplomats' travel in northern Sudan. The restrictions were abolished soon thereafter. Ghazi said these were steps aimed at improving Sudan's relations with the United States. Whether they would have had that effect is impossible to say, because very soon events in the southern city of Juba profoundly worsened the already dismal state of relations between the two countries.

# 5

# The Troubles Begin

Just how little the Sudanese were taking to heart the U.S. government's expressed concerns about human rights violations become abundantly clear that September. Even before then we were getting reports of escalating troubles in Juba, the capital of Equatoria province, part of what once was Sudan's Southern Region.

On August 25 I cabled Washington that "fears are growing here that there is a dark tale of murder and intimidation unfolding in Juba." I cited reports from reliable sources "that the GOS is resorting to extreme measures in Juba to retaliate against southerners who are suspected of supporting the SPLA [Sudan People's Liberation Army, the military arm of the Sudan People's Liberation Movement, SPLM[1]] and to cow the populace into complete submission. Although hard evidence is lacking, at this point, there are sufficient indications to warrant deep concern."

USAID officers were increasingly worried about the agency's Sudanese employees maintaining the USAID compound in Juba. Some two years earlier, after U.S. economic aid to Sudan had been phased out, Washington had decided to keep open the Juba compound, which consisted of an office building and living quarters for USAID employees. I never saw a written rationale for this decision. I understood, however, that USAID and the State Department had agreed with the embassy and the USAID mission in Khartoum that keeping the compound open would signal the U.S. government's continuing concern about the misery of the southern Sudanese. It was also meant to indicate that the United States would resume economic assistance to Sudan once the Sudanese government sufficiently changed its behavior. USAID officials in Washington told me it was important to continue to keep the compound open.

At about the time I arrived in Sudan, the scheduled periodic radio messages from the compound to the USAID office in Khartoum ceased. Embassy and USAID inquiries with the government about the situation at the Juba compound produced no answers, and our anxiety deepened.

Once it was clear that the Ministry of Foreign Affairs and other government offices would be of no help at all, I went with the embassy's political counselor to see Nafi Ali Nafi, a slender, soft-spoken, intense man who had obtained a Ph.D. in botany from the University of California–Riverside. He was now a top official in Sudan's security police and a member of the inner circle of the Bashir government. Nafi told us the authorities at Juba had seized the USAID compound and detained our senior employee there because he had been conspiring with SPLA guerrillas. The compound would be returned to USAID control, but the senior employee, Andrew Tombe, would be tried. Nafi said he had no news of the other twelve USAID employees.

I told him his government's failure to respond to the embassy's requests for information was unacceptable and raised questions about Sudan's seriousness in its dealings with the United States. Nafi said two rebel military penetrations of Juba, one in June and another in July, had revealed that townspeople had collaborated with the enemy. Those involved included members of the army and police forces, clergymen, and others. He said the military had dealt with its own and was also putting on trial the civilians who "had plotted against Sudan."

Very fearful of what might happen to Tombe—a very able and well-liked man, USAID officials told me—I made representations to another security official and to Ghazi. Ghazi, whose relatively light complexion and dark beard led some foreigners who did not know him to wonder if he were an Iranian, was about forty years old at the time and came from a prominent northern Sudanese family. A true revolutionary, he had escaped from the medical profession he had entered at the behest of his family, rapidly risen in the NIF, and become one of the most influential men in the Bashir government. Intelligent and articulate, Ghazi was an able exponent of his government's policies and, as I learned from experience, a formidable opponent of anyone who criticized those policies.

A few days after we met he told me the USAID employees were unharmed. In the meantime, I had written President Bashir to the effect that I was profoundly concerned about Tombe. I asked Bashir to exercise leniency if Tombe had been tried.

Friday, September 18, was a long and difficult day. It started for me at 5:30 A.M., when I went for a seven-mile run along the Blue Nile to the Hilton Hotel and back to the residence. The early morning air was still, oppressively hot, and humid.

At nine o'clock, Julie, Brian, and I went to the compound that housed the embassy's gas pump, maintenance and repair facilities, warehouse, and commissary. There we joined others in a community effort to clean up the commissary, which had almost been destroyed in a fire two nights earlier. Although firefighters had saved our buildings, everything in the commissary was coated with inky black soot. All the canned, boxed, and bottled goods had to be wiped clean and moved elsewhere while the commissary's interior was cleaned and repainted. Not long after we had started working, I got word that I should go to the embassy.

When I arrived there I learned that Bashir had responded to my letter. His message, delivered orally by a military officer on his staff, was that it was too late for him to do anything—the death sentence had been carried out. Later we heard that Tombe had been tried by court-martial (Juba was under martial law) and convicted. We also learned he had been executed weeks earlier, probably about the time I arrived in Sudan.

I called in the director of USAID, Carol Becker, and broke the sad news to her. Even though we had known the odds were high that Tombe had already been killed, confirmation of that fact was an emotional shock to her; she had worked with, liked, and respected him. For the next hour, she and deputy chief of mission[2] Larry Benedict discussed with me what we should do.

Deeply affected by Tombe's death and feeling frustrated after many months of dealing with the government, which had over and over again taken actions adversely affecting the relief program and making life difficult for foreign relief workers, Carol wondered whether we should continue our aid program. Although I understood her feelings, I did not believe we had reached a point yet where we should throw in the towel.

I contacted European Community (EC) representative Charles Brook, British ambassador Peter Streams, and some UN officials and asked them to meet with me at the residence later in the day. The main thing I wanted to do was let them know what had happened to Tombe. This was pertinent to Brook and the UN officials because they also had employees in Juba who had been arrested and whose fate was unknown. We talked about steps our governments and organizations might take later on but came to no firm conclusions.

I wrote a message to Washington and had it sent that afternoon. In it I said we should demand particulars of the government's actions against Tombe, including its evidence concerning the charges against him. Further, we should seek an explanation of why the government evaded informing us much earlier. I also recommended that Carol Becker fly to Nairobi to meet with some USAID officials and discuss her concerns about continuing the USAID program in Sudan. I asked that, to register the U.S. government's anger, I be recalled for consultations in Washington. That would be considered a serious diplomatic step, and I was unsure whether Washington would want to go that far.

Two days later, we learned that another USAID employee in Juba, Baudouin Tally, had also been executed in August. Much later we concluded that two others of the thirteen USAID employees who had been arrested had been executed as well. An employee of the European Community and one of the United Nations were among the other people killed in Juba around the same time.

The State Department agreed with the proposal in my cable except for recalling me to Washington. On September 22, the Department's spokesman said the U.S. government had "learned with sadness and outrage" that Andrew Tombe had been executed by the government of Sudan and that Baudouin Tally had probably been executed. He said, "Several credible sources indicate widespread killing and abuse of the civilian population in Juba by the army and militia of the government of Sudan." The U.S. government condemned Tombe's execution and over the next several days issued additional, stronger denunciations. Khartoum angrily rejected the U.S. assertions.

On September 17 I had written Bashir asking for information about Tombe's execution. I said the embassy wanted to see whatever evidence the Sudanese had that he was guilty of any crime. I referred to the evasions and untruthful responses the embassy had been getting from his government, and I urged that an embassy officer be permitted to fly to Juba to talk to our other Sudanese employees there and to inspect the USAID compound.

On September 22 Foreign Minister Ali Ahmed Sahloul sent me a diplomatic note in which he said my letter to President Bashir constituted interference in Sudan's internal affairs and contained undiplomatic language. I responded to Sahloul's note the same day, denying that what I had done was interference in an internal matter and renewing my request for access to our people in Juba.

A week later, despite continued harsh commentary in the government-controlled media criticizing my actions and Washington's statement, I received a conciliatory diplomatic note. In it I was assured that the information I had requested about what happened in Juba would be provided and that we would be able to send someone down there very soon.

Sahloul and others in the Foreign Ministry probably believed that. Yet the Foreign Ministry carried little if any weight in decisionmaking on security matters, and the embassy ran into a stone wall on our request to fly to Juba. Despite being told repeatedly that we could make the trip, we were kept from doing so. Our only means of getting to Juba was on the UN's aircraft, which was then making flights just once a week. The United Nations canceled a flight scheduled for the last week in September, and in any event the Sudanese security authorities had not given the necessary permission for it to fly.

The government did not formally deny our requests, choosing instead to delay; the effect was the same. The temporizing was making clear to us that the regime did not want us or any other outsiders to go to Juba at that time. We believed there was apprehension within the government that we would learn something about the truth of what had happened there, not only to the USAID employees but also to the many other people who had been arrested and executed in Juba throughout that summer. The delaying tactic finally gave way when a number of factors caused the request to be granted.

First, I informed the ministry that I, instead of Larry Benedict, would be going. Earlier, senior members of my staff and I had decided that I should not go to Juba. Travel there by the U.S. ambassador would be ballyhooed by the government as proof that the rebels were not besieging the area, as indeed they were. By early October, however, the Sudanese press was reporting that the rebels had pulled away from Juba. Therefore the propaganda value the government might get from a visit by me would be of little consequence. We decided I would go. We thought it would be harder for the Sudanese authorities to obstruct the travel of the ambassador than the travel of another officer of the embassy.

Second, we also informed the government that I would be flying with UN officials and James Kunder, the director of USAID's Office of Foreign Disaster Assistance (OFDA), who had come to Sudan to assess the relief situation. Refusal to let them go to Juba would raise further questions about the government's motives.

A final stimulus to the Sudanese decision occurred in mid-October, when in response to the stonewalling I informed the Foreign Ministry that I was going to close the embassy's consular office, which issued visas for travel to the United States. This act would make it impossible for government officials to travel to Washington and New York, which some of them had an urgent need to do.

By October 19 the embassy and the United Nations had received the necessary clearances from the government and assurances from the rebels that they would not fire on our aircraft. So on that day, accompanied by Jim Kunder, Charles Brook, and a Sudanese minister of state, Mustafa Osman Ismail, I flew in the UN plane to El Obeid, where we overnighted.

We landed in Juba at ten o'clock the next morning. Officials there wanted to use most of our time for a meeting with the governor of Eastern Equatoria, a tour of Juba, and a luncheon. We turned them down and said that after a brief meeting with the governor, the Americans wanted to go to the USAID compound and Charles Brook to the Economic Community's compound so we could talk with our respective employees.

At the meeting with the governor I stated I had come primarily to talk to those of the thirteen USAID employees who were still alive and present in Juba. The head of the security police gave the government's version of the circumstances leading to the execution of our employees Andrew Tombe and Baudouin Tally. I replied that we had seen no convincing evidence and that we continued to disbelieve the government's story.

Back in September, Nafi Ali Nafi and General Fatih Irwah, the two security officials who had given me particulars about the detention of Andrew Tombe, had said Tombe had been caught in the act of using the radio on the USAID compound to pass information to the SPLA force that was besieging Juba. I had told Irwah that this was untrue. Because of the suspicion about the radio, Tombe had invited the security people in Juba to the compound, shown it to them, and explained that USAID in Khartoum wanted him to report periodically, whether or not there were problems at the compound. At least one of his subsequent broadcasts was made in the presence of security policemen. Tombe was fully aware that all his broadcasts were monitored. For him to use the radio in aid of the SPLA would have been suicidal. When I related this to Irwah, he insisted nonetheless that, in his words, "Tombe was caught red-handed."

Carol Becker had told me then that even if someone had wanted to use the radio to contact the rebels, it would not have been possible. To reduce the chances that the authorities in Juba might allege that the radio could be or had been used for illegal purposes, it had been modified so that it could transmit on only one frequency, the one used for communicating with USAID Khartoum.

After I began pointing this out to Sudanese officials, I was told Tombe had been using *another* radio, one belonging to the EC office in Juba. But how, I asked, did this square with the assertion that Tombe was apprehended using a radio in the USAID compound? No satisfactory explanation was given. Making the government's case even more contrived, Charles Brook told me the EC radio had been out of operation for some time before the USAID employees were arrested.

One of our talks in Juba on October 20 added to my belief that the government's case against Tombe was based on spurious evidence. The head of security there told Brook, Kunder, and me that Tombe and the EC employee were caught using the radio while sitting under a tree in the market place. I asked him, "Are you telling us that the two men were sitting under a tree, in broad daylight, at the market, in the sight of many people, and using the radio to talk with rebels?"

"Yes," he replied.

I used this ludicrous story, along with the other versions alleging Tombe's guilt, in subsequently telling Sudanese government officials that Tombe had been wrongfully executed and demanding a full, truthful account of what happened to him and the others.

We found four employees at the USAID compound and learned from them that five others were accounted for. In addition to the two who had been executed, two employees were missing. We asked the Sudanese authorities to do all they could to find them or to find out what happened to them. I told the four employees that USAID wanted to transfer them and the others to Khartoum and that within days someone from the embassy would come back to help make arrangements for the transfer. Those who preferred to stay in Juba would continue to be employed by USAID. We gave them their back pay and had a look around the compound, which was in good shape.

We then were taken on the obligatory tour of Juba, designed to show us that all was normal there. We had to cut it short—to about fifteen minutes. After a quick lunch, we left at 1 P.M., the latest we could leave and still get back to Khartoum that night.

As we expected, the next day Khartoum TV aired a piece on the visit, showing me talking to the governor and visiting a market. No mention was made of the purpose of our trip; nothing was shown of our visit to the USAID compound. The theme was that Juba was peaceful (which it seemed to be, except for two loud explosions we heard during the meeting with the governor). But again, because the relatively quiet military situation there was now well known, the government's propaganda about the trip was of little importance.

By November we had learned from various sources, including someone with the security police, that when the security police had detained Tombe they had come into the compound and seized all the employees who were working that day. Most or all were tortured. Those who were released never saw Andrew Tombe or Baudouin Tally again. They heard later that the two men had been executed. Neither they nor anyone else outside the government of Sudan were given any information about the two other USAID employees, Chaplain Lako and Dominic Morris, who were never heard from again after the security police took them away. (During a meeting with Jim Kunder and me on October 19, the day before Kunder and I left for Juba, Ghazi had inadvertently indicated that all four men had been executed. He said that because Tombe and others in Juba had committed acts that caused the deaths of other Sudanese, whether "one, two, three or four" USAID employees were executed or disappeared was, in a sense, immaterial.)

After some weeks, the U.S. government's anger finally began to sink in with the Sudanese. In a step taken to mollify the United States, Bashir replaced his attorney general with a lawyer who was U.S.-educated and had been the embassy's lawyer for a number of years, Abdel Aziz Shiddu.

When I met with him, Shiddu gave assurances that a report on the Juba affair would soon be forthcoming. But it was not, and after more time had passed he met with me again. This time he said the government had established an impartial commission to conduct a thorough investigation of what had taken place in Juba. The commission was composed of well-known and respected men in the legal field. As more months went by, he kept telling me that the commission would soon issue its findings. It never did so. Either the commission was not allowed to do its job, or its findings were damaging to the government and were suppressed.

In addition to its obfuscation in the case of Andrew Tombe, the Sudanese government never stated officially that Baudouin Tally had been executed, even though officials had told me that he had met the same fate as Tombe. Nor did the Sudanese provide any information at all concerning Chaplain Lako and Dominic Morris.

Hasan al-Turabi once told me that in time the U.S. government would forget about Tombe and the others. They were of no importance, and eventually Washington's desire for normalizing relations with Sudan would outweigh any lingering concern about what had happened to them. I told Turabi and others that they were mistaken if they believed this. U.S. officials involved in international affairs, especially those who had served in U.S. embassies and consulates, placed a high premium on the loyalty of foreign nationals working for the U.S. government. The Juba killings, I said, would not be forgotten.

That was true when I said it, and I hope it will continue to be true. The historical record, however, is not encouraging. In June 1974, at the conclusion of the trial of the killers of Cleo Noel, George Moore, and Guy Eid, Sudanese president Numeiry reduced the life sentence they had received to seven years and then immediately had them sent to Cairo to be imprisoned there. Numeiry said he was motivated by fear of terrorist reprisals against Sudanese interests, particularly Sudanese embassies and diplomats abroad. The Nixon administration's reaction was to express outrage at what had been done, recall Ambassador William Brewer, suspend the U.S. aid program, cut off Export-Import Bank loans, and send home some of the Sudanese military officers who were studying in the United States. By mid-November, however, Brewer was back in Khartoum, returned to his post by Secretary of State Henry Kissinger. By 1976 relations had been normalized, and that year President Numeiry paid an official visit to Washington, where he met with President Gerald Ford.

• • •

Although the Juba affair was a central topic of my discussions in those early weeks I was in Sudan, I took every opportunity I could to talk about other aspects of U.S.-Sudanese relations and try to narrow our differences. As in my first calls on officials in late August and early September, I made no headway on this. In a two-hour talk with Turabi on October 3, for example, I failed to get him to concede that Sudan needed to do anything to allay Western concerns about its human rights record and obstruction of the relief effort.

That day and all the other times I saw him in Khartoum, Turabi was dressed elegantly in a gleaming white *jellabiya* and wore an equally immaculate white turban. He was personable and used his ingratiating smile to advantage. In interviews he was impressively adept with words, but his delivery was often interspersed by incongruous bursts of what seemed to be nervous laughter. Turabi, whose opinions carried great weight within the government and the NIF, brushed off the U.S. reaction to the Juba executions by repeating the Sudanese government's theme that Tombe and others had aided the SPLA and were executed on the basis of valid evidence against them.

Stating that Washington made no outcry about political prisoners in Egypt and had a history of violating the rights of African Americans,

"Red Indians," and Japanese Americans, he said U.S. views about human rights in Sudan were hypocritical.

Turabi argued that Sudan needed economic rather than humanitarian aid; displaced southern Sudanese were no worse off than millions of other Sudanese. Relief organizations and donor countries, he charged, had a vested interest in distributing and administering relief supplies. He said he opposed a new world order "dominated by the United States." The United Nations was a tool of the United States and some other UN Security Council permanent members, and the Organization of African Unity was hamstrung by the former colonial powers, which did not want it to be effective.

I took issue with these and other things he said. This was not easy to do. Turabi is a nonstop talker and I had to be aggressive to get him to hear me out.

He spoke of his desire to see better relations with the United States. I told him the U.S. government accepted the opinion of scholars like John Esposito that political Islam need not be in and of itself repressive or contrary to Western interests. But if Sudan, as the only Arab country ruled by Islamic fundamentalists (he made no objection to my use of the term) continued on its present course, it would be held up as a bad example of what happened when Islamists came to power. He made no comment on this, and our meeting ended.

# 6

# The Displaced

The war in southern Sudan had devastated the lives of countless thousands of Sudanese. In the North, it was a principal cause of the severe downturn of the economy, and many young men had been killed or maimed fighting in the South. Between 1983 and 1992, more than a million southerners had died from the effects of the war (a figure that would rise to over two million later in the 1990s). Millions more (estimates ranged from 4 million to 5.3 million) had been displaced from their homes. Of those, over half a million were in refugee camps in Uganda, Kenya, Zaire, Ethiopia, and the Central African Republic. The remainder were living in displaced-persons camps in the South, the transition zone, and the Khartoum area. They survived as best they could, aided by the international relief effort.

Despite continued criticisms of my actions and Washington's statement about what had happened in Juba, the Sudanese allowed me to fly into the transition zone, as I have noted. I traveled with UN and USAID officials to see what the conditions in camps there were like. They were deplorable, but the Sudanese authorities refused to acknowledge this and strenuously resisted requests by aid donors for permission for international NGOs to work in the camps to improve the relief programs in them.

On September 18 I flew to Renk, a town about 330 miles south of Khartoum. There was no commercial air service to Renk, or to many

other places in Sudan, so I traveled in a UN-leased twin-engine Otter, a slow but reliable propeller aircraft capable of getting in and out
of small airstrips in the bush. In the town itself, where newly incoming southerners were initially kept, and at the displaced-persons
camp several miles from the town I saw hundreds of suffering people—adults, many of them terribly emaciated, and similarly malnourished children. Some were being cared for by Concern, a respected Irish relief organization whose work USAID was partially
funding. A few Sudanese aid organizations were also working at
Renk, but Concern was the only foreign relief organization permitted to be there.

When they were able to get out of earshot of the security police,
who tagged along wherever I went that day (and were present at every
camp I visited in the North or in the transition zone), Concern's two
young Irish relief workers told me they had to get prior authorization
whenever they wanted to leave their small compound, even to go to
the feeding center where they worked.

In the previous few months, some 30,000 people who had fled from
towns and villages farther south because of the war had come to Renk
looking for food and shelter. The fittest of the young men among the
displaced were drafted to work in nearby plantations. I was told that
they were paid for their labor, but I was unable to confirm this. Large
acreages near the town were covered with a variety of hibiscus bush
called karkaday. After being harvested, karkaday flowers are dried,
crushed, and packaged for domestic and export sales. Boiled, the prod-
uct becomes a deep-red tea that, with sugar added, is a sweet, pleasant-
tasting drink.

Those who labored on the plantations were a tiny proportion of
Renk's southern immigrants, most of whom were in terrible need of
food and other necessities. Local authorities could not cope with the
influx, and Sudanese relief organizations had neither enough experience nor sufficient resources to provide the kind of care that was
needed. Nevertheless, the government of Sudan was not allowing
nearly enough international relief workers to go to Renk or to other
places inundated by displaced people.

In the town and at the camp I was accompanied by the head of the
local government, who, just before I left, told me there was no serious
problem there. I strongly disagreed with him. A day earlier, when I had

visited a camp for displaced people near Khartoum, I had a similar disagreement with Sudanese officials.

The government's position was that foreign embassies, the United Nations, and international NGOs in Sudan were exaggerating the problems of the displaced. The government had chosen to refuse to acknowledge the existence of what UN officials, the few diplomats who visited displaced camps, and relief workers knew was a situation of widespread suffering. In so doing, Sudanese officials were needlessly intensifying that suffering.

On the twenty-seventh I went to Malakal, which is about 500 miles south of Khartoum on the east bank of the White Nile. The town was depressingly run-down. I was surprised to learn that in colonial days Malakal was such a pleasant, attractive town that it was a favorite recreation spot for Britons who lived and worked in Sudan.

At Malakal, and at Meiram, some 200 miles to the west, where I went a few days later, I found conditions similar to those at Renk. The larger number of displaced at Malakal, an estimated 95,000 at that time, made the task of caring for those in greatest need of help all the more difficult. Most of the displaced people had nothing but the clothes they were wearing when they fled their homes and trekked north. They lacked bedding and adequate shelter and did not get nearly enough food to regain their strength. Many whom I saw were so sick with malaria or some other debilitating disease that they lay inertly on the ground; open sores were common.

There were no international NGOs (INGOs) in Malakal. The area in the vicinity of the town had been divided into five parts, each of which was the responsibility of one of the five Sudanese NGOs working there. This was done without reference to the particular problems of each sector or the ability of the assigned NGO to cope with them. Coordination among the five was poor.

It was only too evident that those NGOs were not up to the task confronting them. One, for example, was conducting a supplementary feeding program for badly malnourished children, yet its director was unable to show me that his organization had a system of registering the children, assessing the extent of their malnourishment, or reevaluating them periodically—standard procedure at a well-run supplementary feeding center. The feeding program was disorganized and primitive in comparison with Concern's program at Renk.

At a camp near Malakal, terribly emaciated children and adults were shockingly prevalent. The people I talked to pleaded for medicines and adequate food. A spokesman for the Upper Nile State Relief Committee gave me a petition stressing an urgent need for mosquito nets, as well as medicines and clothing. Doctors at the Malakal hospital (one of the most dilapidated and poorly equipped of the many hospitals I had seen in Africa) said there was a critical shortage of medicines, especially chloroquine and antibiotics. Malaria and gastrointestinal diseases were rampant.

A local official whispered to me at one point that the Islamic NGOs (four of the five NGOs at Malakal) were using relief supplies as a tool to Islamize people in the camps. The use of food and other inducements to Islamize southerners was a charge that surfaced again and again before, during, and after my years in Sudan. The frequency of firsthand accounts from disparate sources in different parts of the country made a convincing case that efforts at forced Islamization were widespread.

At a meeting attended by the provincial governor and other officials, I told the governor and the relief committee that conditions in the camps were bad and required the combined resources and talents of the United Nations, Sudanese NGOs, and international NGOs. I said USAID, which was providing a high percentage of the food being brought in by the World Food Program (WFP) and distributed through NGOs, could not effectively do its work in Sudan without the international NGOs (INGOs). The Sudanese officials there and back in Khartoum continued to regard the situation in a different light, however. They downplayed the extent of the suffering of the people and refused to concede that the services of INGOs were needed.

Khartoum did not want it known how badly it was failing to meet the needs of the displaced people because of its refusal to give the United Nations and INGOs sufficient access to fully employ their resources and skills. The government detested having to rely on aid donations from Western governments and institutions. This was understandable, especially in light of the bad experience Sudan had had with INGOs in the 1980s, when in response to a disastrous food shortage, there was a heavy influx of INGOs into the country.

According to people involved in the relief program at that time, including the then head of one of the larger INGOs, the government failed to place adequate controls over the activities of the foreign relief organizations. Some of them went where they wanted and operated however they wished without any reference to the government. Adding to the problem, although most or all INGOs refrained from taking sides in the conflict, this was not true of all relief workers themselves. Consequently, "the mantle of altruistic humanitarianism the relief agencies donned was often deeply suspected by the government of Sudan."[1]

All this, of course, infuriated many Sudanese officials at the time, and it continued to rankle years later. However, the anger and defensiveness were carried to an extreme, with tragic results.

Before going to Malakal, I had toured a large displaced-persons camp near Khartoum. Officials of the government and a Sudanese relief agency took my party and me to places they wanted us to see. The officials and a phalanx of armed security guards surrounded us. It was apparent that they did not want us to stray from the itinerary they had prepared or to talk to any displaced southerners. I spied a group of several women about ten yards to the left of where we were headed; obviously angry, they were beckoning me to come talk with them. To the dismay of the officials, I broke away from them and the armed guards so I could hear what the women had to say.

Their leader, a young woman who spoke English, told me conditions in the camp were awful, and she invited me to see where she, the other women, and their children lived. They led me to a small hut that at first glance seemed to be covered by a tarp. Once inside, I saw that the canvas covering was badly torn and offered very little protection from rain. The floor was bare earth, and they had no blankets for themselves or their children. They showed me a bucket of filthy water, which they said was the only kind of water available to them.

The young woman told me her greatest concern was for her children. Medical care was next to nonexistent. The children had no school to attend. They, like herself, needed clothing. She asked that outside aid be allowed to reach people like her, her friends, and their children. I said we and other donors were trying to make that possible. The officials, who were nervously milling about while this was going on, led me back to the prepared tour as soon as I said good-bye to the woman and her friends.

Months later, she made her way to the embassy and asked to see me. In my office, she told me she had paid a price for her audacity at the camp that day. It became harder and harder for her to get food for herself and her children. She was denied any help in replacing the canvas or otherwise improving her shelter. Security policemen frequently harassed her, threatening that one day she would be sorry for having spoken to the American ambassador. She asked me to help her and her children leave Sudan. Before very long I was able to do that, and she and the children made their way to a neighboring country.

# 7

# Hanging In

In some of my earlier assignments in Africa, U.S. relations with the host government were, at one time or another, on a very shaky footing. It had sometimes been hard to see how we could turn things around. Nevertheless, with patience and persistent active diplomacy, along with—in some instances—mistakes by our then Cold War adversaries, we were able to make headway in our efforts to improve relations.

I recall in particular the aftermath of the Zanzibar revolution in the early 1960s. In 1961 the United States opened a consulate in Zanzibar, a British protectorate consisting of the east African islands of Zanzibar and Pemba. The consulate had been established after Washington reached agreement with London to construct and man a space-vehicle tracking station on the main island in conjunction with Project Mercury, the first series of U.S. manned spaceflights.

In July 1963 Julie, our one-year-old daughter, Susan, and I arrived in Zanzibar. On December 9 Zanzibar became an independent republic, with its government dominated by the Arab minority. Of Zanzibar's 300,000 people, 50,000 were Arabs, 20,000 Asians—people having Indian or Pakistani antecedents—and the rest Africans, mostly descendants of mainland Bantu peoples.

At the independence day ceremony, when the British flag was lowered and the Republic of Zanzibar flag raised, there was an ominous lack of enthusiasm on the part of the Africans in attendance. A month later, on January 12, 1964, a bloody revolution toppled the Arab-led government and put into power a predominantly African regime.

A day after the revolution, because of continuing violence and insecurity, all the approximately sixty Americans on the island, except for Chargé d'Affaires Frederick Picard and me, were evacuated to the mainland. On the sixteenth, the revolutionaries arrested us. Picard was accused of interfering in Zanzibar's internal affairs. The next day, he was expelled. I was allowed to remain. Five weeks afterward, because the United States had not yet recognized the new government, I was expelled. A few days later, however, I returned with the new chargé d'affaires, Frank C. Carlucci III.

The revolutionary government coupled this inauspicious beginning of relations with the United States with the establishment of close relations with the Soviet Union, East Germany, and Communist China. Adopting the rhetoric of their new friends, who urged them on, some of the leaders of the Zanzibar government portrayed the United States as an imperialist, neocolonialist enemy of Africa. Even moderates in the government had a less than friendly opinion of the U.S. government. It seemed at the time that our chances of reversing this situation were slim.

However, by the time I left the island two years later, the Zanzibaris' ardor for close ties with the three Communist countries had cooled, and relations with us had warmed up appreciably. Most of the credit belonged to Frank Carlucci, whose intelligence, competence, aggressive diplomacy, and candor projected an image of U.S. intentions very much at odds with the negative views expressed by radical Zanzibaris. Even after Frank was declared persona non grata in January 1965, on false charges that he was working to overthrow the revolutionary government, relations continued to get better.

•  •  •

Thus I knew from experience that bad blood between the United States and another country was not immutable and that efforts to improve a situation could succeed. Yet after several months in Sudan, I had to conclude that circumstances there, and their causes, left little room for optimism that relations could improve in the foreseeable future.

Following the Juba killings, I knew that unless the Sudanese began to show some inclination to move away from the course they were taking, official Washington's displeasure with the Bashir government would intensify. Yet my talks with Bashir, Turabi, Ghazi, and others in the leadership drew little more than repeated denials that any of the U.S. government's concerns were valid.

In all the countries in which I served, even when relations with the United States were bad, people at all societal levels were fascinated by Americans and what they did and what they produced. Sudan was no exception. The November 1992 U.S. elections drew a lot of interest, and an election display at the library of the United States Information Agency (USIA) in Khartoum attracted many Sudanese.

Julie, Brian, and I watched the election returns at the embassy's Blue Nile recreation center, where USIA had a satellite dish to pick up the agency's World Net broadcasts from Washington. We arrived there at 1:45 A.M., about the time polls were closing on the East Coast in the United States. After passing through roadblocks manned by armed personnel enforcing the curfew (I had a curfew pass), we joined others who had arrived before the curfew to spend the night at the recreation center watching the TV broadcast of the election returns.

The next evening I hosted a post-election reception at our house for some seventy people, mainly Sudanese and diplomats. The approach of winter had yet to see a break in the heat. At the end of October, day-time maximum temperatures were 110 or so degrees. Humidity was low, however, and nights were pleasant, and we had an even better than expected turnout for the reception.

Bill Clinton's defeat of President George Bush had led some Sudanese to think that relations with the United States would automatically change for the better. Taking me aside, a friend of mine in the government brought up the possibility of improved relations. I told him he was wrong to assume that a new administration in Washington meant a new, more favorable policy regarding Sudan. After I replied at some length to his question as to why that was so, he said he thought it would be useful if I would talk as frankly to President Bashir. Would I agree to do that? Certainly, I said, whenever the president wanted.

Not long after the U.S. elections, I received a reminder from the director general of the Foreign Service that I had to submit my resignation. The message was sent not just to me but to all ambassadors. For many career ambassadors, submitting their resignation was a pro forma exercise. The real targets were the political appointees, all of whose resignations would be accepted.

It was possible that some career ambassadors would go, too, especially those who were in highly sought-after posts. But people like me, in distinctly less desirable places, were not in much danger of losing our jobs. This was the third time I had had to resign after a U.S. presidential election, and I was fairly sure that once again I would not be asked to leave. It was quite unlikely that any friends of the new president or big financial contributors to his election campaign would want to become ambassador to Sudan. If any did, I never heard about it.

Attacks on the U.S. government and the embassy continued in the Sudanese media. At the same time, however, the tone of the embassy's relations with the government improved. A few days before the U.S. elections, DCM Larry Benedict and Gary Mansavage, the new head of USAID/Khartoum, went to Juba and were able to talk to our Sudanese employees. All of them wanted to be transferred to Khartoum. A few weeks later, after persistent efforts, we obtained the necessary permission for this from the Sudanese government and made arrangements to fly the employees and their families to the North.

Despite the better interaction with the government, the Juba killings always came up in meetings with officials. I would restate that we did not believe the government's story about the guilt of Andrew Tombe and Baudouin Tally nor its claim that it knew nothing about the fate of Chaplain Lako and Dominic Morris. Following those meetings, the government primed the Sudanese media, whose reports invariably twisted what I had said into something favorable about Sudan.

This had happened, for example, following the trip that Jim Kunder, Charles Brook, and I had made to Juba. Media accounts of it were so distorted that I put out a press release to set the record straight. The release said we were grateful for the opportunity the government of Sudan had given us to accomplish our objectives, but nothing government officials had told us altered Kunder's and my "disbelief, and the disbelief of the U.S. government, in the validity of the charges against the three employees." Nor did officials convince us "that the three men had been accorded due process of law. To the contrary, the statements of security officials in Juba added to our conviction that Mr. Tombe and Mr. Tally were wrongfully charged and unjustly tried and executed."

The press release took note of a report in an issue of the Sudan News Agency's *Daily Bulletin* that stated that in a meeting with the Parliament's speaker, Mohamed el-Amin Khalifa, the "U.S. Ambassador said that his country recognizes trial of citizens under the laws of their respective countries." Our press release said, "The SUNA article neglected to report that the ambassador also said that he has seen no convincing evidence of the guilt of the USAID employees, that he disbelieves the charges against them, and that he continues to differ with the Government of Sudan on this issue."

The day after our press release was issued, the Sudanese press misrepresented its content. Obviously, we could not get in the last word, not when the government controlled the media. Embassy press releases, however, did get wide distribution in Khartoum and reached almost everyone who counted in the government and in other influential segments of Sudanese society. Perhaps circulating a message that was bound to anger the government was not the diplomatic thing to do. But my staff and I believed we should not sit silently while the government was purveying distortions of U.S. actions or intentions. As time went on, we learned that our releases were very effective in countering the government's misstatements and occasionally even seemed to have a useful influence on government officials.

On November 10 I met with President Bashir at his office for almost three hours. He said he and his government had "been keen" since taking power for better relations with the United States. Noting that the United States was big and powerful, he said, "Sudan is small and weak and cannot harm the United States, so why can't relations be better?"

I replied, "I will be totally frank, to the point that some of what I say might make you angry." He laughed and said I should go ahead.

I said that first I wanted to address a misconception some Sudanese seemed to have about the outcome of the U.S. elections. "A change of administrations in Washington," I said, "does not mean a change in the basic elements of U.S. foreign policy, including human rights." Then in some detail I recapitulated U.S. concerns about a full range of human rights violations by his government.

At one point I said, "There is a climate of fear in Sudan because of the actions of the security police." People were afraid to speak out or even to meet with foreigners. I knew, I said, that "some people will not come to my embassy because they are afraid they will be picked up by the security police if they do."

"None of this is true," he replied indignantly. The fault lay with "the opposition for trying to isolate the government by spreading false rumors." All Sudanese, he said, were politically aware: "Even my grandmother is a politician." In all the widespread political talk in Sudan, he said, the facts got embroidered.

I told Bashir that as far as I could tell, there had been no movement toward democracy since the military had seized power three years earlier. Later in our discussion I spoke of the frustrations and anger of the United Nations, aid donors, and NGOs over his government's continued obstruction of the humanitarian aid program. And I emphasized that Washington's anger over the execution of our employees in Juba would not blow over.

The essence of his response to me was that the charges against his government were baseless and the West was misinformed about the situation in his country. He defended what had been done in Juba and insisted that there were no violations of human rights in Sudan. He said, "We respect human rights in Sudan. . . . Perhaps our understanding of human rights differs from your government's."

He said that, for example, no prisoners were being tortured. There had been a few instances of torture in the early days after he came to power, but none since then. I said I had to disagree with him, for there was too much testimony from credible sources that torture continued to be inflicted. I told Bashir that, for example, I had talked to a man well known for his probity whose detailed account of how he had been tortured was totally believable.

Bashir said, "Give me the name of that person, and I will put a stop to any torture." "No one," he asserted, "will be harmed for speaking out."

"The man who was tortured might not see it that way," I answered. However, I told him, if a victim of torture gave me permission to use his or her name, I would inform Bashir accordingly.

He said he was astonished by my contention that there had been no progress toward democracy in Sudan over the preceding three years.

He insisted his government was gradually implementing democratic reforms. Totally at variance with detailed information the U.S. government possessed regarding the government's rigging of Sudan's most recent trade union elections, Bashir contended that those elections had been wholly democratic.

I then spent several minutes describing how his government was hampering the effectiveness of the relief program. After describing what I had seen on my trips to the transition zone, I suggested it would be useful for his government to put aside its differences with the INGOs and do everything possible to work together with them, the donors, and the United Nations to make the relief program more effective. Western governments would regard such a development with considerable favor.

President Bashir responded that some INGOs were in league with the Sudan People's Liberation Army. The International Red Cross was the worst offender. Inwardly groaning upon hearing this, I said it was inconceivable that the Red Cross, so respected throughout the world for its work, would take sides in the Sudanese civil war. Its neutrality in armed conflicts was well known. Bashir insisted his government had proof that the Red Cross was actively supporting the SPLA. I said I simply could not believe that.

Further talk about INGOs was similarly unproductive. He said indigenous NGOs had become more effective than their international counterparts. When I defended the competence and integrity of the INGOs, he responded with another sharp attack on them.

Despite lack of agreement on any of the issues we discussed, Bashir called our talk "the start of a dialogue." Commenting in a report to Washington, I said our exchange showed that it would be "a dialogue without much real communication." One positive outcome was his approval for the air evacuation of the USAID employees from Juba. Yet overall, Bashir, like Turabi and others, did "not really hear our message." I said Sudan and the United States continued to be on a collision course and that it remained to be seen whether the Sudanese pragmatists' desire for better relations with Washington would bring about some positive changes. Current circumstances, I said, did "not give rise to optimism on this score."

•  •  •

There had been no letup in the fighting in the South that fall. In fact there was an upsurge in November, although not in the far south around Juba, where rebel military activity had diminished. It appeared that Colonel John Garang, the leader of the largest faction among the rebels, had given up on his objective of capturing Juba. Another faction claimed responsibility for an attack farther north, at Malakal.

Before long the rains would end in the South. It was fully expected that the government would begin a major offensive at the onset of the dry season. The army had to wait until the rains ended because during the rainy season most roads were impassable, especially by large military vehicles. Only a tiny portion of Sudan's 2,500 miles of paved roads, which included the paved streets of Khartoum, were in the South.

The Nigerian government was trying to arrange for a second round of peace talks at Abuja, Nigeria's capital, between the Sudanese government and rebels. The first round of Nigerian-sponsored talks had taken place there in early 1992. Nobody I talked to in Khartoum was optimistic that the talks, known as Abuja II, would be held, much less succeed. However, others in Khartoum, and in Washington as well, believed Sudan's worsening economic situation, and consequent unrest among the people, would compel the government to make the concessions necessary for peace talks to succeed. This did not happen, though, because the government managed to get enough money to keep itself afloat and partially finance the war. Furthermore, Sudanese leaders were confident they had sufficient forces at their disposal to cope with any outbreak of popular discontent. I reported that their confidence was well founded.

From the government's standpoint, maintaining power by means of force would continue to be necessary, since the government lacked much popular support and had no prospects of turning around Sudan's unfavorable economic situation in the foreseeable future. The war would continue to be a drain on the economy. Prospects for significant improvement in agricultural production and commercial activity were poor that year. Aid from former friends, such as Saudi Arabia and Kuwait, had dried up after Sudan spoke out in support of Iraq in the Gulf War.

Khartoum hoped for substantial assistance from other friends. In 1990 Bashir and Libyan ruler Muammar al-Qaddafi signed a declaration calling for an alliance between Libya and Sudan. Although a true alliance was stillborn, Qaddafi's friendship paid off for the Sudanese in the form of subsidized Libyan oil. But in time the friendship waned. Qaddafi feared the spread of political Islam and recognized Sudan's, specifically Turabi's, influence in promoting it. Turabi made no attempt to hide his belief that Islamists in Libya would displace Qaddafi. The subsidized oil shipments ended in 1993.

Suffering from a foreign exchange shortage, the Sudanese government was hard-pressed to pay for oil imports. Each month saw it frantically dredging up enough foreign exchange to buy spot shipments of oil on the open market.

Iraq was Sudan's favored friend among the radical regimes in the Middle East. But the Sudanese were well aware that Iraq, weakened by the Gulf War and its aftermath, was in no position to provide them with substantial economic or military assistance.

Iran was the most promising source of important aid to Sudan. In February 1992 Iranian president Ali Akbar Hashemi Rafsanjani came to Khartoum to strengthen the growing ties between Iran and Sudan. Iran's objective of exporting its fundamentalist revolution was abetted by its relationship with Sudan, a relationship that helped the Iranians spread their ideology and influence in Africa. The Sudanese benefited from Iranian oil shipments, some deliveries of military aid, and Iran's agreement to guarantee payments to China, Sudan's principal source of arms.

However, as Turabi told me repeatedly, Sudan's association with Iran was not as close as many outsiders thought it was. The Sudanese had hoped to get a sweetheart deal on oil from Iran, but the Iranians viewed the oil transaction as strictly business and set a price per barrel that the Sudanese regarded as too high. Indeed, it was more than they could afford. Khartoum's failure to pay on time and in full increasingly annoyed Tehran. The Sudanese were disappointed by what they saw as meager levels of both military and economic aid from Iran, as well as by the tight terms the Iranians put on its oil exports to Sudan.

There was, in addition, a basic incompatibility between Iran and Sudan: Whereas over 90 percent of Iran's Muslims are Shias, almost all of Sudan's Muslims are Sunnis. Turabi and other Sudanese invariably mentioned this in conversations with me when the subject of Iran came up.

Despite their differences, both countries worked to keep relations from suffering any major damage. Sudan needed whatever assistance it could get from Iran, and as its estrangement from the West intensified it valued its ties with the Iranians all the more.

Reports appeared in the media that hundreds, even thousands of Iranians, many of them Revolutionary Guard military and security police advisers, had come to Sudan. Reports also persisted that the Iranians were training Palestinian, Egyptian, Algerian, and other radical Islamist terrorists at sites in Sudan, some of them quite large. The reports were based in part on information provided by Egyptian intelligence sources, which were conducting an assiduous disinformation campaign against Sudan. The truth was something far less alarming. There were Iranian advisers and technicians in Sudan, and Shiite propagandists and clerics as well, yet their numbers were relatively small, certainly nothing like the numbers being reported by the Western press.

• • •

As 1992 drew to a close, there was no discernible improvement in U.S.-Sudanese relations. The differences between the U.S. and Sudanese governments were so pronounced that they seemed to defy resolution. I met with a wide range of Sudanese and had many more talks with Sudanese officials, talks for the most part focusing on the poor state of relations. A lot of these conversations had a numbing repetitive quality to them, and now and then they left me feeling frustrated. Nonetheless, I believed I had to use every forum available to me to counter the flow of anti-American propaganda in the Sudanese media. I wanted to drive home to prominent persons in the government and the NIF the content and rationale of U.S. policy toward Sudan and to seek openings, however small, for reducing the tensions between Washington and Khartoum.

Our talks with knowledgeable Sudanese indicated to us at the embassy that the pressures, all of which I supported, that Washington and other governments were putting on Khartoum had given pause to those in power. They knew the international pressures on Sudan were hindering its economic development. Embassy officers and I used every opportunity to remind the Sudanese of this. Although moderates within the government wanted to do something to reduce or end those pressures, it was unclear how far they would be willing to go to

meet Western conditions. In any case, the moderates did not control
the government, and hard-line Islamists doggedly resisted changes of
the kind the West wanted to see take place.

At the conclusion of my November meeting with President Bashir,
we had agreed that I would set out in writing the U.S. concept of what
needed to be done to improve relations. I knew this would largely be
an exercise of repeating what others and I before me had already expressed to the Sudanese, but I thought something useful might come
from laying it out in written form and in some detail.

I drafted the letter, and after running it by my country team (embassy section heads and heads of other agencies), I cabled it to the
State Department for approval. This came in due course, and I sent the
letter on. At the end of November I got a reply. It came in a letter from
Foreign Minister Sahloul and was essentially a rejection of my suggestions and a reprise of what we had heard so many times from the Sudanese. Sahloul's letter maintained, for example, there were no human
rights violations in Sudan and U.S. information to the contrary was
untrue.

From the Sudanese standpoint, there was an internal logic to the arguments being made by the men running the country: Sudan was at
war, and in wartime the rights of individuals have to be abridged in favor of the survival of the state. History had shown that parliamentary
democracy was unsuitable for Sudan; a new form of democracy that
they deemed suitable for the Sudanese could be fashioned and implemented. The furtherance of Islam was morally correct and a duty.
Opening Sudan's borders to all Muslims was not abetting terrorism.

Nevertheless, this begged the question of their right to arrogate
unto themselves the power to run the country as they saw fit and to
determine its future. And if not ignoring, it passed off very lightly the
crimes committed in the name of state security that took or damaged
the lives of so many human beings.

I wrote the foreign minister that his letter seemed to bar the way to
any possibility for improving relations but that I was willing to keep a
dialogue going with him, as he recommended. Sahloul's letter, which,
from its tone and content, I doubted he had written, indicated that the
hard-liners were calling the shots.

A few days later I met with Sahloul and Sudan's ambassador to the
United States. I had mentioned to a mutual friend my doubts about

the letter's authorship. Sahloul said he was aware that I did not think he wrote it. He said I was correct. He then suggested we stop exchanging letters, which only tended to harden our respective positions. I said that was fine with me, reminding him, though, that it was President Bashir who had asked me to put my thoughts in writing.

He then brought up a resolution condemning Sudan that had been passed the previous day by the UN General Assembly's Committee on Social and Humanitarian Issues. The resolution, which received a vote of 127 for, 7 against, and 27 abstentions, accused Sudan of carrying out collective death sentences, detaining people without trial, hindering the relief effort, and causing thousands to flee to neighboring countries. The Sudanese UN delegation had tried but failed to sidetrack the resolution. The United States had initiated it and lobbied for its passage, but Sahloul refrained from mentioning that. He said the matter was over and done with and Sudan had to look to the future. His reaction was notably in contrast to that of the Sudanese press, which was full of impassioned articles and editorials inveighing against the resolution and against the United States for its role in getting it passed.

At the foreign minister's bidding, I repeated in some detail the reasons, as we saw them, for the bad relations between our two countries. This produced the usual defensive response. But Sahloul and the ambassador seemed to be agreeable to my suggestion for an independent assessment of the human rights situation in Sudan and also for an independent assessment of the elections process.

Later I brought up this suggestion in representations I made to others in the government, including Bashir. Although they indicated that such independent assessments would be possible, nothing ever came of this. It was one thing for the Sudanese to agree with me on this question, but quite another to actually do something about it.

Another idea I raised in the meeting with Sahloul, and repeatedly with other people in the government and the NIF, was that an end to the war would enhance prospects for improved relations with the United States. Many human rights abuses, for example, occurred because of the fighting in the South. Although the Sudanese generally agreed with me, as Sahloul did on this occasion, the government's attitude about the war remained unchanged.

Near the end of our talk, the execution of the USAID employees in Juba came up. I told Sahloul his government had badly mishandled the whole business. I said I was skeptical that the recently appointed commission to investigate what happened in Juba would produce anything more than a whitewash. He assured me the commission would conduct an honest investigation.

As I was leaving his office, Sahloul said he planned to gather together some other high-level officials to continue the kind of discussion we had just had.

• • •

Congressional delegations often are a burden to American embassies in countries of great importance to U.S. interests or located in attractive cities having fine hotels and superior sightseeing opportunities. No doubt most visitors from the House and Senate are serious and want to learn as much as they can. Some, though, are little more than junketeers who show little interest in the issues at hand. Regardless of the circumstances, embassies and consulates have to devote considerable time and resources to making arrangements for the visits of members of Congress. In some places the visits draw heavily on those resources, which have been steadily decreased by congressional budget cuts.

All this notwithstanding, I would have welcomed congressional delegations; it would have been useful to have the Sudanese hear the views of elected U.S. officials. However, Khartoum was not a place that attracted visitors from Capitol Hill, and no congressional delegation came to Khartoum while I was assigned to Sudan. Separately two congressmen, Frank Wolf of Virginia and Harry Johnson of Florida, flew into southern Sudan, but they did not make it to the North. The Sudanese government therefore denounced them.

Also during my time in Sudan, only a handful of senior visitors from the Bush and Clinton administrations came to Khartoum. The State Department believed visits by administration VIPs would be interpreted and publicized by the Sudanese as a sign that relations were on the mend. Sure enough, when visits did take place they were cast in that light by the Sudanese government.

That December the assistant secretary of state for African affairs, Herman Cohen, came to Khartoum. His mission was to get support from the countries of the region for the UN Security Council action that brought a military force, including U.S. troops, to Somalia. The

Sudanese had reacted at first with hostile statements about the U.S. military presence. But not long before Cohen arrived in Khartoum, the foreign minister had assured me Sudan understood the need for U.S. troops and had no objections.

During Cohen's one day in Khartoum, he and I had meetings with the foreign minister, three other top officials, and the president. In each of the five meetings, after a brief discussion of Somalia, the Sudanese turned to the issue of bilateral relations with the United States. Their theme in all these talks was much the same as what I had been hearing: Why was the United States picking on Sudan? Couldn't we understand that they did not commit human rights violations? Our information about Sudan was composed largely of lies and rumors.

Although Bashir told Cohen that he accepted the idea of an independent evaluation of Sudan's human rights performance, nothing of consequence came from the assistant secretary's visit to Khartoum.

•  •  •

Having our families with us was a blessing for embassy Americans who were accompanied by spouses and children. In early 1991, fearing terrorist attacks in retaliation for U.S. actions against Iraq, the State Department had ordered the evacuation of all dependents and almost all U.S. personnel with the embassy. Most who left were angered by the evacuation order, which they believed was totally uncalled-for. Even after they returned, about a year later, Deputy Assistant Secretary of State Robert Houdek, who visited Khartoum, reported to Washington that morale continued to be a problem at the embassy.

After having been in Khartoum for several weeks, I concluded that, as far as I could tell, by then morale was good. However, I knew that Larry Benedict, other embassy officers, and I needed regularly to address this and do all we could to keep the American community's spirits up. Julie, who was happy in her job teaching at the American School, and Larry's wife, Gloria, played key roles in this. For example, they organized a Thanksgiving dinner for seventy people at our house and a Christmas party for all the embassy employees, Sudanese and Americans. About 200 people came to the house at noon for food and drinks.

In January Larry took the lead in arranging a drive out into the desert to the sixth cataract of the Nile, about two hours north of Khartoum. Later, a two-day trip was made to and from the pyramids farther north at MeroEB. These kinds of events helped keep morale high, even in the face of events that seriously disrupted the lives of all of us later on.

•   •   •

That month the dialogue aimed at improving U.S.-Sudanese relations was institutionalized. As he had promised earlier, Foreign Minister Sahloul invited me and members of my staff to a meeting attended by a half-dozen Sudanese officials. At the meeting we agreed to hold formal meetings every two weeks and to focus on one or two problems at a time. From the start it became apparent to Larry Benedict, Political Counselor Lucien Vandenbroucke, and me that the meetings would not iron out any of the major differences between the two governments. We could not understand why the minister and his colleagues seemed to believe that somehow the power of their arguments could prevail, leading the United States to see the wisdom of changing its policies toward Sudan.

The first of the formal talks, chaired by Sahloul, took place in his conference room at the ministry. He was joined by some aides and, a couple of times, by one or two other cabinet ministers. As Benedict, Vandenbroucke, and I had anticipated, neither this nor subsequent meetings produced tangible results. Still, we thought they were a mechanism that might at some point be useful if circumstances changed.

The Sudanese said they saw progress. For example, they told us they now realized Washington was not hostile to Sudan because of the Sudanese government's Islamic character. Why it took them so long to grasp this mystified me, for I had been repeating it over and over again for more than four months. But, I figured, if they seemed to glean from the formal talks that the United States was not anti-Islamic,[1] well and good.

As a rule, the sessions were conducted in a polite atmosphere, yet occasionally there was some heat. At one meeting, after I had brought up the human rights issue, the minister of finance angrily charged that the United States was "engaged in economic warfare" against Sudan and walked out. The series of talks continued, increasingly less frequently, noticeably so after a new foreign minister was appointed. The Sudanese dropped them entirely later in the year, when U.S.-Sudanese relations plunged to a new low.

These and many other discussions with the Sudanese about bilateral relations consumed a fair amount of my time. I put in even more hours on matters relating to the humanitarian assistance program, especially when I chaired the donor group. The chairmanship rotated among the four leading donors—the United States, the European Community, Great Britain, and the Netherlands—and it was my turn in January. As chairman I represented the donors at weekly meetings with UN agencies. I also met with government officials and called the donors together when necessary. Unfortunately, the necessity arose only too often.

To say the least, neither the current and earlier governments nor the rebels had been fully cooperative in the relief effort. Among other things, government officials had denied clearances for relief shipments, charging that food and medicines destined for the displaced in the South ended up in the hands of the rebels. The rebels had also been obstructive, alleging that the Sudanese army had seized relief supplies.

To a degree, both the government and the rebels were right, for some of the relief supplies were stolen by the military of both sides. Most of it, however, was not, and the extent of the delays and obstructions imposed by the government and the rebels was not justified.

The most immediate problem facing us at the beginning of January was the severe difficulties many international NGOs themselves were experiencing in trying to operate in Sudan. The anti-INGO sentiments within the Sudanese leadership had led to harassment of various kinds, causing the local heads of some INGOs to wonder whether they would have to leave Sudan. Some of them complained that the United Nations was not firmly representing INGOs in seeking a relaxation of government restrictions.

In the four months I had been in Sudan, there had been one incident after another involving INGOs: The government withheld travel documents, hampering INGOs from sending workers to projects upcountry. Applications for visas for incoming personnel were delayed or not granted. Some relief workers were under surveillance and at times hassled by the security police. And the government turned down requests to initiate new relief projects in areas where a clear need existed.

The donor countries and UN organizations were confronted with a real dilemma. We all were trying through the relief effort to save the lives of thousands of Sudanese who had been displaced by the war. At times these people, along with many others, were also victims of drought. To help those in need, we had to work with both the Sudanese government and the rebels. Of necessity, this requirement limited the scope of what we could do in response to egregious acts committed by either the government or the rebels in the context of the relief effort.

At one point it seemed that the days of some of the INGOs in Sudan were numbered. But representations by the donors and visiting high-level UN officials, along with the apparent desire of the government to improve its relations with the United States and other Western countries, gave rise to hope that the worst of the problems of the IN-GOs could be resolved. Indeed, in time the overall operating environment for INGOs improved, although some continued to have serious difficulties in dealing with the government. Things got so bad for Concern that finally, months later, it reluctantly decided to leave Sudan.

• • •

January brought more meetings with Turabi, Bashir, and Sahloul, but nothing new came from them. It also brought a momentary return of high temperatures and with them an infestation of crickets at our house. Outside was no problem. Inside was another matter, as dozens of them got into our bedroom a couple of nights. We scurried about, picking up as many as we could and tossing them downstairs. Brian seemed to enjoy the sport. Soon winter reasserted itself and the crickets disappeared.

When Washington says or does something that deeply angers U.S. adversaries in the Middle East, the risks of terrorist attacks on Americans abroad, especially official Americans, are magnified. Generally the danger is most acute in or near the Middle East itself, but embassies and consulates far away from the Middle East can become targets. In 1991 in Harare, when I was chargé d'affaires, Iraqi terrorists were apprehended while making preparations to strike at the embassy. In 1998 terrorists succeeded in carrying out the terrible bombings of the U.S. embassies in Nairobi and Dar es Salaam. Those tragedies revealed once again the vulnerability of the U.S. and foreign national employees working in our embassies and consulates throughout the world.

In Khartoum in early January 1993 we had to do what we could to make our tight security precautions even tighter, following a U.S. attack on antiaircraft missile sites in Iraq. I had the embassy's emergency action committee consider what additional measures we could take to bolster security. We implemented their findings after I reviewed them. Because we had to live in a tight security environment, the new situation did not mean any changes for me, Julie, or Brian, except that Brian had to stay away from the Blue Nile recreation center, where he went to swim and get together with friends. The embassy advised all Americans to avoid gathering together there or elsewhere for the time being.

Later that month I accepted an invitation to speak to the Sudanese Center for Strategic Studies about U.S. foreign policy, with an emphasis on U.S.-Sudanese relations. I saw this as an opportunity to reach a wider audience of influential Sudanese and to present them with a candid exposition of why the U.S. and Sudanese governments differed so much on a variety of issues. There was a large turnout at Friendship Hall when I gave the talk. Apart from some predictable attacks on what I said, most of the questions and comments from the audience were objective and not posed antagonistically. Later I heard from Sudanese friends, several of whom were there, that many in the audience were surprised and favorably impressed that I had spoken as candidly as I had.

We continued to get indications that the government wanted better relations with the United States and that some officials understood this would not happen unless there were significant changes in the way Sudan was governed. A few people in the government and even the NIF were telling me I was making a difference. That may have been nice to hear, but I did not put much stock in it. In reality, whether or not influential Sudanese were listening to me and sincerely wanted better relations with the United States, the deep freeze in relations that took place following the killings in Juba had not yet begun to thaw.

There were times when I briefly wondered if it was worthwhile continuing in a job that had such great frustrations when Julie and Brian and I could have been settling down somewhere back in the States. Yet there were other times, much more frequent, when I was stimulated by my work, such as when I was faced with difficult circumstances and made a decision that only I, as the ambassador, could make; or when I thought something through and made a proposal to Washington and, in so doing, was satisfied with my reasoning and conclusions; or when I traveled to places like the transition zone to see, assess, and report what was happening there.

In short, I was glad to be in Sudan and to be engaged, to be doing something that for me and for Julie still had considerable meaning. Moreover, even in a difficult place like Sudan, we still felt at home in Africa.

# 8

# Into Southern Sudan

The situation of many of the hundreds of thousands of southern Sudanese displaced by the war, awful to begin with in late 1992, worsened as the months went by. This caught the attention of the international press every once in a while, although usually not for long. In February 1993 *Washington Post* correspondent Keith Richburg wrote that "relief workers, U.S. officials and others are calling strife-torn southern Sudan 'another Somalia.' . . . Television pictures emerging from southern Sudan are eerily similar to the images that six months ago made Somali towns such as Baidoa and Baadheere synonymous with mass starvation; emaciated people, stick-like limbs, the hollow eyes of malnourished children."[1]

Some of the increased suffering was a result of advances made by the Sudanese army, as it took towns and villages that had fallen to the rebels during the SPLA's military successes of 1990–1991. However, most of the new additions to the toll of death, destruction, and displacement of southerners came about because of internecine fighting among southerners themselves. In the early 1990s some of SPLA leader John Garang's officers broke away from him and the SPLA and formed a rival political and military force. For a time the two opposing armies were known as SPLA-Torit, headed by Garang, and SPLA-Nasir, led by Riek Machar. Later the two factions changed their names to SPLA-Mainstream and SPLA-United, respectively.[2] (Even later, dissension within the two factions spawned more divisions within the rebel movement.) In 1992–1993 battles between the two factions not only directly led to increased civilian casualties but also indirectly caused the deaths of thousands, for the relief operation was hampered by both the fighting and the restrictions on access imposed by the two rebel forces and the government of Sudan.

Early in February my ailing mother's health took a turn for the worse, and I went to California for a couple of weeks. Shortly after my return to Khartoum I flew to Nairobi and from there into southern Sudan. I had given a lot of thought to the southern Sudan problem while I was flying to Khartoum from Washington and had decided that I should travel into the South.

This would be breaking new ground, for diplomats in Khartoum did not travel to the war zone in the South or to areas held by the SPLA.

I needed to see conditions there at firsthand to be able to give Washington, and my donor-country colleagues in Khartoum, a better appreciation of what was happening. I also thought that by going to the South I would be in a better position to advise Washington on how to respond more effectively to the humanitarian needs arising from the war. Perhaps, as well, media coverage of an ambassador's trips into southern Sudan would focus more attention on the true extent of the disaster there. I and others felt there was a hidden crisis in southern Sudan that was being ignored by the outside world.

Accompanied by Philip O'Brien[3]—the UN official in charge of Operation Lifeline Sudan (OLS), the relief program in southern Sudan[4]— and five other people, I went to nine places in Equatoria and Upper Nile provinces between February 27 and March 3. We saw thousands of people displaced by the war, many of them close to death from starvation or disease. We met with the leaders of the SPLA-Mainstream and SPLA-United factions, local officials, Sudanese army officers, church people, relief workers, and UN personnel. By plane and car, we covered hundreds of miles. We encountered human misery of the worst kind and an aid program that needed improvement. I had seen this kind of tragedy before—in Somalia—and knew what to expect. Yet that did not make it any easier to witness the awful physical condition of so many people, and so many of them little children.

Our planned four-day trip turned into five when the chartered airplane that was going to pick us up at a village in northern Uganda did not show up. This forced us to spend the night there and then drive back into southern Sudan, where a UN plane was able to locate us and take us back to Kenya.

In a cable sent from Nairobi on March 4, I told Washington that the trip "into Equatoria and Upper Nile provinces has confirmed my belief that a more intense and effective humanitarian relief program is urgently needed." The USAID cable reporting on the trip noted that in Ayod, Upper Nile, "About ten people were dying each day and . . . there were very few children under five years of age still alive." In the nearby town of Kongor, the approximately 300 people there "were all suffering from severe malnutrition. . . . There is little hope that those remaining in Kongor can survive unless an intensive feeding program is established right away."

In Upper Nile province there was a triangular area whose base ran west to east between Ayod and Waat in the north and whose apex was at Kongor in the south. This area began to be called the "starvation triangle." The most recent fighting in the triangle, which resulted in the starvation of thousands of civilians, was between the two SPLA factions.

In my March 4 cable I reported that during a meeting at a village called Ulang six days earlier "Riek Machar and his colleagues with whom we spoke were categorical in stating that his faction [would] not budge from its insistence on total separation of the South from the North." For their part, John Garang and his followers were arguing for fundamental changes in the relationship between the North and the South, but within the framework of a united Sudan.

The heart of the animosity between Garang and Riek, though, was not their political views. It was their mutual dislike and distrust. Riek had been with Garang for eight years when in 1991, after a failed bid to supplant the SPLA leader, Riek split from Garang and he and his followers formed their own military-political organization. Neither of the two SPLA factions was ethnically exclusive, although the majority of Garang's faction were Dinka, the largest ethnic group in southern Sudan, and Riek's were Nuer, the second largest.

As I sat talking with Riek in Ulang, just thirty yards away from us about 100 terribly emaciated women, children, and old men were huddled. A group brought a man's body a few feet closer to us and laid it on the ground. As my party and I were walking back to our airplane, I said to Riek's well-fed and well-clothed lieutenants that surely ending the factional fighting and thereby relieving the suffering of people like those we had seen was more important than continuing to fight over political or ideological differences. Not so, they replied; adhering to principles outweighed any other considerations. Angered, I said I totally disagreed with them.

Their response was hypocritical as well as callous. It illustrated that the root cause of the factional dispute was a struggle for power—to seize or retain the leadership of the rebel movement. When I saw Garang in Uganda, on the night of February 28, I found him to be as inflexible as Riek on the question of putting aside their differences in order to end the fighting. Fighting the enemy, whether the government or another rebel faction, took precedence, and neither Garang nor Riek saw anything wrong with taking relief food meant for starving civilians and using it to feed soldiers and officials.

In Nairobi on March 4 I held a press conference. My purpose was to underline the need for an accelerated and improved relief program and to stress the need for a negotiated settlement of the war. Some of what I said, taken out of context and appearing in media reports that reached Khartoum, gave Sudanese officials heartburn, adding to their irritation that I had gone into the South without asking them first (I had informed the Foreign Ministry but had not asked for permission).[5] When they saw the full text of what I said to the press in Nairobi, however, their annoyance dissipated.

I was disappointed that the correspondents for major U.S. newspapers who were based in Nairobi were out of town, for I knew that as a result there would not be much coverage of the trip in the U.S. press. BBC coverage was good, though, and Canadian and U.S. public radio interviewed me. Apparently influenced by what I had done, other ambassadors in Khartoum were saying they intended to try to go to the South. So in a limited way my trip was useful in directing more attention to the problem. And Washington had my report and recommendations, which would be considered in a policy review later that month.

Throughout my years in Africa I had enjoyed useful, symbiotic relations with journalists. Generally, anything I said to them was either for background or off the record. In Sudan, however, I decided I could more ably counter the Sudanese government's propaganda and also be more effective in drawing attention to the dreadful situation in south-ern Sudan by going on record when journalists interviewed me.

Because of an emergency involving one of our children, Julie had gone to the United States. It became clear to me that while I was away on the trip to southern Sudan, thirteen-year-old Brian had been lonely, even though he had stayed with a nice family in my absence. He needed me around while Julie was gone. For that reason, the next time I traveled—later that month to Cairo, where I had to go to confer with the ambassador and other officers of our embassy there and some offi-cials of the Egyptian government—I limited my stay to two days.

My talks with the Egyptians highlighted for me that the Egyptian government had ambivalent feelings about Sudan. In 1989 they had welcomed the ouster of Sadiq al-Mahdi, whose foreign policy they dis-liked and whose aims they distrusted. But before long they changed their attitude about Sudan's new rulers. They deplored the arrests of politicians who had favored close ties to Egypt. As the Islamist lean-ings of the military junta became apparent, the Egyptians worried that Khartoum might foster the spread of political Islam to Egypt as well as to other Middle Eastern countries. And they regularly condemned Su-dan for abetting Iranian terrorism. They detested Turabi and, appar-ently either not knowing or unwilling to admit to themselves how powerful Turabi was, urged Bashir to dissociate himself from Turabi and the NIF.

At the same time, however, the Egyptians did not want to see the advent of an independent state in southern Sudan. Their historical concern about control of the Nile and their uncertainty about what policies a southern Sudanese government might develop about the use of Nile waters in its territory came through loud and clear in talks I had with a foreign ministry official and with the head of Egypt's secu-rity apparatus.

Because of its concerns about the Nile, Egypt did not provide mili-tary aid to the southern rebels (at least not during my three years in Sudan), despite Cairo's distaste for the Islamist government in Khar-toum.

• • •

On March 9, a few days after I returned from southern Sudan and Kenya, I went to the office of the new foreign minister, Hussein

Suleiman Abu Salih. I wasn't looking forward to the meeting. I had dealt with him before on noncontentious issues when he was minister of social welfare. On those occasions he had done nothing that gave substance to his reputation for having a short fuse. For this first meeting with him in his new job, I would have preferred to stay within the bounds of a courtesy call in order to start off on a cordial basis. However, the State Department, responding to inquiries from Congress, instructed me to raise with him two human rights cases. I knew I was going to take some heat.

After briefing him on my trip to the South and discussing the less than glowing prospects for the Nigerian peace talks, I turned to human rights issues. As instructed, I brought up the case of retired Brigadier General Camillo Odong N. Loyak, who had been tortured and beaten to death while in detention in Khartoum. I had sent a letter earlier to President Bashir requesting information about Camillo, as he was known, but had received no response.

I told Abu Salih the U.S. government had credible evidence of how Camillo had been killed. Showing some annoyance, the minister said he had no information on this and did not know whether Camillo was killed in battle or had died in some other manner. I said it was clear that he had been beaten to death, and I asked for a reply to the letter to Bashir.

Continuing, I said, "We also have reliable information that Father David Tombe, a Catholic priest, was tortured while he was being held by security police in Juba."

"Has he been released?" Abu Salih asked. I replied that he had been but that the issue was one of his mistreatment while he was in detention.

Bristling, Abu Salih said any Sudanese who claimed to be mistreated by the authorities was free to make a formal complaint using existing legal procedures. I said the Camillo and Tombe cases added to the weight of the human rights accusations against Sudan. Testily, he declared, "The government of Sudan will never accept outside political pressures designed to make Sudan get down on its knees." He said Sudan was being singled out unjustly, that there were human rights violations everywhere in the world. Why the discrimination against Sudan?

I was frequently confronted with this argument when the topic of human rights came up, and my response was to emphasize that Sudan's human rights record was deplorable by any standard and that the Sudanese government should look to its own practices and stop citing the records of other countries. I told Abu Salih this and also told him it was a fact that the Sudanese government continued to allow serious violations to occur, as shown by the cases of Camillo, Father Tombe, and a journalist recently arrested.

Angrily and bitterly, Abu Salih insisted that Sudan was "far better than other countries." He said, "There is a conspiracy against Sudan." When I denied that, he declared, "The times of colonialism are over," and, by maintaining a frosty silence, he indicated the meeting was over. He did not shake my hand or even say good-bye when I left his office.

Démarches of this kind, on specific human rights violations, sometimes apparently had a positive effect. I say "apparently" because as a rule we were unable to be sure that our representations were a factor when the government's maltreatment of individuals was ended or reduced. But there were times when improvements took place very soon after our démarches.

My relationship with Abu Salih suffered no lasting damage from our first encounter. He blew up at me on other occasions, in reaction to some of the topics I raised, but he usually cooled down before the particular meeting was over. For the most part, we had reasonably agreeable discussions carried out in a cordial atmosphere. When I saw him at receptions I made it a point to seek him out and talk about noncontroversial matters. I was genuinely interested in his political and medical careers—he had been a neurosurgeon when he entered politics—and asked him questions about his training and life as a surgeon, as well as about his rise in politics. He seemed pleased by my show of interest.

Human rights came up again on April 5, when Larry Benedict and I met with President Bashir and Abu Salih at Bashir's office at Friendship Hall. I called their attention to a passage in a letter to Bashir from President Clinton that had made a positive reference to the peace talks and had asked Bashir if a date had been set for Abuja II. This attempt at opening the meeting on a high note fell flat, for Bashir's response was to accuse European Community countries of pressing Garang to sabotage the peace talks.

The rest of our talk, which centered on points the Clinton letter had raised about the problems in U.S.-Sudanese relations, was largely unproductive. Bashir said the specific human rights violations I cited to him were fabrications of opponents of his government, and he denied that any such violations at all occurred in Sudan. When I urged, as I had done previously, that outside observers be allowed to come to Sudan to look into the human rights situation, Bashir replied that Gaspar Biro, the UN Human Rights Commission's special rapporteur for Sudan, would be coming. (Biro did come to Sudan. His report on his findings was highly critical of what was happening there. The government denounced Biro and eventually labeled him an enemy of Islam and proscribed him from reentering Sudan.)

Bashir's distaste for the OLS relief program headquartered in Kenya was evident. When I said I might soon travel into the South via the UN base at the Kenyan town of Lokichokio, close to Sudan's southeastern border, he suggested it would be more cost-effective to deliver relief supplies to the South by barge and road through northern Sudan rather than by air from Kenya and Uganda. I agreed but pointed out that this could be done only if a permanent cease-fire was in place, permitting the establishment of the necessary infrastructure for increased operations from the North.

During that meeting with Bashir, Abu Salih said that agreement had been reached within the government to speed up implementation of an NGO agreement. A circular was being sent to all NGOs, inviting them to sign individual agreements with the newly created Commission on Voluntary Agencies. This was welcome news, and for a time it seemed that UN and Western representations to the Sudanese government regarding the overall humanitarian aid program were beginning to have an effect.

The more cooperative attitude was flawed, particularly with regard to the need for INGOs to operate in the transition zone. Still, things appeared to be moving in a better direction. Unfortunately, however, a new outbreak of fighting among rebel factions broke out in late March, further complicating the difficult task of getting food and medicines into the South.

• • •

That spring, Western news media again gave some brief attention to Sudan. In part this came about because the United Nations and donor countries were giving prominence to the humanitarian crisis in the South. It was also a result of a decision by the Sudanese government, which, in an attempt to improve its image, for a time eased its restrictions on the entry of Western print and television journalists into the country.

Just about every reporter who came to Khartoum wanted to see Hasan al-Turabi, and most got the interviews they sought. Doug Struck of the *Baltimore Sun* wrote that Turabi "clearly relishes thumbing his nose at the West, which he blames for spreading lies about Sudan." Struck reported that

> Sudan's leaders chafe at the West's complaints about human rights violations. "Americans don't know much about the world," said Mr. al-Turabi, who holds no title but is the acknowledged leader behind the military government of Gen. Omar Hassan Ahmed al-Bashir. "If someone tells them something, they publish it. There are no massacres. These are just tribal fights. It's not serious."

According to Struck, however, what he heard from other Sudanese and what he saw for himself gave lie to what Turabi had said.[6]

Most reporters focused less on Turabi than on the suffering of southerners. For example, Kim Murphy of the *Los Angeles Times* wrote of the plight of the people of Bor, about 100 miles south of Kongor. After floods and cattle disease had left them destitute, "In December last year, the raids began—vicious fighting between rival tribal factions that led to the theft of the rest of the cattle and the slaughter of most of Bor's remaining men. The women, children and elders remaining there were walking bones, people on the brink of starvation."[7]

This kind of reporting was a reflection of a reality that UN experts were describing as the most urgent need for emergency assistance in the world.[8]

The increased press coverage soon ended, however, and the conflict in southern Sudan again became the "forgotten war," as some termed it. Yet the greater attention, however short-lived, may have helped keep the flow of emergency aid coming in. Many officials in Washington, especially in the Office of Foreign Disaster Assistance but others as well, were unstinting in their efforts to come up with adequate resources for Sudan. The United States, by far the largest donor of humanitarian assistance, had good reason to be proud of its role in the relief program, which was keeping countless thousands of southern Sudanese, mainly women and children, alive.

In late April I made another trip to Kenya and southern Sudan, accompanied again by OFDA director Jim Kunder, USAID Khartoum's director, Gary Mansavage, USAID officers from Washington and Kenya, and UN officials. On the twenty-third, before leaving Nairobi for southern Sudan, Kunder and I, along with American embassy officers, met separately with leaders of the two major SPLA factions. Alarmed by the enormity of the disaster in southern Sudan and the sometimes precarious situation of relief workers, State Department and USAID officials in Washington had put together talking points for me to draw on in discussions with the rebels.

I told both groups that I was speaking to them on instructions from Washington, where there was growing concern about the situation in the South. I said the greatest threat to southerners currently was intra-SPLA fighting. To ensure delivery of relief assistance, all fighting had to come to an end; otherwise additional thousands of innocent civilians would die.

John Garang had come to Nairobi and was present when we met with the SPLA-Mainstream delegation. Like most Dinka, he is tall, well over six feet, but unlike most Dinka, he is not thin. Garang was born in Upper Nile in 1945 and attended high school in Tanzania, where he made a lifelong friend in Yoweri Museveni, now president of Uganda. After getting a bachelor of science degree at Grinnel College in Iowa in 1971, Garang returned to Sudan to join the rebels in their war against the central government.

When a peace agreement was signed in 1972 he became a captain in the Sudanese army. He went back to the United States in 1977 and four years later earned a Ph.D. from Iowa State University. Returning to Sudan again, he was an active-duty colonel when the civil war broke out again. Sent to Bor in May 1983 to put down a revolt of an army unit, Garang instead joined the rebels. Very soon afterward, he became the leader of the SPLA.

Kunder and I told Garang that because of their attack on Kongor, he and his organization were being strongly criticized in the United States. The SPLA-Mainstream's destruction of UN compounds in Kongor, Ayod, and nearby Yuai was yet another sign of a total disregard for the relief program and the needs of his own people. I said continued fighting in the area was nothing less than criminal.

Garang, a well-spoken man, is a master at avoiding answering difficult questions. He devoted most of his response to revisiting the past sins of Khartoum, attacking his SPLA rivals, and accusing the United Nations and INGOs of partiality. Finally, in response to a specific request, he said he would guarantee security for a proposed convoy of trucks carrying relief supplies from Lokichokio to Kongor.⁹

I passed on to Garang Washington's urging that he attend the Abuja II talks. Although the State Department was not sanguine about the talks' prospects, it considered the Nigerian effort the only viable chance to end the Sudanese war. When Garang equivocated, I pressed him, and he finally admitted he had no plans to attend and preferred to remain "in reserve" unless Bashir attended. I said this seemed to be gamesmanship and that he should do whatever he could to end the fighting. Washington, I said, perceived him as being disinclined to negotiate seriously. He insisted he was but said Khartoum's intentions could not be trusted. (Garang did attend the tail end of the Abuja II talks, but like the earlier round at Abuja, the talks failed.)¹⁰

Simon Mori Didumo, SPLA-United's humanitarian affairs secretary, headed the other rebel delegation that Jim Kunder and I met with in Nairobi. Like Garang, Mori seemed more interested in casting blame than in helping find ways to end the fighting. He expressed total distrust of Garang. Also like Garang, Mori accused INGOs of partiality, telling us that a Norwegian Peoples' Aid (NPA) convoy had delivered food to help feed Garang's army. Having spent time in the field with NPA workers and seen how much they were helping destitute people, I told Mori he was mistaken.¹¹

Again I could see that neither faction was interested in making any concession to the other side in order to end the fighting and save many of their own people's lives as a result.

Kunder and I and our party left Nairobi early the next morning. Our first stop was Torit, a town in Equatoria that had been under the control of the Sudanese army since they retook it from the SPLA the previous October. At that time, the provincial commissioner told us, the only inhabitants remaining in Torit were fifty-three elderly people too infirm to flee. Once convinced it would be safe and that some food might be obtained there, some 12,000 people filtered back into the town and its immediately surrounding area.

The commissioner said there was hunger in Torit but no starvation. Compared to other people I had seen in the South, the inhabitants of Torit appeared to be in relatively good physical condition. Nevertheless, they were far from well-off and were totally dependent on food brought in from nearby Juba or by air from Kenya.

From Torit we flew north to Kongor in Upper Nile, where I had visited six weeks earlier. In the interval, Garang's SPLA-Mainstream had driven Riek's SPLA-United force out of Kongor. It was likely that the starving displaced people I saw there in March were now dead. They had been replaced by thousands of Dinka, mostly from the Bor area, who had come for food and whatever else international relief workers had available. They badly needed clothing, for instance; most were scantily clad in rags.

In Kongor the relief workers, who belonged to Concern and Goal, another Irish INGO, were doing heroic work. Because of the lack of security in the area, they could not stay there overnight and were flown in and out from Lokichokio. Kunder and I wanted to fly to the nearby town of Waat, but because one of the rebel commanders said he would shoot down any aircraft that approached Waat, the United Nations decided we should not go there.

The next day we flew back to Equatoria, to the town of Nimule, just north of the Ugandan border. From there we drove an hour north to a displaced-persons camp, one that I had gone to on my previous visit. It was sad to see that the poor conditions in the camp—insufficient food and shelter and an extreme scarcity of medicines, for example—had not improved. The United Nations and some INGOs had completed a plan of action and were on the verge of implementing it. One reason it had taken so much time to get the plan underway was that the United Nations had pulled out of the area several months earlier when three UN relief workers and a journalist were killed by a rebel force. Only now were UN personnel returning.

Back in Nairobi on April 26, I held a press conference, as I had in March. I leveled most of my criticism at the rebel factions, emphasizing that their attacks on each other were interrupting the relief effort and that as a result many people had starved to death.

Sudanese newspapers, reflecting the government's views, chose to put a negative slant on my remarks, however. They zeroed in on the last sentence of my press statement. I had said that if there was no progress toward a negotiated settlement at Abuja, "the international community will have to consider what can and should be done to end the awful suffering of the people of southern Sudan." The papers accused me of calling for outside military intervention, and one of them suggested I should be declared persona non grata. But once again when I got back to Khartoum, I found government officials' anger had cooled after they had seen the full text of my remarks.

• • •

Julie returned from California on May 3, and of course Brian and I were happy to have her back home. The day before I had gone back to the transition zone. I flew to two towns, Abyei and Meiram, in southern Kordofan province about 400 or 500 miles southwest of Khartoum. The return trip was a bit wearing; for some reason the convection currents generated by the heat were stronger than usual, tossing the airplane about more than the passengers liked.

I wanted to see if conditions in the displaced-persons camps near the two towns warranted making another plea to the government to allow international relief workers to go there. The donors, as well as the United Nations and INGOs, continued to have every reason to believe that the displaced in the transition zone were suffering unnecessarily as a result of government restrictions on the INGOs.

As I expected, conditions at Abyei and Meiram were not good: Food deliveries had been delayed, serious malnutrition was prevalent, and health clinics were short of medicines and trained personnel. The mortality rate among new arrivals from the South was high. The situation of the people in these towns was better than the worst of what I saw in my trips to southern Sudan, yet it was bad enough to spur me to try again to get the government to change its policy on INGO access. It took many months before those of us who persisted in this finally had some limited success: The government at last permitted several INGO personnel to carry out relief work in the transition zone. However, they were far too few to meet the needs adequately.

• • •

No agreement was reached at the Abuja II peace talks, which opened April 26 and lasted into May. Instead of flying from Kenya to Nigeria to participate in the talks, John Garang went to the United States. His visit included a few days in Washington, where he saw the new assistant secretary of state for African affairs, George Moose, as well as other officials and two members of Congress. Moose appealed to Garang to attend the Abuja talks, and Garang agreed. But when he got to Abuja, he did not take part in the negotiations, which ended in failure again.

Soon thereafter the Sudanese government claimed the SPLA-Mainstream delegation had been on the point of signing an agreement when Garang arrived and vetoed the deal. Ignoring what I told them about the Moose-Garang meeting in Washington, the government concluded that the U.S. government had given Garang instructions to scuttle the talks. No matter how often and how insistently I told them this was false, they repeated the allegation throughout the rest of my assignment in Sudan, and they continued to do so after I departed.

With the failure of Abuja II, there seemed to be no way soon to end either the overall war or the fighting between the Garang's SPLA-Mainstream and Riek's SPLA-United factions, still the current cause of the worst suffering in the South. The most acute problem continued to be in the starvation triangle in Upper Nile, where interfactional fighting had virtually closed down relief operations.

In Khartoum in mid-May I met with leading figures among the southerners who lived in the city. At one meeting, Abel Alier, a vice president in the national government during the Numeiry years, said he feared the unsuccessful ending to the Abuja talks would result in a heating up of the war in the South, where a temporary cease-fire between the government and the SPLA was in place. I told him and the others at the meeting that the rumors around town of outside intervention to end the war had no basis in fact. They said that they and other influential southerners would renew efforts to get the SPLA factions to stop their infighting.[12]

Alier said he thought it would be useful for me to talk again with the leaders of the two factions, especially Riek. He said, however, that although I had successfully made "two risky trips to the South," I should not go see Riek if doing so would put me in danger. I replied that on my previous trips I had flown in UN aircraft, which did not fly

into any areas that UN authorities or the pilots considered too dangerous. If I went to the South again, the same precautions would apply.

In a cable to the State Department I proposed to make the trip. I said
that before leaving I would meet with the foreign minister to urge the
Sudanese government to forgo new military activities, which would
have a drastic effect on civilians. Also, I would inform him of my intention to go to Nairobi and into the South to try to get the SPLA factions to honor the current cease-fire fully and stop their infighting,
which was causing so much suffering to civilians. The Department
agreed with my proposal.

I told Abu Salih of my intention to try to broker a cease-fire in the
starvation triangle. I said this was a further indication of Washington's
deep desire to see an end to the fighting in the South so that the humanitarian relief effort could be carried out as effectively as possible.
Abu Salih indicated he approved, adding that the government of Sudan
would prefer to deal with a reunited SPLA rather than with different
factions.

Some in the government seemed to support reunification of the
SPLA, and this became the government's announced policy. Other,
more powerful individuals, whose will prevailed in the end, did not
want an end to the SPLA split, which was favorable to the ruling
elite's military and political objectives. Those leaders did not want to
see interventions of any sort aimed at reconciliation.

On May 23 I arrived in Nairobi. At the American embassy the next
morning, following a talk with the UN's Philip O'Brien, I met separately with representatives of the two factions. In sessions lasting
most of the day, we covered a lot of ground, including issues relating
to relief operations, such as the need for airdrops of food. I stressed
that outside military intervention to end the war (which they were
hoping for) was most unlikely and that their infighting was eroding
sympathy in the United States for the SPLA. I appealed to them to accept an agreement for a simultaneous cease-fire and pullback of their
military forces from Kongor, Ayod, Waat, and Yuai so that humanitarian relief could proceed.

As usual, each side concentrated on making accusations against the
other, and I had to tell them I had not come to Nairobi to hear all that
again. The SPLA-Mainstream delegation, headed by Salva Kiir,

Garang's top military commander, tried to make agreement condi-
tional on an end to what he claimed were weapons supplies from
Khartoum to the SPLA-United[13] and a commitment by SPLA-United
not to move its troops out of a designated area. The SPLA-United delegation, led by Simon Mori Didumo, said Garang should stop using
Kongor as a launching pad for attacks on areas held by United. I told
the two sides that their preconditions would block agreement and
therefore were unacceptable.

After a lot of back-and-forth, late that afternoon both sides agreed in
principle to the cease-fire and military pullback. Garang had autho-
rized the Mainstream delegation to sign an agreement, but the United
delegation was unable to sign without Riek Machar's prior approval.

Accordingly, the next day I flew to Ulang, a village in Upper Nile,
where Riek was then headquartered. Along with the UN officials who
came with me, I sat with Riek under a tree in an open field. Flies were
swarming about, and those landing on my face in large numbers momentarily distracted me. Once I saw they did not bother Riek or the
others sitting with us and realized they were not the biting kind, I put
them out of my mind and let them crawl where they wanted, except
up my nostrils. I made my presentation. Riek rejected it. He said
Garang could not be trusted to honor any agreement. Finally, after I
had made some additional arguments, he said he would agree to the
plan I had outlined.

Two days later, following a trip west to Thiet in Bahr al-Ghazal
province, yet another area in desperate need of food and medical care, I
went back to Nairobi and met again with the two sides. I gave them a
draft agreement I had written during the flight from Thiet to Nairobi.
The gist of it was that at 6:00 P.M. on May 28 the two sides would com-
mence a complete withdrawal of all their military personnel from an
area encompassed within a forty-five-mile radius from the landing
strips at Ayod, Kongor, Waat, and Yuai. The withdrawal would be
completed by 6:00 P.M., June 5. No military personnel would be permitted to come into the demilitarized area, and there would be no hin-
drance to humanitarian relief operations there.

When they said that the wording of the draft agreement was acceptable, I got each side to agree to have a three-man delegation come to
the embassy the next day for a joint meeting to agree on the final
wording and to sign the agreement.

Next morning, at what I thought would be the signing session, the Mainstream faction insisted on adding two more locations north of the four cited in the draft. The United faction absolutely refused to accept any changes. Things looked bleak as we broke for a two-hour adjournment. I reminded them of the press conference the previous day in which I had told journalists that the two sides had agreed to stop fighting and to create a safe haven for the people of the triangle. I said the side that blocked agreement would be subjected to severe international criticism. When we reconvened, Salva Kiir, leader of the Mainstream delegation, said that after having consulted with Garang, his delegation now agreed to my proposal. After we made some minor changes in the wording, the two sides signed the agreement.

I was pleased, for it appeared the United Nations and voluntary agencies could now go into the area and stay there to administer the relief program. As a result, some people, perhaps many, who would have died would be saved. But there was an obvious weakness in the agreement: It did not provide a mechanism for monitoring.

During the talks I was asked who would guarantee the cease-fire, and I suggested that UN and INGO personnel, whose numbers would increase significantly, would be alert to and report on any resumption of military activity in the area. I knew that lacking strong public and congressional support, the U.S. government would not send any Americans into southern Sudan to monitor the agreement. Nor would any other Western country participate. Furthermore, Khartoum would emphatically oppose placement of a monitoring group inside southern Sudan. As it was, then, the agreement would succeed or fail depending on the goodwill and cooperation of the two rebel factions. And that was the problem: Their mutual distrust and antagonism ran very deep.

Concerned about the monitoring problem, three days earlier I had telephoned the State Department and asked for ideas on possible next steps to implement the agreement. The Department cabled back a suggestion that the UN's newly appointed special coordinator for Sudan could fly to Nairobi to assist in the negotiations and announce the signing of the agreement. Implicit in this was that he would make recommendations on the means of monitoring. However, nothing came of this because the UN chose not to become directly involved in helping implement the agreement.

As it turned out, the agreement lasted only a short time. Suspicious of each other's intentions and afraid of giving the other side a military edge in the triangle, neither side ever fully honored it. If it had had an enforcement mechanism, it might have held. But none was in the offing.

When I got back to Khartoum I found the Sudanese government was unhappy with me yet again, having gotten the impression that a UN force would come in to monitor the cease-fire. I met with Foreign Minister Abu Salih, who initially was belligerent. After I explained that there would be no outside intervention and that the only UN personnel in the triangle would be relief workers, he calmed down. Nevertheless, I saw again that the government and NIF leaders really did not like my trips into the South. This time they were particularly incensed, understandably from their viewpoint, that I had worked out an agreement between the rebels.

Despite this displeasure, my American embassy colleagues and I continued to have amicable relations with most Sudanese officials. The security police were the most notable exception to this. They had recently intensified their game-playing with us. They picked up one of our people and held him for a short while, and they detained some Sudanese employees of a moving company who were packing the household effects of an American who was leaving Sudan. The security policemen asked questions about what was being packed and let it be known they were deliberately harassing Americans. This kind of aggravation ended after I complained to the foreign ministry.

• • •

The strains in U.S.-Sudanese relations were exacerbated by an outcry in the U.S. Congress against the practices of the Sudanese government. In April the Senate Foreign Relations Committee issued the text of a "sense of the Senate" resolution on Sudan. The full Senate adopted it in May. The resolution condemned "the egregious human rights abuses of the Sudan government," deplored the SPLA's internecine fighting, and urged the government and the SPLA to grant relief organizations full access to the needy. It called upon President Clinton to expand relief operations in Sudan, increase U.S. financial assistance to INGOs working there, and "appoint a United Nations Special Representative for Sudan."

That it was a nonbinding sense of the Senate resolution, rather than legislation, made no difference to the Sudanese government, which characterized it as another example of U.S. bias against Muslim Sudan.

The words of Congressman Frank Wolf seemed to sting the Sudanese more than the Senate resolution. Wolf was appalled by the human misery he encountered when he visited southern Sudan and he had become the most vocal critic of Sudan in the Congress. In May, made aware of an embassy report to Washington about government troops' involvement in massacres of civilians, in kidnappings, and in transporting forced labor into Libya,[14] Wolf demanded that the report be declassified so he could cite it publicly. The administration complied, and Wolf introduced the document in the House of Representatives.

Rhetorically, Wolf asked, "Where's the Congress on this issue? Where's the Clinton administration on this issue? Where's the media on this issue?" He urged the administration to appoint a special envoy to Sudan.

In publicizing the embassy's report, Wolf heightened the attention given to slavery in Sudan. The practice of seizing women and children and using them as slaves was nothing new. It was associated mainly with cattle raids, primarily in Bahr al-Ghazal province, and it had been taking place for years. It took on a new dimension during the Numeiry years when the government armed the *murahileen*, as the Baqqara Arab raiders were called. Now, with intensification of military activity in that area, slave taking seemed to be increasing, mostly in *murahileen* raids on Dinka villages. Khartoum was still arming the *murahileen*, who cooperated with the Sudanese military.

The government did nothing to interfere with the slavery and bore ultimate responsibility for it. Nevertheless, Khartoum angrily and categorically denied that slavery existed in Sudan. As time went on, accusations that slavery was being practiced in Sudan increased, buttressed by credible evidence published by different European and U.S. human rights organizations. As for our report, the one cited by Congressman Wolf, it had been sent to Washington only after we had carefully corroborated the authenticity of the information we had received from various sources.

Despite Wolf's outrage at what was occurring in Sudan and the passionate concerns expressed by some senators and members of the

House, congressional interventions had, at most, a marginal impact on U.S. policy toward Sudan. Congressional antipathy for human rights abuses of both the government and the rebels mirrored that of the administration and, as such, was consistent with existing policy. Eventually, the administration responded to the recommendation for the appointment of a special envoy for Sudan, but little else of a practical nature came from congressional calls for specific actions (like massive increases in international aid) that were unaccompanied by appropriations of funds or any other kind of enabling legislation.

Various special interest groups weighed in. They were not opposed to the administration's overall approach to Sudan, yet they wanted more dramatic actions to terminate the war or to force Khartoum and the rebels to end restrictions on humanitarian aid and to cooperate fully with the United Nations and INGOs. Human rights groups and prominent relief organizations lobbied a great deal. However, with only occasional and ephemeral reporting on Sudan in the U.S. media, events in Sudan did not arouse much public notice.[15] The U.S. public was not interested in an expanded U.S. role in Sudan and would not have supported direct intervention there. This would be acutely so after the U.S. military debacle in Mogadishu in October 1993.

While I was in Sudan, except for Congressman Donald Payne, the congressional Black Caucus paid little attention to the situation there and seemed to have ambivalent feelings about it. The ambivalence was easy to fathom: Both sides in the war were African, even though much of the North was identified as Arab.

Like most other ordinary Americans, African Americans generally knew little about Sudan and its problems. The Sudanese government courted African Americans, mostly Muslims, bringing dozens to Khartoum to meet with Bashir, Turabi, and other prominent Sudanese. This effort, though, paid few dividends, despite some lobbying by individuals who returned to the United States apparently convinced by the Bashir government's argument that it had unjustly been accused of wrongdoing and was being subjected to an anti-Islamic bias of the U.S. government.

•   •   •

The traditionally low level of attention given to Africa by U.S. presidents has caused policy formulation to be delegated in considerable measure to African specialists, particularly in the State Department's African Bureau. In some crisis situations, the president and his top advisers, including the secretary of state and the national security adviser, will take direct control of policy. This was very evident during the Cold War, when East-West considerations were major determinants of U.S., as well as Soviet, actions in Africa.

But in the 1990s the Cold War was over, Sudan was of no strategic interest to the United States (except in the negative sense that it was a nesting ground for Islamic terrorist organizations), and the upper reaches of the Bush and Clinton administrations were focused on other international problems. The African bureau was the primary locus of policymaking for Sudan, and the embassy in Khartoum, through our analyses and recommendations, played an important role.

# 9

# From Bad to Worse

During the year before I arrived in Sudan, the State Department began expressing concern about Sudan's links with known terrorists. President Bashir and other officials in his government, and Hasan al-Turabi as well, denied any association with terrorists and insisted Washington was wrongly informed. Beginning with the first talk I had with Bashir after presenting my credentials, I repeated Washington's position on this matter. Reactions ranged from disdain to anger. Time and again I was asked to provide proof that the U.S. allegation was true. Unfortunately, Washington had not given me a strong hand to play. When pressed by Sudanese, all I could say was that the U.S. government had firm evidence of Sudan's involvement but that the evidence was from sensitive sources and could not be disclosed. However true, it was a lame argument, and more than once I asked Washington for some convincing information that could be divulged. Intelligence agencies, which had the last word on what could and could not be disclosed, were unwilling to provide anything of the kind I needed.

I knew we had evidence of collusion between some elements of the Sudanese government and terrorist organizations in Khartoum. But I did not think this evidence was sufficiently conclusive to put Sudan on the U.S. government's list of state sponsors of terrorism, which Washington was considering doing.

I was, therefore, surprised to learn in August 1993, as Julie, Brian, and I were preparing to return to Sudan from leave in California, that Secretary of State Warren Christopher might soon make the decision to put Sudan on the list. I called Assistant Secretary George Moose in Washington; he assured me that new evidence was conclusive. I asked that the Sudanese government not be informed Sudan was being added to the list until I returned to Khartoum. Knowing that the Sudanese would react angrily, I told Moose that I, rather than Larry Benedict, should be one to deliver the message and take the brunt of the reaction. He agreed. The next day, Julie, Brian, and I departed for Sudan and an uncertain future.

On August 15, the day after we reached Khartoum, Washington instructed me to convey Secretary Christopher's decision to President Bashir or some other appropriate senior official. The decision would not be announced in Washington until after I had delivered the message in Khartoum. I was unable to get an appointment with President Bashir, whose calendar was full, until the eighteenth.

On the sixteenth ABC television reported there was strong evidence linking the Sudanese government to the bombing of the World Trade Center building in New York. ABC also said Washington was expected to put Sudan on the list of state sponsors of terrorism. The telecast caused considerable commotion within the Sudanese government. Officials angrily denounced the United States for slandering Sudan, and the media began producing a steady stream of vitriolic anti-American articles, editorials, and broadcasts. Now knowing the crux of what I would tell him, Bashir declined to meet with me, and on the eighteenth I delivered Washington's message to the Foreign Ministry's first under secretary, Omar Berido.

With that done, the State Department announced the decision. In a statement issued August 18 the Department said that after it and other U.S. government agencies had concluded "a systematic review," Secretary Christopher had

> decided to designate Sudan a state sponsor of acts of international terrorism. . . . The decision on Sudan was reached after carefully weighing all available information and U.S. law. . . . The Secretary's decision reflects an assessment of facts, not a bias against Sudan because of the ideological or religious orientations of its government.

The Sudanese government was incensed. As reported in the August 19 issue of *Horizon*, an English-language newspaper, the Foreign Ministry released a statement expressing "astonishment over the American decision," which it said was based on unfounded allegations. "Enmity to the Islamic civilizational orientation of Sudan" was the "sole reason behind the U.S. decision." Changing its subject but not its intention, the statement condemned "the U.S. silence over the current massacres in Bosnia-Herzegovina and the occupied Arab lands."

As it unfolded, the Bashir government's reaction was definitely more one of anger than of sorrow. The media maintained an incessant flow of anti-American denunciations. Organized demonstrations took place. The first, on August 20, occurred in front of our house. Through the media, the government let it be known that on the twenty-fourth demonstrations against the United States would he held throughout the country. The largest of these would take place in front of the embassy. That day, I gave the embassy's Sudanese employees the day off and told the Americans to stay home until after the demonstration.

Only the Marines, security officers, and I (Larry Benedict was on leave) were in the embassy to observe the show. About 10,000 people (the government claimed there were over 100,000) were gathered together—many of them government workers and many of them people bused in from the outskirts of the city—for the "spontaneous" demonstration. They marched on the embassy but were not allowed by the army and police to get closer than fifty yards from the entrance to our building. Although at one point the crowd surged forward, the police-army line held, and we were in no danger. I later heard that a creative CNN telecast made it appear that the demonstration was far more threatening than it really was.

Even before the demonstration Washington had become alarmed at the anti-American propaganda's content and its increasingly frenzied tone. This and information about a plan to harm American officials led the State Department to order an evacuation of our spouses and children and a reduction of my American staff by one-third. At first, I thought Washington was overreacting. We at the embassy had seen or heard nothing manifesting a clear and present danger from either terrorists or the Sudanese government. But the order was firm and irrevocable.

The word on the ordered evacuation reached me fairly late at night on August 21, so I waited until the next morning to inform first the embassy's Americans, then our Sudanese employees. In the afternoon—at an American community meeting at the residence—my senior staff and I informed all the Americans in Khartoum whom we could gather together: the families of embassy employees, Americans with the INGOs and the United Nations, and private Americans not associated with the relief program or directly with the embassy, such as teachers at the American School. After explaining what the embassy staff reduction would entail, I told the private citizens that whether they stayed or left was a personal matter for them to decide. I said there was no immediate, discernible threat to Americans but in view of the implications of Sudan's being placed on the list of state sponsors of terrorism, it was prudent to reduce the number of embassy Americans.

The news shocked many of them. Hardest hit were embassy Americans with school-age children who had just finished their first day of school. The children would have to go back to the United States and start school there, perhaps for a short time, but perhaps for months— we simply did not know for how long. Some of the private Americans who had children in the American School wondered what would happen to it. The school principal and I said there was no plan to close the school. Only 9 students of the 150 in the school would be departing.

I went to the Foreign Ministry to see First Under Secretary Berido to tell him about the evacuation and talk about the anti-American propaganda campaign. I told him that Sudanese government leaders were contributing to an anti-American climate. For example, President Bashir had said Washington supported John Garang's SPLA. This, I said, was inflammatory and absolutely false. I also noted that Ghazi had stated flatly that the United States was the enemy of Sudan. Those kinds of statements and the hostile media campaign could lead some Sudanese to conclude that Americans were fair game for retaliation.

I said the Sudanese government was arranging for, and doing all it could to stimulate participation in, the demonstrations. All this was contributing to a heightened concern about the safety of Americans, and Washington had decided to order the evacuation of the dependents of embassy Americans and to reduce the American staff. I said I trusted that the current anti-American campaign would not make it difficult for us to get the required exit permits or in any other way hinder the departure of American citizens or the continued operation of the embassy.

Berido denied that the government had anything to do with the demonstrations, which he said would not be permitted to get out of control. As for the official statements, he said they reflected the "bitterness and disappointment" of Sudanese leaders over their nation's placement on the terrorism list. American citizens would not be mistreated or put in any danger. Our decision to evacuate dependents and reduce the size of the embassy staff was within the rights of the U.S. government and even understandable under the circumstances. His government, he said, would "give all help to facilitate the departure of those who are leaving."

• • •

I had very little time to decide who on the U.S. mission[1] staff would stay and who would go. The State Department wanted our numbers reduced from fifty-two direct-hire Americans to thirty-eight by the end of the first week in September. My decision was not an easy one, for the transfers would probably be permanent and would consequently disrupt the professional and personal lives of those who left.

To make matters worse, within a week we acquired new information indicating, if not immediate danger, at least an increasingly precarious situation for Americans in Khartoum. From this I determined that I should reduce the American staff even further. In communications with George Moose and the African Bureau and with Under Secretary of State for Management Richard Moose, I recommended that this be done.

Most dependents had already gone by September 3 when Julie and Brian left. Brian, who continued going to school until the day they departed, was unhappy about leaving but seemed excited about entering school in Ashland, Oregon, where they were bound. Julie, who had been looking forward to another year of teaching at the American School, was very upset. She did not agree with Washington's decision to evacuate dependents. Having been evacuated from a post before, she knew it was uncertain when we would be reunited. Nevertheless, she remained cheerful, kept teaching at the school, and found time to make arrangements for a dinner party we held for about fifteen people—friends of ours in the diplomatic corps and the Sudanese business community. We spent the evening of the third at home. Just before midnight we drove to the airport, where Julie and Brian boarded their flight for Europe.

The families affected by the evacuation and the employees who had to leave because of the reduction in the embassy staff reacted calmly and professionally. However, it was not easy for anyone. Families would be split up. All who were going would have to leave most of their possessions behind. Employees saw their assignments suddenly broken with no indication of what lay ahead.

By the end of the first week of September there was little improvement in our situation in Khartoum. We had made no progress in reducing the differences between us and the Sudanese government. The anti-American campaign went on without letup. The government continued organizing demonstrations. There was another one in front of the embassy on the fifteenth, and at least two more were slated to take place in the coming week. If the campaign was designed to provoke the Sudanese people to show real anger against Americans, it failed. There were rarely any signs, and only one incident—when two American teachers driving to work were harassed by several young bearded men following them in a car—of genuine hostility directed against any Americans, official or nonofficial, in Sudan.

In fact, except for militant Islamists, the Sudanese continued to show friendliness to Americans. Time and again when I drove through the streets of Khartoum, people showed by smiles and gestures their positive feelings about the United States. Occasionally bearded young men gazed stonily at me as I passed. But I can remember only once when someone—and it was an Iranian, not a Sudanese—was distinctly hostile. Standing on a corner, he glared at me and drew his finger across his throat.

Because of the distortions and outright lies in the media, on September 10 the embassy released a statement, which the State Department had approved in advance, refuting as "baseless" the accusations that the United States was working for the secession of southern Sudan, supported the rebellion, and wanted to foil the cause of peace in Sudan. Our statement said that, contrary to the Sudanese government's assertion that the United States had no basis for putting Sudan on the terrorism list and did it only in compliance with SPLA wishes, there was sufficient evidence that the government gave official sanction to the use of its territory as a sanctuary for terrorists, some of whom trained in Sudan.

The statement denied the allegation that the United States was "hostile to Islam and was plotting against Sudan because of the Islamic nature of its government." The United States respected Islam as "one of the world's great faiths, whose followers include millions of American citizens." It was concerned, however, "about those who use religion—any religion—as a pretext for violence, intolerance, intimidation, or terror."

A day earlier Omar Berido had called me into his office for a long discussion. I told him about the statement, but he said nothing about it. And in fact, the way our talk went indicated that after more than two weeks of holding me at arm's length, the government wanted to resume a more normal relationship. This prospect was short-lived. Soon I was confronted with a new development that was clearly going to put an even greater strain on U.S.-Sudanese relations and close the door that seemed about to open for me. I received instructions from Washington to deliver a very harsh message to President Bashir and to Hasan al-Turabi. I got appointments to see them on September 12, Bashir first, then Turabi shortly afterward.

The message was devoid of diplomatic niceties. Washington, deeply concerned about continuing indications that embassy Americans in Sudan were in danger, warned Bashir and Turabi that if any harm came to Americans, the U.S. government would retaliate in a manner that "could result in the international isolation of Sudan, in the destruction of your economy, and in military measures that would make you pay a high price." As I knew they would, both Bashir and Turabi reacted in fury, Turabi in particular. The best I could tell Washington was that the two Sudanese leaders assured me I should have no fear for the safety of Americans in Sudan. I had told Turabi I knew the tenets of Islam, Arab tradition, and Sudanese hospitality all assured that guests in Sudan would be protected from any harm. He had indicated his full agreement with that.

Although Washington and the embassy honored the confidentiality of the message I had delivered, some of the Sudanese who were privy to its contents revealed them to a variety of people, including some of my ambassadorial colleagues. In a very short time, many people in Khartoum knew the message's main points.

One result of this affair was an end to my access to Bashir for many months. The Sudanese ambassador in Washington, to whom the State Department had given essentially the same message I gave to Bashir and Turabi, had led his government to believe I would be delivering a friendly communication from President Clinton. Why he did this was best known to himself; no one in Khartoum with whom I talked about this could give an explanation to account for his action.

Shortly after I had asked to see Bashir, a Foreign Ministry official called to ask if I was bringing a message from President Clinton. I said that I was not, but that the message represented the views of the highest levels of the U.S. government. Despite what I told the official, when I saw Bashir and his advisers they were still expecting a friendly message from Clinton. Consequently, they were taken aback by what I read to them, and their outrage was directed not only at the message but also at the messenger for having, as they thought, deceived them.

Later, when I learned why so much of their anger had focused on me, I explained to officials what had actually happened. Although they said they believed me, I was still kept from meeting with Bashir because of the lingering deep anger at the tough words from Washington.

•  •  •

I do not want to leave an impression that my interaction with Sudanese leaders and officials was one of almost constant conflict. That was not the case. On a personal level, I found almost all Sudanese congenial and pleasant to deal with. There were some notable exceptions to this. But overall the Sudanese deserved their reputation as the nicest people in the eastern half of the African continent. Although sometimes my conversations with government officials and NIF leaders became argumentative, and tempers were frayed, almost never did anger or animosity color an entire meeting or persist afterward.

Some in the government and the NIF were undeviating in their hostility toward the U.S. government. That being said, I believe that most of the northern Sudanese whom I knew genuinely wanted to see an improvement in relations between Sudan and the United States. And my impression was that they recognized that I did, too.

There were many northerners who were deeply concerned about the problems that the country and all its people were facing and who strove to overcome them. One example of many comes to mind. Throughout my time in Sudan, I worked closely with Ibrahim Abu Ouf, who was the government's leading official in overseeing the Sudanese part of the humanitarian aid program and interacting with UN agencies, NGOs, and donor-country ambassadors. He was fiercely loyal to the government he served. There were occasions when we disagreed, sometimes strongly, on aspects of the program, but we both knew we shared the desire to help relieve the suffering of the victims of war and drought. Abu Ouf was only one of many Sudanese, inside and outside the government, who worked on behalf of the Sudanese people.

•   •   •

On September 17 we completed our plans for the additional drawdown of embassy staff. I had stayed in close touch with George Moose and on the fifteenth had sent my recommendations to him and to Under Secretary Richard Moose, who on the sixteenth chaired an interagency meeting on Khartoum staffing. The result was the adoption of the recommendations. On the morning of the seventeenth, I met with Larry Benedict and the rest of the country team to draw up a final plan for the reduction. In the afternoon I had the embassy's American employees and their spouses come to the house to let them know what the decision was. This latest cutback, of fifteen people, which we had to complete by the first of October, brought our numbers down to twenty-three, from fifty-two when the reduction process began.

It was important for me to do whatever I could to keep all the Americans in Khartoum, and those elsewhere in Sudan whom we could reach, as well informed as possible. On the eighteenth I made a special point of going to the American School to speak with the American teachers. I let them know about the staff reductions and reassured them that we saw no signs of danger to nonofficial Americans.

Two days later I met again at the residence with the American community. The meeting was well attended. More people were there than at the previous community meeting. No one was panicking, and it seemed doubtful that any non-embassy people would choose to leave. I told them the reduction in the embassy staff was a precautionary move based on continuing concerns that official Americans might be targeted. I emphasized, as I had done with the teachers, that there was no information, and we had no reason to suspect, that nonofficial Americans were in any danger. Later, I continued to find it useful to invite the American community to the residence from time to time to keep them informed of developments and also to ease the fears that grew out of the many wild rumors that were circulating.

In addition to regular sessions with the country team, I held fairly frequent meetings with all the mission's American personnel to ensure that everyone was kept informed on what was happening and was aware of my thinking and Washington's intentions.

The country team and I also met with our Sudanese and other non-American employees to brief them on such things as why U.S. relations with Sudan were so bad, what U.S. objectives were and how we hoped to achieve them, and how what was taking place (for example, the decrease in American employees) might affect them. I wanted to be sure that they were informed as fully as could be.

I knew that among them were a few government informants. This is true at many of our diplomatic and consular posts; governments sometimes put unbearable pressures on foreign-national employees to supply information about what goes on in the embassy or consulate or manage to get persons loyal to the government on the American payroll. Knowing this, obviously I avoided imparting any sensitive information to the employees. At the same time, I passed on to them words that both kept them informed and might have done some good if they reached the government.

As the month wore on the Blue Nile continued to run full and to cause the White Nile to back up and flood some of the low-lying ground in the southern part of town. It was very hot and somewhat humid. Except for the anti-American demonstrations, the city was fairly somnolent.

On September 20 we had the last of the demonstrations, for the time being at least. It was billed as a demonstration by southern Sudanese angered by U.S. actions against Sudan, but of course it was organized by the government. The demonstration was a bust. The organizers had trouble getting southerners to participate. Southern leaders put the word out that people should not cooperate with the government. A few of the southerners whom the government paid to urge others to participate were beaten up. When the great day arrived, only about 500 people showed up, and of those, many were northerners. Thousands of people had ignored the bribes and the threats to take part.

With tension still in the air, for a time I called off all gatherings of Americans—even relatively small dinner parties. Jim Burke, the regional security officer, told me, quite rightly, that it would not be right for me to cancel gatherings and yet still go running, as I thought of doing. Later, when things got back to a more normal footing, I resumed running, with my security detail in attendance, of course. We had to be sure to vary the days, times, and routes of the runs.

The staff reduction went forward smoothly, with everyone working together and responding in a professional way. Morale remained high, in spite of the circumstances. By this time we knew it was unlikely that dependents would be returning before Christmas. We had no way of knowing that it would not be until well after yet another Christmas that the restriction on dependents in Khartoum would be lifted.

# 10

# Making Adjustments

Although we weren't sure how long those who were evacuated would be away from Sudan, I believed it would be at least a few months before they could come back. From my experience as director of the Liberia task force in 1990, when an evacuation from Monrovia took place, I knew the State Department took a very conservative view on allowing the return of dependents who had been evacuated.

The under secretary for management, as the official in the State Department most directly responsible for decisions on evacuations and returns, would want to be as sure as possible that returning spouses and children would not be going back into a potentially dangerous situation. Both Ivan Selin, the under secretary I worked with in the Bush administration, and Richard Moose were imaginative administrators but, not surprisingly, exceedingly cautious when it came to decisions affecting the safety of the personnel and their dependents at our diplomatic posts.

As the weeks after the evacuation turned into months, I became concerned about morale and our ability to carry out our responsibilities effectively. The extra workload the smaller staff had to assume and the tensions arising from our situation in Khartoum were bound to have some adverse effects. When it became evident to us in Khartoum which of the positions that had been abolished needed to be restored, I asked Dick Moose for their restoration. Because of his strong feelings about putting additional people at risk by assigning them to Khartoum, he resisted all but the most compelling arguments I made for augmenting the embassy's American staff.

As the months went by, with the backing of pertinent offices in the State Department, I got his assent for a few positions. Eventually our permanent American complement was increased to about thirty from the twenty-three positions remaining immediately after the reduction.

Six of the positions were filled by Marines. The function of a Marine security guard detachment is to keep the chancery, or embassy building, secure from intrusion by hostile or otherwise unauthorized persons and in other ways to ensure that classified information in the chancery is not compromised. The Marines do not provide routine off-site protection for the ambassador or other officials of the embassy. The State Department's Bureau for Diplomatic Security has that responsibility. Several security officers trained and supervised the Sudanese bodyguard units for the ambassador and DCM and managed the security programs for all the buildings and grounds of the U.S. mission and the residences of the mission's Americans.

With twelve of the mission's American employees devoted to security matters and nine more providing administrative, communications, or secretarial services, there were only a handful of us to provide executive management; to interact with Sudan's political leadership, the opposition, religious leaders, academics, businesspeople, the media, and other important sectors of Sudanese society, and non-Sudanese as well; to report on political and economic matters; to carry out the public information function; to do consular work; and to oversee humanitarian aid.

It is one thing to have positions and another to have people assigned to them. At any given time, some of the thirty positions we now had were not filled. A position might go unfilled for long periods of time while we waited for Washington to supply us with a body. We were stretched very thin.

Nothing materialized from the perceived threat to embassy Americans. In answer to inquiries from our families, the State Department said we were safe. Still wondering what the danger was, Julie asked me, "Safe from what?"

I wrote her that we in Khartoum were not aware of any present danger to us, except for the usual risks Americans face from attacks by individual fanatics or lunatics incensed by U.S. policies, such as support for Israel. The malicious anti-American campaign that the government waged for several weeks had increased the possibility that something like that could happen, but nothing did. The continued presence in Sudan of terrorist groups like Hizbollah was nothing new. So was our situation now more perilous than it had been before the events of August and September? Probably so, but again, there was nothing to indicate that we now faced any specific danger.

Sudanese officials assured me Americans would not be harmed. Certainly, it would have been illogical for the government to foster or approve any violent action against us—the message I had delivered to Bashir and Turabi September 12 made it clear that such action would bring retaliation of a kind distinctly inimical to their interests.

My relationship with the government fluctuated, apparently on the mend one day, then taking another turn for the worse the next. In early October my access to Sudanese officials got better. Some in the government remained antagonistic. Others, believing that Sudan had to have better relations with the United States, favored at least talking with us to see if there was any way to improve relations. At about this time we learned from a reliable source that the extremely tough message I had delivered a month earlier had caused some Sudanese leaders to worry that Washington might decide to take some steps to damage the regime.

In a meeting with Foreign Minister Abu Salih at his office on October 14 I brought up the continuing anti-American campaign in the media. He said it would abate soon. He also let me know the Foreign Ministry wanted to resume the formal dialogue. There was still no reason to believe that dialogue sessions would lead anywhere, yet at the same time there was no good reason not to use every opportunity for discourse between the Sudanese and us.

It was my turn to be chairman of the donors again, and as such I had a couple of sometimes acrimonious meetings with Sudanese government relief officials. One issue at hand was where the United Nations could fly and which INGOs could take part in assessments of the need for aid projects in Malakal and elsewhere in the transition zone. Still harboring a strong mistrust of INGOs, the government persistently delayed the initiation of the assessments.

The government refused to let the United Nations fly aid into Nimule for delivery to nearby displaced-persons camps—the "Triple-

A" camps (Ame, Atepi, and Aswa)—where 100,000 people, mainly Bor
Dinka, were located. The situation of these people was increasingly
precarious, but the government took no heed of that and gave no ratio-
nal excuse for not allowing UN aircraft to go to Nimule. Behind the
government's obduracy lay the fact that the Sudanese did not want
any UN flights into that area, especially flights originating in Uganda,
because they believed the United Nations might carry supplies or
weapons for the SPLA.

Near the end of October U.S.-Sudanese relations lurched downward
again. At that time a symposium on Sudan was held in Washington
under the auspices of the Institute of Peace and the Africa Subcommittee of the House Foreign Affairs Committee. The symposium organizers invited scholars and other experts on Sudan and senior members of the government of Sudan, of the northern opposition, and of
the main rebel factions. The government chose not to attend. Afterward it was provoked less by the symposium than by the private meetings organized by the subcommittee's chairman, Congressman Harry
Johnson, and attended by John Garang and Riek Machar.

State Department officials also attended the private meetings, but
only as observers. This distinction made no difference to Khartoum,
which chose to view the meetings as a hostile act by the U.S. government. Whether or not the attendance by State Department officials
was a good idea—and I did not think it was—it made it more difficult
for us in Khartoum to deny that the administration had a role in organizing and holding the symposium and the private meetings.

The affair inculcated more firmly in the minds of some Sudanese
that Washington supported the SPLA. For all the fuss about the meetings, they did not achieve anything of value for either the rebel movement or the cause of peace. Garang and Riek reached a tentative agreement to stop fighting and reunify the southern rebel movement, but
the agreement never went into effect.

The Sudanese government's unhappiness with the symposium and
the private meetings was expressed through the media. The U.S. government was accused of working with the SPLA to keep the war going
and thereby harm Sudan. President Bashir himself joined in with a
public attack on U.S. policy toward Sudan. Once more, however, as
the anti-American campaign seemed about to rise to a potentially dangerous level, it began to subside. Ironically, at the same time the me-

dia were denouncing the United States Abu Salih resumed the dialogue sessions.

Just about anything I did in public was subject to scrutiny and frequently to misinterpretation. One example: After meeting with Abu Salih on October 25, I went across the river to Omdurman, where the president gave a speech to the Parliament. I could understand some, but not a lot, of what he said. Arabic-speaking ambassadors told me there was not much advantage to understanding the president that day because he did not really say anything of interest.

I spent part of the two hours I was there writing a cable reporting what had transpired in my meeting with Abu Salih. Some non-Arabic-speaking ambassadors were impressed, thinking that I seemed to understand everything the president was saying and was taking extensive notes on the speech.

The next day's issue of one of Khartoum's newspapers contained an article very critical of my actions at Parliament. It implied there was something sinister about my taking notes on what the president was saying. For some reason, it was also considered suspicious that I was seen looking around at the thousand or so people who were at the Parliament that day and that I was "conferring with an aide" (I was talking to one of the ambassadors seated next to me in the diplomatic gallery).

Attacks on me intensified when I made public comments about matters such as the causes of the poor relations between Sudan and the United States. An interview I had with a correspondent for a French news agency (Alliance Français Presse, AFP) at the end of October is a case in point. I said relations between Sudan and the United States would remain bad unless the Sudanese government began to show respect for human rights, renewed a democratic process, and stopped supporting terrorism. This was nothing I had not said before both publicly and privately. But after the AFP article appeared in Europe—it did not appear in the Sudanese press—a government spokesman berated me, and an editorial in one of the papers, *Al Engaz al Watani*, said perhaps I should "pack my effects and go back to the paradise of human rights and oasis of democracy."

Three weeks later, another newspaper, *As Sudan Al Hadith*, editorialized that "the American ambassador failed in his mission" of enhancing relations between the United States and Sudan, a "failure similar to his country's government's drunk imaginations of supremacy in Bosnia . . . and its miserable failure in Sudan." It said, "He took his ideas and information from the remnants of the jobless sectarianism,"[1] and the SPLA. The U.S. government and I were enemies of Islam and Muslims. Sudan did not follow the path of the United States because "that path might lead our army to gays. American society recognizes this practice. . . . even your rulers come to power by defending and supporting" gays. Sudanese, the paper said, "think that your democracy is absolutely similar to this practice, which we consider a social crime."

Sudanese friends laughed about the editorials, telling me they represented the thinking of only the extreme fringes of the NIF. Some said ruefully, however, that the extremists were not without influence in the government.

As a matter of course, other officers of the embassy and I met with government opponents, just as we met with its officials and supporters. Not surprisingly, this elicited additional media criticism. Former prime minister Sadiq al-Mahdi was one of those we saw. Born in 1935, the great-grandson of the Mahdi, Sadiq was Sudan's prime minister in 1966–1967 and again from 1985 until 1989, when the military-NIF coup ousted him. He was imprisoned several times by military governments, the Bashir government being no exception.

I generally saw Sadiq at his home in Omdurman. We sat and talked in the garden behind his house. As always with Sudanese, an occasion for talk was an occasion for hospitality, and at Sadiq's home I had fruit juices and pastries to choose from and tea. Sadiq is a tall, expansive man who exhibits great self-confidence. In our talks, he was contemptuous of the NIF and disparaging of Turabi, his brother-in-law. Sadiq was invariably upbeat, predicting that the government would fall in the near future. In this he, and many other Sudanese, underestimated the abilities and staying power of the government.

In early November the Revolutionary Command Council (RCC) (once, but no longer, the ruling body of the Bashir government) dissolved itself and proclaimed Bashir president, a formality, since he was already using the title. As usual, there was no explanation in the media as to how and why the change was made. This contributed to rampant rumors that a coup was imminent. We reported to Washington that the change in the government's structure did not mean a change in where power resided—within the National Islamic Front. Because of disagreement between civilian and military members of the NIF, it took them a few days to decide who would be in the cabinet. There were only three changes, and the newcomers were all staunch adherents of the NIF.

Apparently the inner circle decided to abolish the RCC to show the outside world that military officers no longer ruled Sudan and to exert a firmer control over the government. We soon learned that Turabi had engineered the whole thing.

Intelligence analysts and other users of the embassy's political reports and analyses were interested in any light we could shed on who was in charge of Sudan's governing apparatus and how decisions were made. Some observers in Khartoum wrote off Bashir as a mere puppet of Turabi and the NIF; others saw Turabi being supplanted by younger men in his organization. Both speculations were inaccurate.

During the two years preceding my assignment to Khartoum, information from a variety of sources showed that Bashir did not dominate the government he nominally headed. This led some to believe that he was merely a figurehead. The truth, at least as the other officers in the embassy who did political reporting and I came to see it, was something else. Bashir was entirely in tune with the ideology, aims, and methods of the NIF. He relied on Turabi in particular for guidance. Turabi and his colleagues relied on him, in turn, as a man highly esteemed in the army, to help ensure the military's loyalty to the government.

The dominance of the NIF and the men in the army who had close ties to it grew as they steadily expanded their control of the security police and, mainly by means of purges, the army. Nothing suggested that Bashir resisted the NIF's power, even though there had been indications he was not entirely comfortable with it. He once came close to saying as much in a talk with the president of a neighboring country. Nevertheless, for years nothing he said or did in public gave any indication that he really wanted to alter his relationship with Turabi and the NIF. Nor did the other Islamists in the military who were powerful figures in the ruling establishment. Some of these men—like the ruthless Colonel Ibrahim Shams al-Din, who was known to use extreme measures against persons suspected of being security threats to the government—kept in the shadows.

Now and then it was rumored that Turabi would be displaced by some of his NIF colleagues, such as Ali Osman Taha, Turabi's putative heir apparent, and Ghazi Salah Eddin. Because several years later the rumor would become fact, perhaps in 1993 it was not baseless. But if that was the case, it was not apparent, as the younger men, who were playing increasingly prominent roles in the government, continued to defer to Turabi, who had been their mentor for years.

A Sudanese who was about the same age as Ghazi, Mustafa Osman Ismail, and other prominent members of the NIF who were in their early forties, once told me these men had gone to school together. Under the leadership of Ali Osman Taha, who was a few years older than they, they were committed Islamists before they went abroad for undergraduate or postgraduate studies. Like Taha, they revered Hassan al-Turabi. Another Sudanese who was in a position to know told me that when they were teenagers Taha and Ghazi had come under Turabi's direct tutelage. I saw no reason to question the belief of well-informed Sudanese and others that Turabi was the most influential man in the country.

This did not mean he exercised close control over the daily affairs of the government or by himself made the major decisions affecting its direction. Important decisions were apparently reached collectively through discussions about particular subjects by knowledgeable individuals. Often the presentation made by the most articulate and best informed on the matter at hand formed the basis for the decision reached, though major decisions would rarely if ever be at odds with Turabi's expressed beliefs and opinions. When Turabi himself participated in deliberations, his words carried very heavy weight.

Even before I came to Sudan many people believed Turabi was the primary figure in the Sudanese power structure. The basis for this assumption was largely anecdotal—sufficient evidence for some but not for the U.S. intelligence community, which required something more solid before making a firm judgment on the matter. By the latter half of 1993 I believed we had acquired adequate information to reach a definitive verdict about Turabi's role, and from then on embassy reporting explicitly acknowledged his preeminence.

•  •  •

Sudan's economy steadily worsened. City dwellers in particular were finding it increasingly hard to make ends meet. Unemployment was high and retail prices were soaring. People were especially upset because of the extremely high prices for basic food items. In addition, they hated the regime's curbs on any form of opposition to its policies and its hold on power. Although there was no widespread popular uprising of the kind that had toppled two previous dictatorships, outbreaks of resistance did occur from time to time.

In mid-October secondary school students demonstrated in Omdurman, protesting a shortage of gasoline and the sharp rise in the cost of living. The government responded with force, and in the course of three days of demonstrations two people were killed and many arrested. There were riots in other towns, the worst in El Obeid, where a bank and a gasoline station were burned down and seven people were killed.

On the night of November 10 tear gas drifted into my yard from the nearby University of Khartoum. An hour earlier university students had gathered to demonstrate. They were angry because Islamists, with the complicity of the NIF and the government, had rigged the student body election. The demonstrators were met by armed policemen and by security toughs armed with guns and clubs. When the students refused to disperse, the police fired some shots and threw tear gas. Many students were beaten, and some were arrested. In its handling of the demonstrations, the government showed that it would employ whatever force it believed necessary to maintain order and keep the populace under control. The Sudanese press made no mention of this affray or of the earlier riots.

The Sudanese remembered that an unarmed civilian uprising in 1964 had led military officers to pressure the junta then in power to resign and that Numeiry's rule ended in 1985 when the military stepped in after people went into the streets and immobilized the country with a general strike. Many believed the Bashir government would suffer the same fate. But those who were hoping that manifestations of popular discontent would lead the army to intervene and overthrow the government were disappointed.

The government and NIF leaders also remembered what civilian uprisings had accomplished in previous years and were determined that this would not happen to them. They successfully cleansed the army of possibly disloyal elements and demoralized those remaining members who did not like the Islamist regime. Once aware that the military would not intervene, and having seen how ruthless the government could be in suppressing demonstrations, most people were unwilling to run the risks involved in overtly opposing the government.

• • •

In early November, the EC's Charles Brook, the UNICEF representative, the French ambassador, and I flew south to Malakal to look at the displaced-persons camps in the town and surrounding area. Thanks to the efforts of four UNICEF and four International Red Cross workers who had been allowed to go there, the high death rate in the camps caused by inadequate health and nutrition programs had been reduced.

When we arrived we found that Sudanese officials had prepared a schedule that would have kept us in town for the entire day. We turned it down and insisted that we wanted to visit the camps at Obel, south of Malakal. We drove an hour to the first camp at Obel, where we found a familiar situation. The Sudanese NGO Da'wa Islamia, which had links to the NIF and the government, was making an ineffectual effort to provide feeding and health services. As had been the case at other places I visited, Da'wa Islamia's main focus was on providing schools so the displaced children could be exposed to the Islam-oriented national curriculum of the Sudanese government.

We crossed the Sobat River in dugout canoes to reach a displaced-persons camp at an abandoned construction site of the Jonglai Canal, a French project to dig a canal through the great Sudd swamp, which was shut down in 1983 by the war. The care provided for the people at this camp was also woefully inadequate. Sanitation at both camps was awful.

Back on the other side of the river I was interviewed by Sudan television and said the services of INGOs were desperately needed. When we returned to Malakal, Brook and I told local officials and government representatives from Khartoum that, as I had said in Malakal more than a year earlier, the feeding programs and rudimentary medical clinics were poorly managed and sanitation was virtually nonexistent. Conditions at Malakal and other displaced-persons camps in the transition zone cried out for the experience and resources of INGOs, and I urged the Sudanese (once again) to allow INGOs to come and do their work. Many lives could be saved. The government officials replied (once again) that there was no need for INGOs.

It was a frustrating business. The donor countries and the United Nations had been pushing for INGO access to the transition zone's displaced-persons camps for over a year now, with meager results. Later on, by mid-1995, Khartoum had grudgingly permitted the handful of relief workers in the transition zone to be augmented by a few more, but not nearly enough considering the continued high rates of malnutrition and disease.

Equally frustrating was the inability of the United Nations and donors to get the government to stop razing dwellings in parts of Khartoum and forcing their occupants to go to makeshift camps in the desert outside town. In late November I made another visit to some of those camps. Conditions had not improved in any perceptible way. The Khartoum state minister of housing, the man in charge of the removals, had said he would make some changes in his policies in order to enable the United Nations and INGOs to help the displaced people more effectively. He sought UN, USAID, and British and Dutch funding for a rehabilitation project. With a UN official who was keen on the idea, I went to see him. What he told us was disappointing, for it became clear that the forcible removals to inadequately prepared sites would continue. Needless to say, no funds were provided for his project.

Neither the United Nations nor the donor countries could prevail on the issues of the transition zone and the Khartoum displaced. We had influence, to be sure. As much as the Islamists in power in Sudan disliked the West and only tolerated the United Nations, they knew there would be a price to pay for going too far, for totally alienating much of the international community. But they had learned that although the United Nations would cajole, urge, even plead, it would stop short of applying strong pressures to get Sudan to agree more fully to what it wanted to do. A friend of mine who had been with the United Nations for more than twenty years and who had come with a UN mission to Khartoum while I was there explained to me that Sudan was a member of the United Nations, and the UN bureaucracy was not disposed to be very aggressive with member states.

Although Western countries were not constrained in the same way the United Nations was, they too were reluctant to go much beyond condemnations when Khartoum did not respond to entreaties or prodding to improve the effectiveness of the relief program. The United States, for its part, had force to spare that could have been applied to Sudan if the political will to use it existed. I knew, from talks I had with senior officials in the State Department, Anthony Lake and some of his staff at the National Security Council, and Under Secretary of Defense Frank Wisner—a Foreign Service officer who was outraged by the killings of U.S. government employees at Juba and the behavior of the Sudanese government—that there was a desire to do something to force Sudan to behave better. However, once faced with options that amounted to active U.S. intervention, policymakers backed off. They had no choice. They knew the administration was not in a position to advocate measures on Sudan that would be most unlikely to find favor in the Congress or be understood and supported by the American people.

•  •  •

As 1993 drew to a close U.S.-Sudanese relations remained sour. In early December the Sudanese government organized a demonstration in front of the embassy. The theme was anger at the Washington meeting in October between John Garang and Riek Machar. The Sudanese continued to assert that the meeting had been organized by the U.S. government as part of a U.S. conspiracy to achieve the separation of the South from the rest of Sudan.

Media attacks on the United States waxed and waned but never ceased. Because of my openness in expressing U.S. policy toward Sudan and discussing subjects such as new occurrences of human rights abuses and Sudan's continued support for international terrorism and because of my belief that we should reply publicly when the government made untrue statements about U.S. policy or about actions by Washington or the embassy, I handed the media opportunities to criticize me. On the positive side, I continued to have good access to government officials, although the president and some of the ministers were still off-limits to me.

We in the embassy looked forward to the next year with some hope that it would see a return of dependents to Khartoum. As far as Larry Benedict and I could tell, embassy Americans continued to have a positive attitude. Everyone who was able to attend turned up for Thanksgiving dinner at the residence, to which I had invited non-Americans as well. An in-house tennis tournament in December may not have produced much good tennis, but everyone had a good time. Other social events, frequently at Larry and Gloria Benedict's[2] home, were equally successful. State Department inspectors who came to Khartoum many months later commented that Khartoum was a "very collegial post" and that "despite the post's extremely adverse physical and danger-pay environment, morale is high."

•  •  •

Periodically the administration in Washington reexamined its Sudan policy. In the last half of my assignment to Sudan, policy reevaluations generated no new suggestions of ways to alter the barren status quo. The White House and the State Department judged that the costs of possible options outweighed potential gains.

One problem we faced was that the Sudanese gave us no lasting opportunity to do anything positive toward them to demonstrate that we were not locked into unremitting hostility regardless of circumstances. I told Washington that leading figures in the NIF complained to me that no matter what Sudan might do to meet U.S. demands, Washington, instead of giving it credit, would continue to apply pressure. Although there was something to what the Sudanese said, there was a sound reason for Washington to be cautious about giving even slight praise to the regime.

For example, when Khartoum had signed agreements with Operation Lifeline Sudan and INGOs earlier in the year, the United States had acknowledged the accords in less than ringing terms. As it soon turned out, we had been right to show restraint, for the two agreements were only gradually and partially implemented, and the obstruction of relief operations by both Khartoum and the SPLA persisted. Furthermore, at the same time, there were new instances of government oppression of the Sudanese people.

Government leaders seemed to fail to understand that unless they began to make some convincing moves away from their policies and actions, they could not expect the administration in Washington to go out on a limb and publicly laud the regime for such small, and sometimes transitory, gestures in the right direction. Were the administration to do so, it would come under vociferous criticism from Congress and groups ranging from human rights organizations to the Christian Right.

And so we had a catch–22 situation: Washington would stint on praise unless the Sudanese made major changes, and the Sudanese wanted more up-front praise from Washington before they would consider going in the direction Washington was stipulating.

In November, feeling stymied by the continued absence of any progress toward an improvement in relations with Sudan, I made a proposal that included a few very modest steps to elicit a reaction from the Sudanese. I suggested, for instance, that because of the government's current improved attitude about the relief program, the United States could hold off criticizing Sudan in the United Nations for obstructing the relief effort. But shortly after I sent the proposal to Washington the Sudanese military began a new offensive in the South that was sure to have harmful effects on civilians. The State Department cabled that in view of the offensive, there could be no change for the time being in our public posture toward the Sudanese government.

In mid-January 1994, after having been in Oregon for the Christmas and New Year holidays with Julie, Brian, and other members of our family, I was in Washington on consultations. A few hours before leaving for Sudan I met with Under Secretary of State for Political Affairs Peter Tarnoff, Dick Moose, and George Moose. At their request I gave them my thoughts on where we were in our relations with Sudan, what I believed was likely to happen, and what we should do. I urged that the Clinton administration make one last diplomatic effort to see if we could begin to come to some understanding with the Sudanese government. Acknowledging that a positive outcome was unlikely, I said there would be no harm in trying. I suggested the effort be initiated by a letter from President Clinton. Peter asked me to draft the letter as soon as I got back to Khartoum, so that it would be ready for an interagency meeting he would chair at the White House later in the month.

I told them I was opposed to a presidential appointment of a special envoy for Sudan, an idea that continued to have currency. I said conditions for ending the war in Sudan did not exist now nor would they for the indefinite future; none of the parties was ready for serious negotiations. I saw no good reason to lend the president's prestige to an endeavor that would fail. Someday a legitimate need for a special envoy might arise, but there was none now. Tarnoff and the others indicated their agreement with this.

The interagency meeting on Sudan took place at the White House about a week later. From it came a decision to take no new initiatives either to try to improve relations or to put additional pressure on the Sudanese government. New accounts of the continued prosecution of the war, with increased suffering by civilians and an absence of any serious effort by Khartoum to respond to U.S. concerns about terrorism, human rights, and other major issues had led to the conclusion that any gesture toward the Sudanese government would be inappropriate. As for new pressures, the administration saw insufficient domestic or international support for more active intervention in Sudan.

I wrote Julie and Brian that the policy decision meant dependents would not be returning to Khartoum now or for the immediate future. Julie's anger with the State Department's decision to evacuate families from Khartoum was rekindled. From the beginning she had held that the decision was unjustified. In time she was proven right. The months wore on, no credible threat to embassy Americans materialized, and eventually serious doubt was raised about the validity of the information that had led to the evacuation.

# 11

# Terrorism

The plot to kill Americans may have been made of whole cloth, but there was no doubt at all about the continued presence of foreign terrorists in Khartoum. The information about the terrorists and their organizations that the embassy had painstakingly gathered over time was first-hand. It was not obtained in a manner that would have lent itself to disinformation or in any other way have been manipulated or altered by intelligence sources in Sudan.

The end of the career of the infamous terrorist Ilich Ramirez Sanchez, better known as Carlos the Jackal, was a good example of the accuracy and value of the kind of information we were collecting. A spent force in the world of terrorism, in 1993 Carlos had failed to get sanctuary in Iraq and Libya. He finally found refuge in Khartoum in August of that year. Around town, under an assumed name he stood out as a heavy drinking, womanizing playboy.

His true identity and his presence became known to the embassy. There were no charges pending against him in the United States, but he was wanted elsewhere for his crimes, which included a multiple murder charge against him in France. Therefore, we passed our information about Carlos to the French. They in turn notified the Sudanese government that they wanted him apprehended for extradition to France. The Sudanese stalled on taking action. Frustrated and annoyed, the French told the Sudanese that if they did not do as the

French wanted, there would be a serious political cost to pay. The Sudanese agreed to play ball.

An opportunity to seize Carlos with no risk of violence arose in mid-August 1994, when he checked into Khartoum's Ibu Khalmud hospital for minor surgery. After the surgery, while Carlos was still groggy from the anesthetic, Sudanese government security police agents persuaded him to transfer to a military hospital for his own security. They then proceeded to hand him over to the French, who whisked him off to Paris, where later he was tried, convicted, and imprisoned.

The Bashir government was quick to take credit for having handed Carlos over to the French. The Sudanese professed to be miffed when the U.S. government did not give them credit for helping put Carlos out of action. During a meeting I had with Turabi on August 28, in expressing his displeasure over the lack of American praise, he went so far as to accuse the CIA of having had a hand in bringing Carlos to Khartoum. I told him that this was totally untrue. I said the embassy knew full well that Carlos was in Sudan with the knowledge and consent of the Sudanese government and that the Sudanese had let the French have Carlos only after the French put heavy pressure on them to hand him over.

A man who would later be more infamous than Carlos was living in Khartoum at this time. Osama bin Laden had come to Sudan from Saudi Arabia in 1991, when he was thirty-four years old. One of the many children of an immensely wealthy Yemeni-born Saudi construction contractor who died at the end of the 1960s, bin Laden inherited a fortune from his father. While studying economics and management at King Abdulaziz University in Jeddah, he was deeply impressed by the Islamic teachings of two Muslim scholars, one of whom was Abdullah Azzam, a Palestinian from Jordan.

Very soon after the Soviets invaded Afghanistan in 1979, bin Laden went to Pakistan and expressed his faith by working for their expulsion. He formed a close association with Abdullah Azzam. Working together they established the *Maktab al-Khidamat* (MAK) or Afghan Service Bureau, through which they oversaw the recruitment, indoctrination, and training of foreign *mujahidin*. In time the MAK would evolve into Al Qaeda, conceptualized by Azzam as the vanguard of an international movement to further the Islamist reformist aims that he had laid down. He saw it as "an organization that would channel the energies of the *mujahidin* into fighting on behalf of oppressed Muslims worldwide."[1] Azzam and bin Laden would come to disagree on tactics for Al Qaeda. After Azzam was assassinated, possibly with bin Laden's acquiescence, bin Laden became the undisputed leader of Al Qaeda and molded it into a worldwide terrorist organization. It developed close links with many extremist Islamist terrorist groups in the Arab world and elsewhere.

In the early 1980s in Pakistan, along with his work with the MAK, bin Laden had provided logistical support and money to build schools and shelters for Afghan refugees. Then he moved to Afghanistan, helping the Afghani and foreign *mujahidin* in various ways and finally taking up arms himself.

In 1989 he returned to Saudi Arabia after the Soviet withdrawal from Afghanistan. Treated with respect for what he had accomplished in Afghanistan, he rejoined the family business and founded a welfare organization for veterans of the war in Afghanistan. But he broke with the Saudi royal family for inviting the American military to the country for protection after Saddam Hussein invaded and occupied Kuwait. His strong and vocal criticism of the royal family led to his confinement to Jedda. In 1991 he managed to leave the country, flying in his personal jet aircraft to Peshawar, Pakistan. However, he did not feel safe in Pakistan, which had close relations with Saudi Arabia. He was, therefore, amenable to an invitation from Hasan al-Turabi to come to Sudan and establish an Al Qaeda presence there.

The Bashir government, hard-pressed for outside capital investments, welcomed bin Laden. With much in common ideologically, he and Turabi formed a close association. Bin Laden provided financial backing for Turabi's Popular Arab and Islamic Conference (PAIC), an umbrella organization for Islamist political movements which Turabi established in 1991. Turabi shared bin Laden's hatred for Jews and the United States and his antipathy to the Saudi royal family and rulers of other Arab countries whom they regarded as having strayed from the true path of Islam. Bin Laden's support for Islamist extremists' terrorist organizations paralleled the clandestine support the Sudanese were providing.

Speaking for the record, years later Sudanese officials would insist that bin Laden was engaging only in business activities during his stay in Sudan. In 2001, Gutbi al-Mahdi, then a leading figure in Sudan's intelligence services and later a cabinet minister, told a reporter: "Whatever his views when he was here, he was just doing business. We were watching him and he was under control."[2]

But in truth, while he did create and run a wide variety of business enterprises, bin Laden also worked hard at strengthening Al Qaeda and forging ties between it and other terrorist organizations. The support he received from Bashir, Turabi, and the Sudanese intelligence services and military was crucial to both his business and his terrorist activities. For instance, Bashir directed that bin Laden's imports would not be subject to inspection or taxation. Among the help bin Laden gave to the Sudanese were weapons and funding for the war in southern Sudan.

Bin Laden established some thirty companies in Sudan. Among them was a construction company whose projects included a road from the vicinity of Khartoum to Port Sudan. Other enterprises included farms, a fruit and vegetable company, a trucking firm, a company engaged in processing and distributing the products of bin Laden's farms, export-import companies, and an investment company. But however much his time was spent on his business activities, his main interest continued to be furthering his political aims through Al Qaeda. He brought many of his fighters to Sudan. At least one of his farms was used as a site by Al Qaeda members and terrorists of other organizations for refresher training in explosives and weapons use. The Sudanese authorities were of great help in arranging for the arrival and departure of hundreds of these people and the shipment of weapons that bin Laden sent to various terrorists groups outside Sudan.

While he was in Sudan, bin Laden widened and strengthened Al Qaeda's worldwide network and developed its communications capabilities. It has been alleged that bin Laden and Al Qaeda launched various terrorist operations, including an attempt to assassinate Egypt's President Hosni Mubarak in Ethiopia in 1994 and bombings in Saudi Arabia in 1995. Bin Laden continued to issue statements harshly critical of the Saudi government. In 1994, Riyadh stripped him of his Saudi citizenship and froze the assets he still had in Saudi Arabia. His family disowned him.

The U.S. government was well aware of bin Laden's presence in Sudan. Through covert means, the embassy kept tabs on him and his Al Qaeda followers. For several years Washington regarded him as an important financier of terrorist organizations but did not consider him to be directly involved in terrorist operations. The State Department did not include him or Al Qaeda in the list of terrorist organizations it provided to me for the various démarches I made to the Sudanese government on the terrorism issue during my three years in Sudan. Washington's view of him, however, changed not long after I left Sudan.

By the end of 1995, the Egyptians, Saudis, and Americans were pressuring the Bashir government to expel bin Laden from Sudan. In 1996 the Sudanese gave in to the pressure and came to agreement with bin Laden for his departure. Much later the Sudanese would claim that they offered to turn him over to Saudis but that the Saudis, fearing retaliation, declined. In any event, bin Laden left Sudan for Afghanistan in the spring of 1996. From there he would continue to direct Al Qaeda's terrorist activities, now concentrated on American targets, including the U.S. embassies in Kenya and Tanzania, which were bombed in 1998. He would become a household name in the United States and elsewhere after the 9/11 attacks.

The American aim to get the Sudanese to end their support for terrorism was not directed just at Al Qaeda. While I was ambassador and afterward, the United States had irrefutable evidence of the presence in Khartoum of a variety of terrorist organizations. We at the embassy knew, and reported to Washington, the names of many of the terrorists in town and where their organizations' offices were located. Among them were the Abu Nidal Organization, Hizbollah, Palestine Islamic Jihad, Egypt's al-Gama'at al-Islamiyya, the Islamic Resistance Movement (Hamas), and others from Algeria, Eritrea, and other countries. In addition to refuge in Sudan, the Sudanese government provided the terrorists with travel documentation and safe passage out of Sudan.

In my remaining time in Sudan, I continued to bring up the terrorism issue, only to hear again and again from Bashir, Turabi, and others denials of any association whatsoever of the Sudanese government with terrorism. One could argue that their definition of terrorism was different from ours. But their denials rang hollow in Washington in view of our knowledge that the organizations we cited and individuals belonging to them were indeed present in Khartoum. Only some years later, when the value of the Sudanese support for the terrorists was outweighed by negative consequences for that support and by the Bashir government's growing need for the advantages of better relations with the United States, would the Sudanese change their tune.

# 12

# Tragedy in Southern Sudan Deepens

The situation in southern Sudan had deteriorated even further in the short time I had been away in Oregon and Washington, D.C., between late December 1993 and mid-January 1994. A drought in parts of the South and further displacements of civilians compounded the widespread misery. At least 1.5 million people were at risk of starvation unless the relief program could reach them, and continued warfare was making that difficult. Air raids on towns were a major reason civilians were fleeing into the countryside.

In late January preparations for the government's military offensive were continuing, despite a peace effort being mounted by East African heads of government and Western appeals that the military action be postponed.

In a January 28, 1994, article entitled "Sudan's Hidden Disaster" the *Washington Post*'s Jennifer Parmelee aptly summed up the situation. She wrote that the war

continues apace in virtual silence by the outside world, without any of the attention received by the nearby Somali disaster, slipping only occasionally into world view when Khartoum is accused of supporting terrorists. . . . Even by the tortured yardstick of Africa, a continent riven by

armed conflict, the scarcely visible war ravaging southern Sudan has sur-
passed most measures. . . . The conflict rates as the continent's most
deadly—an estimated one million people have died from war or war-related famine in the last decade alone, according to aid workers."[1]

The images of the dead and dying I had seen in southern Sudan were
etched in my mind, and I feared a new plague of violence was imminent. One arm of the Sudanese army's offensive would thrust south
from Juba toward the Ugandan border. It would head straight for the
area of the Triple-A camps, and the tens of thousands of people in
those camps would be at risk.

The basic situation in Khartoum had not changed much from when
I had gone on leave three weeks earlier. The weather had been unsea-
sonably hot, so hot, in fact, that the winter wheat crop had been severely damaged, adding further to Sudan's economic woes. Food prices
in the city continued to soar.

Peter Streams, the British ambassador, had been declared persona
non grata and left Khartoum two days before my return. He was a valued colleague and friend, and I was sorry I had not been there to say
good-bye when he left. Outspoken and forthrightly critical of the
regime, Streams had told me several months earlier that he would not
be surprised if the Sudanese told him to leave the country.

In the last week of January I proposed to Washington that the embassy release a statement calling for a cease-fire and asking Khartoum
not to start the military offensive. In the statement we would support
the mediation attempt by the presidents of Eritrea, Ethiopia, Kenya,
and Uganda. They had chosen to work under the umbrella of an East
African regional organization, the Intergovernmental Agency for
Drought and Desertification (IGADD). Washington agreed with my
proposal, and the embassy released the statement.

I met with the foreign minister a day later. I thought the government would react adversely to the statement, since it did not like being told to stop fighting in the South. However, he surprised me by
saying his government was pleased that the United States supported
the IGADD mediation. Later there was some relatively low-key criticism in the press.

I took advantage of an interview by a Reuters correspondent on January 31 to restate U.S. concern about the effects of a new military offensive. Although the Reuters article did not appear in Sudanese news-

papers, people in the government became aware of its contents, and a minister made a public statement criticizing me for what he said were erroneous and provocative words.

In the interview I said that if Khartoum went ahead with its planned offensive, "the consequences to the people in the area would be devastating." I said the United States hoped the Sudanese government would not go forward with its offensive but had no leverage with Khartoum. Commenting on the article, a government official stated to the press in one breath that there was no famine in the South and in the next that the rebels were responsible for the food shortage. He said the West, led by the United States, was trying to "destabilize the situation inside Sudan."

The first round of IGADD-sponsored peace talks had taken place in Nairobi earlier in January. In messages to Washington before the talks began, I was pessimistic about their chances for success. Just getting the sides to come to the negotiating table had taken months of effort. I pointed out that the Sudanese government and the rebels were miles apart on basic issues, in particular the place of religion in the state and the right of the South to self-determination.

The government insisted Islamic law (*sharia*²) should be the main underpinning of Sudan's legal system and legislation. The SPLA said this meant Sudan would become, if not in name, in fact an Islamic state, which it wholly opposed. As for self-determination, the SPLA was adamant that the South had the right to become independent if it so chose. (Self-determination, I should note, was not synonymous with independence. It meant, rather, that southerners would have the right to choose their political future, which could include a greater degree of autonomy for the South in a united Sudan, or a confederation, or separation and full independence.) The North was equally insistent that southern Sudan was an integral part of the country as a whole. With neither side showing any willingness to compromise on these issues, the prospects for peace were bleak. After several days, the session in Nairobi ended, with no measurable progress.

The second round of IGADD talks was held in Nairobi in March. It failed, like the first round, to produce any long-term results, again justifying skepticism that the IGADD effort would bring about an end to the war. After a couple of days, the talks were adjourned until mid-May. The disagreement between the government and the SPLA on self-determination and *sharia* was as deep as ever. One good thing came out of the abbreviated talks: an agreement in principle by the government and the SPLA to forgo any military activity during the last half of April and all of May and June in areas designated as "zones of tranquillity" by UNICEF. If the two sides could reach agreement with the United Nations, UNICEF would be able to give the basic childhood vaccinations to children in those specific areas. This had but limited success, for the war went on and the zones of tranquillity in which UNICEF was actually able to do its work were relatively few.

• • •

I flew to Nairobi on February 3 to attend a USAID-sponsored conference on humanitarian aid to the Horn of Africa. Three other U.S. ambassadors to countries in the area (Robert Houdek from Eritrea, Mark Baas from Ethiopia, and Aurelia Brazeal from Kenya) and officials from the State Department and USAID participated. It was a useful conference, focusing on the need for an integrated policy for aid to the Horn countries.

We spent one entire day talking about Sudan. This yielded, I thought, a greater realization by the USAID people from Washington of the severe problems we faced in our relations with Sudan and in getting food and other assistance to the people in southern Sudan. I appealed for U.S. funding to increase the airlift capacity of OLS, which was heavily dependent on air deliveries and airdrops to get food and other supplies into the South. (Additional funds were made available not long afterward.)

At the close of the conference on the fifth, a U.S. government statement was released in Nairobi condemning the air raids in southern Sudan and sounding an alarm about their consequences.

• • •

The Clinton administration's continuing criticism of Sudan, its call for a cease-fire, and the lead it had taken in the United Nations to bring about the adoption of resolutions condemning Sudan put additional strains on U.S.-Sudanese relations. One result was that most of the cabinet, as well as the president, were again off-limits to me. In a span of six weeks after I had made an official request to meet various ministers and three people in the NIF, I had been able to see only one minister and Hasan al-Turabi. If my meeting with Turabi was an indication, however, the ban had little practical effect: There appeared to be no give whatsoever in Sudanese policy, and any meetings I might have had would not have been productive.

This certainly was the case when I met with Turabi. We talked for two hours, but nothing new emerged; he merely restated the Sudanese leadership's hostility toward the U.S. government and its unwillingness to change its stance on human rights and terrorism. Among other things, Turabi again charged that the United States supported John Garang's SPLA faction, and he said that Washington's failure to intervene against the Serbs in Yugoslavia and its hostility toward Sudan were manifestations of its militant anti-Islam bias.

Conditions in southern Sudan continued to worsen. In most of the southeastern part of the South, the harvest had failed and food stocks were exhausted. OLS head Philip O'Brien said a "colossal humanitarian crisis" was developing there. In addition to the drought, the effect that bombings and other military activities were having on the people in displaced-persons camps was very worrisome. The United Nations verified that all the people in the Triple-A camps were, or soon would be, moving to new locations to get out of harm's way.

On February 5 the White House press secretary made a statement, the same one released in Nairobi, condemning "the new military offensive by the armed forces of the government of Sudan on populations in the South." He said the military activity demonstrated "a callous lack of concern for the lives of innocent Sudanese and a disregard for efforts to promote peace." The State Department called in the Sudanese ambassador to underscore the U.S. government's concern and anger regarding, in particular, the "indiscriminate bombing of civilians," and I was instructed to lodge a protest in Khartoum.

I did that on February 7 in a note I delivered to the Foreign Ministry. The note included the text of the White House statement. I told Omar Berido that the statement's tough language was justified, given the harm the raids were doing to thousands of southern Sudanese. Berido said that since the ministry had no information about any "bombing incidents," he could not accept the assertions made in the statement. I told him U.S. fears were being borne out, that military activity at or near the Triple-A camps would lead to an exodus of the displaced people in those camps.

The next day newspapers reported the government's rejection of the U.S. statement. The government said no raids had been or were being carried out and claimed the Sudanese army was only reacting to attacks by the rebels. Once again, truth took a backseat to propaganda.

In another meeting with Berido on February 12, I told him I was "amazed and dismayed" by his government's response to the note I had given him five days earlier. I said the Sudanese denial that air raids were being carried out was untrue, and I cited eyewitness accounts of bombings at Arapi, Maridi, Pariang, and Parajok (towns between Juba and the Ugandan border). I told him how many people had been killed and wounded and what was being done to evacuate the wounded. With the outside world now more aware of the awful extent of the tragedy in southern Sudan, I said, there would be growing pressure for something to be done.

Berido asserted again that the U.S. statement and press reports of bombings were inaccurate. I said eyewitness accounts were incontrovertible and could not be brushed aside. Instead of responding to that, he said the U.S. Congress and others were not evenhanded in their criticisms, for they "ignored SPLA crimes."

I reported to Washington that the Sudanese government would "continue to pursue its military objectives regardless of the urging of other governments unless more compelling pressures are applied." None were.

In another message, I informed the State Department that I soon would go to southern Sudan to assess the effects the air raids and ground attacks were having on the civilian population. On February 14 I met again with Berido at the ministry. When I told him I planned to go to Nairobi on February 16 and from there to southern Sudan, he said the Sudanese government would want me to go to the South through Juba.

I replied that, since I wanted to talk to USAID in Nairobi before going into the South, passing through Juba was out of the question. He said he would talk to the minister and get back to me. I was determined to make the trip and equally determined that I could not allow the Sudanese government to tell me when and how I should travel. Berido did not get back to me the next day, and so on the sixteenth I left for Nairobi.

On the seventeenth, together with a USAID officer and a UN official, I flew to Nimule. Khartoum had not given permission for a UN flight to Nimule or to Maridi, where we went later, so we traveled in a civilian charter aircraft. From Nimule we drove north to the Triple-A camps. On the way, we stopped to see the damage from an air raid on the town of Pageri. It had been bombed on February 8, and eight people had been killed. I saw bomb fragments and damaged and burned structures.

The Triple-A camps, which I had visited twice before, were to the north of Pageri. I found that Ame, which had developed into a well-run camp of about 40,000 people (Dinka displaced by the war from their home area) at the time of my first visit, was now a ghost town. Frightened by the nearby air raids and an attack by marauders, all the people at Ame had fled, leaving much of their possessions behind. The marauders had been led by William Nyuon, Riek Machar's principal deputy, who had received arms from the Sudanese government.

Nyuon seemed to be operating independently, and there was no hard evidence that Riek was also getting arms from the government. Whether he was or not, his SPLA-United was no longer fighting against the Sudanese army. Its military operations were directed solely against the SPLA-Mainstream.

The people who fled from Ame went to Atepi camp. From there most of the people of the two camps trekked about thirty miles east to a place called Parajok, which reportedly had also been bombed on the eighth. In Nimule that night, I talked to relief workers about getting food and other supplies to the 50,000 displaced people at Parajok.

The next day our party flew west to Yambio in western Equatoria, where we met with the SPLA-Mainstream military commander of that area and the few relief workers who had not been evacuated. They were nervous about reports of a Sudanese government military force approaching from across the border in the Central African Republic. The attack never materialized.

From Yambio we drove farther west to Nzara, then flew northeast to Maridi, also in western Equatoria. We proceeded by car toward Mundri, where a battle between government troops and the SPLA[3] had taken place a week earlier. We wanted to have a look at how the 35,000 Dinka who had fled from their camp at Kotobi, just south of Mundri, were doing.

About half way to Mundri, at a place called Bahr Olo, we came upon them. They had been walking for two days and had another five days' walk ahead of them. They were organized into groups of about 2,000 that set off separately in order to avoid congestion at places along the way where a relief organization had pre-positioned food. From what we observed, most people (by no means everyone, however) seemed to be in relatively good physical condition. Dehydration, malnutrition, and diarrhea were prevalent but not severe. I saw my first case of guinea worm—an elderly man who had a foot-long worm emerging from his leg.

I talked to the SPLA military commander at Bahr Olo. He said the fighting had moved to fifteen miles north of Mundri. There had been an air raid that morning. Refusing to be used for SPLA propaganda, I declined to talk to a prisoner whom his men had on display or to examine the weapons they had captured.

We stayed at Maridi that night at a former government guest house. It had no electricity or running water, but buckets of water were available for a bath to remove the red dust of the dirt road. The next morning we drove to the site being prepared for a new camp for the people from Kotobi, then boarded our plane and flew back to Nairobi.

• • •

The flights I made in light aircraft in Sudan, usually a Twin Otter or a single-engine Cessna Caravan, afforded me a great opportunity to see at relatively low altitudes large swaths of the variegated countryside, which ranges from sere desert in the north to vivid green forests in the southern mountains. We flew over parts of the Sudd, the vast swamp where the White Nile, blocked by papyrus and floating water plants, is dispersed into a myriad of sluggish watercourses. I sat next to the pilot whenever I could, relishing the great view and, as a former pilot, enjoying the sensations of flight in a light plane.

Landings on the short dirt airstrips at the villages and towns we visited were interesting. Before landing, the pilot reconnoitered the strips, sometimes by flying their perimeters a couple hundred feet or so off the ground. Only once did this make me apprehensive. Our pilot on that flight flew the perimeter at an altitude of about 100 feet, in itself no cause for alarm. But this was done at a 90-degree bank, and as I looked out my window straight down at the ground, I fervently hoped the engine would not hiccup, abruptly ending our flight and existence right then and there.

I believed we had little to fear from the government or rebel military forces on the ground, since we had cleared our flights beforehand. I can recall only a couple of times when we found out that firing from the ground could have occurred. Once, as we started our landing approach, we saw military vehicles speeding from the town to the airstrip. The local military commander, who was at the airstrip that morning, had not received notification of our impending arrival and had taken steps to prevent our landing. Fortunately we were on the ground before the vehicles carrying armed troops got there. After accosting us and hearing our story, the commander made us welcome.

· · ·

On my February 19 return to Nairobi from the Triple-A camps, Yambio, Nzara, Maridi, and Bahr Olo, I held a press conference and gave an interview to BBC radio. Knowing the Sudanese government would probably be angry with me for having gone to the South again, I avoided direct answers to those questions that were aimed at getting me to say something provocative against either the government or the SPLA.

Nevertheless, on February 21, the day after I got back to Khartoum, I was attacked in the Sudanese press. The day before, a government source told the press that my visit to "some parts of southern Sudan without the consent of the Sudanese government" was "an uncordial act in violation of the national sovereignty and exceeding his responsibilities." I was accused of being biased in favor of the rebels and of trying to ensure "delivery of arms and military hardware to the rebel fighting forces." The source said I "could at least [have] sought an official permission from the Sudan government" to make the visit. One newspaper, *As Sudan Al Hadith*, after noting that I had gone to the South without the government's prior permission, said, "Expel this man!"

On the same day the press attacks appeared I met with Foreign Minister Abu Salih. It was a cordial meeting. I described what I saw and did in the South, and we discussed U.S.-Sudanese relations. He made no complaint about my trip. On February 22 the press carried a statement that Abu Salih issued after our meeting. In it he said my trip to the South "took place with the knowledge of the Sudan Foreign Ministry" and that what I had said at the press conference in Nairobi was "balanced." He also said that he "thanked the American Ambassador for the diplomatic efforts he has been exerting for resolution of the South problem and his support for the IGADD peace initiative."

Picking up on the contradiction within the government, one newspaper said that it was surprised by Abu Salih's statement and that it owed me an apology for the unkind words it had printed about me. It went on to ask, "Who was responsible for these contradictory positions and policies?"[4]

Hard-liners' true feelings about this latest trip were expressed in an editorial in *As Sudan Al Hadith*. It said any diplomat traveling in Sudan should be accompanied by a government official. As for the U.S. ambassador, it wrote, "We do not expect such an ambassador who represents a country that is hostile to the people and government of Sudan to be fair and to contradict the American policy toward an Islamic state." The ministry, the paper said, should have considered this "bias in favor of the rebel movement" before giving me permission to travel.

Within the government there were two conflicting opinions about what I did. The hard-line Islamists were unhappy, whereas the moderates were trying to present a better image of Sudan.

Because the weather in Khartoum in July is usually so bad, we held our national-day celebration[5] on Presidents' Day, February 21. In 1993 Julie had organized the party, and she and our cook, Bushra, prepared all the food. This year, with Julie gone, I had a caterer help Bushra do the food and serve it and the drinks. The reception in the garden of our house went well. The weather that night was good, the catered food was fine, and the turnout, which included some government officials, not bad, all things considered.

•  •  •

It was at about this time that our consular problems became so serious that I asked Dick Moose to approve an increase in our staff by one full-time consular officer. Officers who had had only rudimentary consular training were doing the consular work part-time. They were having trouble doing their primary job and coping with the consular workload, which consisted mainly of examining and processing applications for visas to enter the United States. Things came to a head when a case of visa fraud was not handled well. Nevertheless, Moose turned me down, saying in no uncertain terms that because of the security situation in Khartoum, he was not going to permit any permanent additions to our staff. Later, when he better understood the seriousness of the consular problem, he relented and we got the position.

With the strains between the U.S. and Sudanese governments still pronounced, and with the recent violence in Omdurman and Khartoum, the State Department was even more inclined than before to keep our staffing level at a minimum and dependents away from post. We did get a doctor, but after a time we lost the position. Owing to our diminished numbers, I could not justify having a doctor at post. We reverted to the same medical care available to many U.S. diplomatic posts in Third World countries where medical care is not good: State Department regional physicians would occasionally make short visits to the post.

At our embassy, however, we were blessed with a great asset in a very capable nurse, Fiona Hamid, and an equally able laboratory technician, Alison Imam, the former a Scot and the latter a New Zealander, both married to Sudanese. Their advice and professional skills were invaluable, especially when we had a medical emergency, as we did in November 1993 when one of our employees came down with a life-threatening bout of malaria. On the basis of their diagnosis and strong recommendation to the State Department's Medical Division, he was evacuated by air to Holland, where after two weeks or so his kidneys, shut down by the disease, began functioning again. Had he stayed in Khartoum, he would have died.

The medical hazards of living in Khartoum were sadly brought home to us again in May 1995. Three months earlier Alison had had a seizure of some sort; she had passed out and had convulsions. Lacking the most technically advanced diagnostic equipment, doctors in Khartoum could find nothing wrong, and she seemed to get better. But her headaches persisted, and she went on leave to New Zealand with her husband and young daughter. A short while later Fiona got word that Alison had had an operation to remove a cancerous brain tumor; she had perhaps a few months to a year to live. It is not certain she would have lived had the tumor been found earlier, but she might have.

Fiona and Alison were like sisters, and Fiona was devastated by the news. I asked Gloria Benedict to find out how much it would cost for an air ticket to New Zealand and to see if the Americans in the embassy would join me in contributing to a fund to pay for a round-trip ticket so Fiona could go to see her friend. Once I knew we could manage it, I asked Fiona if she would like to go. She was overjoyed, and flew to Auckland the next week.

• • •

In late February and early March 1994 I had a number of talks with the foreign minister and, separately, with representatives of the southern Sudanese leadership in Khartoum. I was trying to capitalize on the good reputation I seemed to have with southerners because of my travels into the South and the at least momentary goodwill that the foreign minister was exhibiting toward me. My aim was to see if I could begin to find some common ground between the two sides so that a better basis for peace talks could be found.

I would have been quite prepared to carry this further if the Sudanese government was interested, but the White House was on the verge of naming a special envoy to try to mediate an end to the Sudanese conflict. For domestic political purposes the administration had decided to go along with a call from a few legislators on Capitol Hill for the appointment of a special envoy for Sudan. And it now appeared that the Sudanese were ready to agree to work with the special envoy, whereas a few weeks earlier they were declaring they would not receive anyone in that capacity.

I was not sure what had changed their minds. Perhaps it was because the war was not going well for them; the dry season offensive had been a failure so far, and the army and militia (the People's Defense Force, PDF[6]) had taken fairly heavy casualties. Perhaps, too, the international condemnation of Sudan was beginning to have some effect. In any case, through talks with the government and representatives of the rebels, I hoped to be able in the days immediately ahead to help pave the way for the envoy.

In the meantime, the war went on. In the first week of March the Sudanese air force bombed Nimule and the displaced-persons camp at Aswa, both of which I had visited less than two weeks earlier. This was the first raid affecting civilians since February 12, and it dashed any hopes that the government was heeding the international outcry for a halt to the bombings. Casualties in the two places were light.

Only civilians were hurt. Both the State Department and the House Foreign Affairs Committee denounced the raids.

I was planning to attend a ceremony at which President Bashir was going to honor governors of the ten or so new states that had recently been created,[7] but as soon as I heard about the air raids, I decided not to go. I could not be present at a government ceremony shortly after that same government had allowed its air force to drop bombs on civilians. I had no intention of isolating myself from the government, however, so a week later I went to a post-Ramadan *iftar* (breaking of the fast) that the president gave for heads of diplomatic missions. And I planned to go to the *Eid al Fitr* reception he was going to have a few days later.

When I spoke briefly with Bashir at the *iftar*, he said we should have a talk soon. I had not met with him since the previous September, when I delivered the very harsh warning from Washington. By seeing Turabi, the foreign minister, and other notables I had been able to convey what I wanted to get across to the government and the NIF. Access to Sudan's president was important, however, and I was glad that the door to resuming talks with Bashir was open to me again.

On March 13 I was one of the few diplomats to whom Bashir gave an audience at his *Eid al Fitr* reception. Part of my cable on our meeting gives a flavor of how it went:

> I noted that it had been seven months since we last met. He nodded and said that I had, however, met with the Foreign Minister frequently during that time. Acknowledging that, I mentioned that in recent days Abu Salih and I had been talking about the IGADD peace effort. He indicated he had been fully briefed on [those] meetings.
>
> He went on to say his government wanted the IGADD mediation to succeed in ending the war. He expected to meet with [Kenyan] President Moi on March 16, and a GOS delegation would go to Nairobi for talks with the SPLA beginning on the 17th. He said Sudan was suffering enormously because of the war, which in his view was the cause of most of its problems with the West. However, some outside forces were bent on keeping the war going so that his government would be weakened and toppled.
>
> I said I hoped he did not include the United States among those forces, as some in Sudan are alleging. We supported the IGADD mediation and were not providing any military assistance to the SPLA. He said he had

information that the U.S. government had given 80 military trucks to the SPLA. "Absolutely untrue," I said. "What about stinger missiles?" he asked. I answered that this was equally false information.

Commenting at the end of the reporting cable, I told Washington that the conversation revealed again the poor quality of the data the Sudanese intelligence services were passing on to Bashir and other Sudanese leaders. This, I said, fed their tendency to believe the worst about the U.S. government and its intentions.

On March 16 I received word from the State Department that the U.S. permanent representative to the United Nations, Ambassador Madeleine Albright, would be coming to Khartoum on March 31 to deliver a message to President Bashir. She was traveling to several countries and had wanted to come to Khartoum on the twenty-fifth. When the U.S. Mission to the United Nations learned from me that Bashir would not be available on that date, the visit was canceled. But after I sent a message that Bashir could meet with her on the thirty-first, it was decided to revamp her entire itinerary to enable her to come to Sudan. The administration decided it was that important that she come to Khartoum.

The immediate upshot of this for me was that I would be unable to attend a regional chiefs-of-mission conference at Zanzibar at the end of March. Because Ambassador Albright would be the first senior official of the Clinton administration to come to Khartoum, and the only cabinet member to set foot in Sudan in years, I needed to be present for her visit.

She arrived March 31, as planned. I accompanied her and some of her staff to a meeting with President Bashir and several of his principal advisers. She forcefully reiterated the administration's Sudan policy, emphasizing our concerns about human rights, the war, the relief program, and terrorism. Bashir responded as he always did, denying that his government was guilty of any wrongdoing and accusing Washington of being hostile to Sudan solely because of its Islamic orientation. Ambassador Albright flatly rejected this.

The exchange between Albright, Bashir, and some of his advisers got heated a few times. Nevertheless, it ended cordially, and, somewhat to the bemusement of the Americans, Foreign Minister Abu Salih and other officials who accompanied the Albright party to the airport to see them off proclaimed their pleasure about the meeting. They chose to ignore her message and focus on the fact that a cabinet-level American had come to Sudan on an official visit.

The next day the Sudanese media downplayed the differences between the two governments and featured remarks by Abu Salih that the Albright visit was "a real start of a serious dialogue with the United States administration."

The upbeat Sudanese interpretation of the visit lasted only a day. Speaking at a press conference in Addis Ababa on April 1, Ambassador Albright said that at the meeting with Bashir she had "stated that Sudan has set itself apart from the community of nations by its support for international terrorism, its gross human rights violations, and its failure to take steps to resolve the civil war that has created a massive humanitarian crisis throughout Sudan." She said she had "stressed our profound concern over the compelling evidence that elements of the Sudanese government continue to assist international terrorist groups." In addition, she "expressed revulsion of the international community over the arbitrary detentions, torture, and repression of political opposition and unions."

The Sudanese leaders, furious that she had made public the central points of the severe message she had delivered to them the night before in Khartoum, lashed out at her through the media and, for good measure, excoriated the government she represented.

• • •

I had no trouble bearing in mind the true picture in Sudan regarding the government's abuses of human rights. Embassy officers and I had frequent cogent reminders of what was happening. Two examples:

A few days before the Albright visit, I met with two women who belonged to a group calling itself the "Martyrs' Association." The members of the Martyrs' Association were relatives, mainly wives or mothers, of army officers who had been summarily executed by the Bashir government not long after it had come to power. Since that time, the relatives had been trying to find out where the men were buried. For doing this, they had been under surveillance, some had been arrested, some had been beaten, and some had their houses taken away from them.

When Gaspar Biro, the UN's special rapporteur on human rights for Sudan, came to Khartoum in 1993, women who belonged to the Mar-

tyrs' Association gathered in front of the UN compound in an attempt
to have an audience with him to tell him about their plight. Security
police came and, in front of Biro, flogged the women and arrested
them.

The two women who came to see me wanted simply to tell their
story. The younger of the two had been detained four times; the elder
was once beaten and trampled on and, as a result, suffered a heart attack. They asked that the U.S. government keep pressure on the Sudanese government to stop oppressing people like themselves. I told
them what we had been doing—the condemnations in the United Nations and the economic pressures we exerted the previous year, for example—and said Washington would not relent and begin to have a
normal relationship with Khartoum until the regime changed its behavior toward the people of Sudan.

Earlier, in February, I had gone to the house of a man I had met several times. Before the military overthrew the government of Sadiq al-
Mahdi in 1989, he had been a leading figure of one of the country's
three main political parties. He was a man much respected for his
honesty and courage. Since the Bashir government came to power, he
had been imprisoned several times. He had been out of detention a little over a week when he asked me to come see him at his house. I got
word to him that I was worried this could add to his problems with
the government. He repeated his request for a meeting.

When I saw him, he said he didn't care what the regime did to him
and that he was overjoyed the American ambassador had come to his
house. I told him I was honored to talk to a man of his courage and
convictions.

He described his latest imprisonment in a "ghost house." Ghost
houses were residences in Khartoum or Omdurman that had been
converted into small prisons. Many or most political detainees were
taken to these houses, which were called ghost houses because the
government denied they existed. Some detainees were kept in them
for months before being released or put into a regular prison. They had
no access to family or legal representation. Many were tortured. As
time went by and the existence, and even the location, of ghost houses
became widely known, their use diminished.

Unlike at least one of his earlier imprisonments, this time my
friend was not tortured. However, others who were in the ghost house

while he was there were tortured, he said. He told me he had been detained after giving a speech at the university. He intended to continue to speak out. "All they can do," he said, "is kill me." He said this quietly, without false bravado. A month after I met with him, he was arrested once more, shortly after again speaking out against the government.

In addition to drawing on the body of evidence that Amnesty International, the American embassy, and other organizations had accumulated on human rights abuses, I used firsthand experiences like these—talking to victims—when I spoke to government and NIF officials about the human rights issue. Their standard line continued to be that the charges against Sudan were no more than lies put out by the regime's political enemies. But when I described firsthand accounts of people whom I had met, they tended to change the subject by, for example, accusing the U.S. government of wholesale human rights violations.

•   •   •

It was inevitable that sooner or later we would have to reduce the number of the embassy's Sudanese employees to be more in line with the diminished number of Americans. In March the State Department made it clear that the embassy had to carry out a "rif" (reduction in force). I had wanted to delay this as long as possible because I knew that, owing to the terrible state of the Sudanese economy, most of those who would be cut would find it difficult or impossible to get other work. By holding off as long as we did before carrying out the rif in May, at least we were able to ensure that those who lost their jobs would get severance pay at the new pay rate, induced by rampant inflation, that had just gone into effect.

# 13

# A Spring of Little Promise

Hasan al-Turabi is a fascinating man. A lawyer educated in Sudan, Britain, and France who speaks classical Arabic, French, and excellent English, and a world-renowned Islamic scholar, Turabi is also a politician whose ambition to lead his country has, many believe, been fulfilled. He sees himself at the center of an Islamic revival that he believes will sweep away the old order in Muslim countries throughout the world. Some believe his vision of a new Islamic order is the driving force of his political involvement; others say he is motivated by ego and personal ambition.

The son of an Islamic judge, Turabi was born in 1932. He became a member of the Muslim Brotherhood in the early 1950s when he was a student at the University of Khartoum. He was a brilliant student and became the leader of Islamic activists at the university. By 1965, after having received a master's degree at the University of London and his doctorate at the University of Paris, he was dean of the school of law at the University of Khartoum. He became dissatisfied with the more traditional Muslim Brothers' nonparticipation in politics and formed the Islamic Charter Front, which later became the National Islamic Front.

When Numeiry was in power, Turabi spent time in prison, under house arrest, and in exile before joining Numeiry's Sudan Socialist Union in 1976. When he was attorney general in Numeiry's government, Turabi played an influential part in the controversial introduction of *sharia*. In 1985 he was jailed again, but after three months was freed when Numeiry was deposed.

Turabi's National Islamic Front became a strong political force, and during the unstable politics of Sadiq al-Mahdi's six successive coalition governments he was in and out of the government. In 1988 Turabi became minister of justice, and in 1989 minister of foreign affairs and deputy prime minister. He was dropped from the government over his opposition to suspending *sharia* until the convening of a constitutional conference. Then, in June of that year came the coup that toppled Sadiq and brought Turabi to his place of power.

I first met Turabi in April 1992, when he was visiting Washington, D.C. I was in attendance when he gave an address before a small group at the Institute of Peace and took questions afterward. He was adept at avoiding answering tough questions about Sudan's human rights record. But his responses, although deftly worded, were utterly unconvincing to his well-informed audience.

He was more impressive in a private conversation the two of us had after dinner one night at the Sudanese embassy. However, an occurrence later that night offset this favorable impression. Another dinner guest, Andrew Natsios, Jim Kunder's predecessor as director of the U.S. Office of Foreign Disaster Assistance, had been to Sudan recently and had gone to the displaced-persons camps on the outskirts of Khartoum. Natsios described what he saw and heard. He said people had been forcibly taken to areas lacking any basic facilities, such as water and housing. Turabi told him he was wrong; people went voluntarily to the camps, which were well situated and had adequate facilities. When Natsios replied that he had seen with his own eyes the deplorable conditions in the camps, Turabi impassively told him he was mistaken.

A few days later, at an airport in Canada, Turabi was assaulted by a young Sudanese and beaten unconscious. Months later, in early September 1992 at our first meeting in Khartoum, he told me he still suffered from effects of the beating, such as fatigue and a diminished sense of taste. I could detect, however, no obvious impairment of his mental faculties, contrary to reports to that effect. After that meeting I told Washington, "An apparently only slightly impaired Hasan Turabi has come through his ordeal in Canada with his leadership of the NIF intact and his objective of promoting the cause of Islamic revivalism throughout Sudan and elsewhere unchanged. Unchanged also are his animus for other Arab regimes and his opposition to U.S. policies in the Middle East."

Others who knew Turabi said he was not as sharp mentally as he once had been. Often there were rumors that he was behaving bizarrely, that he was dying, or that he had gone abroad for treatment. But on the many occasions we met, even as the rumors flew, he always seemed in good health, both physically and mentally. His health aside, I noted some very flawed thinking on Turabi's part. For a man of his education, sophistication, and intelligence, Turabi harbored eccentric ideas and repugnant prejudices, anti-Semitism in particular.

Nevertheless, Turabi could be impressive when holding forth on many aspects of Islam. He would explain the currents in modern Islam and the power of the Islamic Resurgence. I appreciated his discourses on political Islam in different parts of the Muslim world, for example. Too often, however, he focused on pet themes and lashed out intemperately on such things as the evils of the West, the stupidity of those in the Arab world who resisted change, and the hopelessly ignorant Americans and other benighted enemies of Sudan.

Given his importance in Sudan and because his views diverged so much from Washington's on matters such as human rights, political freedoms, and the presence of terrorist organizations in Sudan, it was all the more difficult to see how relations could be materially improved. In two conversations we had in the early months of 1994, Turabi stated several such views:

- U.S. antagonism toward Sudan reflected an anti-Islam policy, not concerns about human rights or any other issues we cited. Out of hostility toward Muslims, the United States aligned itself with the "pro-Serbia" policy of the Europeans.
- The United States was a racist and godless society with no moral compass and a philosophy of "whatever works goes."
- The "Jewish-Zionist" lobby controlled every instrument of power in the United States—the executive branch of government, the Congress, the media, and so on.
- This lobby, in concert with "the Christian-fundamentalist lobby," dictated the anti-Islamic bias of U.S. policy.

- American police routinely beat suspects.
- The United States was the leading terrorist state in the world.
- Hamas was not a terrorist organization.
- There was no need for the Clinton administration to appoint a special representative for Sudan, but at least it was not going to appoint "that Jew" (former congressman Steven Solarz).[1]
- Western intelligence organizations were behind the attack on him in Canada. The Canadian government definitely had a hand in it, probably at the direction of the CIA.

• • •

In late April 1994 there seemed to be some sentiment within the Sudanese government and the NIF to try again to improve relations with the United States. On the night of the twenty-sixth I had a three-hour meeting at the house of a prominent member of the NIF, Mustafa Osman Ismail, then a junior minister in the cabinet (in 1998 he would become Sudan's foreign minister). I did my best to explain to him and the other three men there that night that they were deluding themselves if they thought there could be any progress toward a better relationship if their government did not begin to clean up its human rights record and meet other U.S. concerns. I was pleasantly surprised when they admitted, if only grudgingly, that there might be some substance to what the U.S. government was saying.

They asked whether the United States would reciprocate if the government did begin to do some of the things we wanted to see done. Yes, I replied, but only if real changes occurred, not the kind of hollow gestures the government had made in the past.

They promised to arrange a meeting with President Bashir. I told Washington that even if the meeting took place, I would be astonished if Bashir conceded, as the four did last night, that his government was guilty of any wrongdoing.

In the meantime we were getting reliable reports of increased human rights violations. In early May the embassy learned of more cases of torture, more-frequent floggings for violations of *sharia*, theft of donated food in Malakal by the Islamic "relief agency" Da'wa Islamia and the Sudanese military, and increasing numbers of people being detained. As for the SPLA, it was interfering with barge shipments at times and stealing food from them and from trains carrying desperately needed food destined for displaced people.

The knowledge that peace talks were about to reopen in Nairobi had not led to any lessening of military activity in the South. For two weeks the northern army had been breaking through SPLA defenses in various places, primarily north of Nimule and near Kajo Keji (west of Nimule).

If the government forces took those two objectives, they would seal off from the SPLA two very important border access points through which the rebels received supplies. At the same time, Khartoum would have a stronger bargaining position at the negotiating table. In addition, it could proclaim to the people that the North had won a great victory, justifying the sacrifices made for the war, including the heavy casualties of recent weeks. But the offensive slowed down. It seemed unlikely the government could capture either Nimule or Kajo Keji by May 16, when the Nairobi talks were set to begin.

Even if Nimule and Kajo Keji fell, it was doubtful that the SPLA would give in. Militarily, they would just change over to guerrilla warfare. The fighting would go on, and the people of the South would continue to suffer. In talks with southerners and government officials, I urged both sides to be flexible in the peace talks and to do all they could to overcome differences and reach a settlement.

• • •

As soon as I could, I went back to southern Sudan. The worsening plight of displaced southerners and a consequent need to reexamine the relief effort to deliver vitally needed food, medicines, and other supplies to them demanded that I go there, see what was happening, confer with relief workers and UN officials, and report on what I learned.

Before leaving Khartoum I met with four prominent southerners: Abel Alier; Martin Malwal, a former member of the Revolutionary Command Council; Eliaba Surur; and Hilary Logale. I told them that UN negotiators and some other participants in recent talks in Nairobi on relief operations reported that the Sudanese government had been more flexible than the SPLA. The government delegation had accepted the UN's proposals for opening certain roads to relief convoys. In contrast, the SPLA had rejected them out of hand. More generally, the

SPLA seemed poorly prepared for the talks and uninterested in them once they started.

Alier defended SPLA-Mainstream's view that opening land routes from Lokichokio in Kenya to Kapoeta and Torit would allow Khartoum to relieve the beleaguered garrisons in the two towns. I noted that the government was already resupplying Kapoeta and Torit by air and that the arrival of some food by land would not substantially alter the military situation. It was imperative that all parties to the conflict bend over backward to improve the delivery of humanitarian aid. There was another important factor: Land access routes would be much cheaper than the exorbitantly expensive air deliveries. After more discussion, Alier agreed the SPLA should show maximum concern for the welfare of the southern people and said he would pass on to the SPLA what I had told him.

Khartoum had stated repeatedly, I said, that everything except self-determination was negotiable. I therefore questioned the SPLA's practice of stating publicly on the verge of going into peace talks that their objective was self-determination. Instead, the SPLA ought to focus on the substance of its agenda: an interim arrangement for southern Sudan during a cooling-off period, followed by a referendum in which southerners would determine their own future. This would be the same thing as self-determination, but the use of the controversial term would be avoided.

Alier, Surur, and Logale responded that southerners deeply distrusted Khartoum and felt the need to call for nothing less than self-determination. However, following more exchanges on this, they conceded that it might be better for the SPLA to drop its use of "self-determination" if the government would agree to the principle of a referendum.

About a week later, I was on my way again to southern Sudan. In an unclassified cable sent from Nairobi, I reported on the two-day (May 13–14) tour of places in Equatoria and Bahr al-Ghazal:

1. Summary:[2] For tens of the thousands of southern Sudanese, their hold on life remains precarious because of the continuing effects of the war and the shortage of the resources for the relief effort. I believe that we and other donors need to rethink what must be done—what additional help we can scrape up—at the very least

to keep the civilian death rate from climbing higher. The global [moderate to severe] malnutrition rate at Labone camp (60,000 displaced) has reached an alarming 31 percent, the same level measured by an MSF [Médecins sans Frontières]-France team in the Akon area of Bahr al Ghazal. With access to displaced and other desperately needy people in Bahr al Ghazal limited almost entirely to aircraft and with not enough planes available to the UN to adequately cover the relief needs of southern Sudan, either more money for aircraft is provided or a lot of people who could have been saved will die.

2. Unless the GOS decides for political reasons to declare a cease-fire at the outset of the peace talks, the war will go on, diminished in intensity but not halted by the rains. For other reasons, the Sudanese army's advances on Nimule and Kajo Keji seem to be stalled, at least momentarily. Thirty-two international relief workers and several missionaries remain at Nimule, hoping to be able to stay there but poised to depart at a moment's notice. End Summary.

3. On Friday, May 13, UN Program Officer Paulette Nichols and I flew to Nimule in a chartered aircraft (because of the GOS ban on UN flights into Nimule, we had to take a civilian plane). We traveled via Lokichokio, where we were joined by Trevor Harvey, the UN's security officer.

4. From Nimule we drove 30 kilometers over a dirt road, damaged by the rains but still open, to Monghale Camp. Established five weeks ago, the camp is inhabited by 30,000 Dinka from Aswa camp, the last of the "Triple-A" camps to be evacuated, and some 20,000 residents of towns extending south from the Triple-A area to Nimule. Donated food is relatively abundant, but gastro-intestinal diseases resulting from the unsafe water supply are raising the malnutrition rate. There is a lot of malaria. Medical supplies are wholly inadequate. The relief organization AICN is hoping to be able to drill bore holes between the camp and the river to stop the people from using the now-polluted Aswa river.

5. Relief workers who recently traveled farther east to Labone camp, where 60,000 former residents of Ame and Atepi camps are now located, told us that delivering food there from Gulu [in Uganda] is extremely difficult because of the poor condition of

some stretches of the road. The 31 percent moderate-to-severe malnutrition rate is of deep concern. The unhealthy sources of water (small streams in the area) and insufficient medical services add to the problem. It is imperative that AICN's work to supply potable water be completed and that the road into Labone be improved. ($80,000 dollars of a $625,000 USAID grant to the World Food Program for road improvements in Equatoria will be used for the Labone road. Repairs are slated to begin early next month.)

6. I met with Kuol Manyang, the SPLA's acting military commander of the area, at his command post a few miles east of Nimule. He claimed that in fighting on April 23–24 and again on May 4, the SPLA inflicted heavy casualties on the government force north of Nimule and halted their advance. He said the ability of the northern Sudanese forces to advance in this sector depends to a significant extent on use of the Antonov aircraft, not to inflict casualties on SPLA troops but to locate troop dispositions. When the aircrews spot troop concentrations, they drop bombs on the area. Smoke from the explosions guides Sudanese army artillery batteries, whose concentrated fire forces the SPLA to withdraw.

7. Lately the Antonovs have not been flying. Manyang believes a shortage of fuel and bombs accounts for this. He said the northern army's supply problems will not last much longer, and he intimated that the northern advance toward Nimule will resume. It should be noted that the road from Moli (about 35 miles north of Nimule), where the northern forces currently are stalled, is useable in the rains.

8. Manyang said the northern forces will not be able to cross the Aswa river (about 20 kilometers north of Nimule), which although not yet at flood is fairly deep and wide (over 100 yards). I said that even if they do not cross, they can shell Nimule from there. Not so, he replied. They will be unable to occupy positions near the north bank of the Aswa because the terrain on that side is considerably lower than the bluffs of the south bank. The northern forces will be dangerously exposed to southern fire, he said. However, later an ex–British army officer told me that the northerners could pull back to protected positions a mile or two from the river and shell Nimule from there.

9. At Nimule, Nichols and I talked with a group of about 15 relief workers. They and the other relief workers in town have sent a lot of their gear and some of their vehicles to Gulu in northern Uganda. At this time, though, they have no intention of leaving the Nimule area. If the Sudanese army advances farther south to a point that would trigger a UN order for an evacuation, the relief workers can literally strike their tents, collect their belongings and be out of Nimule very quickly.

10. From Nimule we flew back to Lokichokio instead of proceeding to Akon, north of Wau in Bahr al Ghazal. We had to scrub our plan to overnight at Akon, partly because it was getting late in the day, but mainly because Harvey was firmly opposed to having me overnight at a "level-3" location. [Level 3 on the UN security scale indicates some danger but not quite enough to warrant evacuation of UN and NGO relief workers.]

11. The next morning [on the way to Akon] we flew to Maridi to pick up USAID staffer Gordon Wagner. During the brief stop there, I talked to Commander Geir, the officer in charge of the SPLA troops who drove the "Mujahidin" (northern militia) unit that briefly occupied Mundri out of the town and north to Amadi, where it remains. [In the rest of this paragraph I described military developments as related to me by Geir.]

12. Akon has had but little rain this season and the people there have been increasingly worried about drought. When we arrived, tribal elders asked me to participate in a ceremony they reserve for high-ranking guests. Several men hold a cow down on the ground, and the honored guest steps (or jumps, depending on the size of the cow) over the cow. This brings good fortune to the guest and, I believe, to the people. But not to the cow, which is dispatched after the ceremony. Sure enough, about an hour after I had walked over the cow, we had a heavy rain shower. The downside, for us, was that the landing strip was too muddy for us to take off. However, three hours after the shower ended, and with another squall line approaching, the pilot figured the strip was dry enough, and off we went.

13. Some 1500 children at Akon, recent arrivals, are badly, some severely, malnourished and are receiving special feeding. We saw the depressing sight (only too common in parts of southern Su-

dan) of children, and adults too, emaciated, dull-eyed, listless from their malnourishment. Thanks to the MSF-France team, almost all the afflicted will survive. The situation in much or most of Bahr al Ghazal is ominous as a consequence of last year's drought and the effects of the war. Indications are that there has been a steady increase in malnutrition. A survey that MSF-France made of people within a radius of about forty miles from Akon showed a 32 percent rate of global malnutrition (ten percent severe). This is unlikely to improve and could get worse, because the relief program reaches only a very small proportion of the people of Bahr al Ghazal. For the most part, access at this time is limited to aircraft, and the UN does not have the resources to markedly improve food deliveries.

14. The amount of food delivered by barge and by road into southern Sudan has been far less than the UN and donors had hoped for. The OLS met only about forty percent of its goal for the first three months of this year. The figure is about 25 percent for the Sudan relief program as a whole. Unless the air delivery system is improved, this record cannot be improved by much. It is vital that between now and the end of the harvest (late October), the Sudan relief effort have sufficient aircraft to increase the delivery of food and medicines. Too many people will die if this does not happen.

15. OLS Coordinator Philip O'Brien told me this morning [in Nairobi] that to do its job, the UN needs three Buffalo aircraft and two C-130s operating out of Lokichokio and an Ilyushin out of Khartoum. Right now one Buffalo and one C-130 are at Loki. The U.S. C-130 is paid for through mid-June. A Belgian C-130, funded by the European Union, should be coming on line about now and be available for six months.

16. I request that State and AID consider on an urgent basis what the USG can do. If we are absolutely unable to help fund the additional air-delivery capability, we should do all possible to coordinate with other donors and urge them to provide funding.

Back in Nairobi on May 15 and 16 I met separately with the foreign ministers of Ethiopia, Uganda, and Kenya, who had gathered for the third round of IGADD peace talks. Except for the Kenyan, they were pessimistic about the prospects for successful negotiations. The Kenyan's main point was to renew his government's request for financial aid to pay for the expenses of running the negotiations. One of the reasons the United States was reluctant to help in this way was that the Kenyans, who had taken the lead among the IGADD governments in making arrangements for the negotiations, had done such a poor job of it.

The next day, a few hours before leaving for Khartoum, I met with the Sudanese government's chief negotiator at the peace talks, Ali al-Haj, and with three members of John Garang's SPLA negotiating team. In both meetings I reiterated some specific suggestions I had made earlier about ways to make the peace talks productive. As far as I could tell, I was wasting my time; both sides remained unwilling to give an inch on the basic issues that divided them.

I had planned to go back into the South before returning to Khartoum but had to scrub the second trip because it was taking too long to get the Sudanese government's clearance to go to the government-held town of Torit. Without a clearance from Khartoum, the United Nations would not fly to a town controlled by the northern military, just as it would not go to a rebel-held town absent prior clearance from the SPLA. Considering that local military commanders had orders to fire on uncleared aircraft, this was only prudent.

· · ·

Eliaba Surur, one of the southerners with whom I met at the residence before I went to Nairobi and the South, was picked up by security police in mid-May. Surur, a wisp of a man who was about seventy and walked with the aid of a cane, was clubbed and threatened with death if he did not tell security what was said when he met with me and agree to spy on the Americans for the Sudanese government. I could have sent a protest note to the government or sought to see the president, but I did not want to do anything that might jeopardize Surur and the others. Several southerners, including Surur, got word to me that they wanted to meet. I agreed on the condition that Abel Alier would be with them and that he judged it safe for them to meet with me, in the full knowledge that my house was under surveillance.

After reflecting on what I said, Surur and his friends decided it would be better not to come see me. They let me know they had decided Surur would stand a better chance of not being mistreated again, or killed, if I took his case up with the government. This I did on June 19 by lodging a formal protest with the Foreign Ministry. All I could really hope for from this démarche was that Surur would be left alone. He later managed to leave Sudan and go to Nairobi, where he survived an operation on his brain to remove swelling that had been caused by the beating.

• • •

Over the Memorial Day weekend I traveled to Nairobi again, this time to take part in briefings of a U.S. presidential delegation led by Brian Atwood, the head of USAID. I briefed Atwood and his party on the state of play in our relations with Sudan, what was happening in Khartoum, the poor prospects for a successful end to the peace process (the May talks ended with no progress after a few days and were adjourned until mid-July), and the difficulties that lay ahead for the humanitarian aid program. Pointing to the increasing incidence of rising rates of malnutrition and the less than expected amount of food deliveries by river, railroad, and roads, I said, as I had done in February at the meeting in Nairobi and in subsequent cables, that unless someone put up money for additional aircraft for the relief program, many people would starve.

Atwood and Nan Borton, the new director of OFDA, gave a sympathetic hearing to what I said but warned that they were faced with many crises worldwide and a shortage of resources to deal with them. Not long afterwards, however, OFDA funds were made available to help increase Operation Lifeline Sudan's air-delivery capacity. Other donor countries also provided some funding.

On May 24 the State Department announced that President Clinton had appointed Melissa F. Wells "as his special representative on Sudan." Her mission was "to assist regional efforts to achieve a cease-fire and permanent peace agreement to end the long civil war in southern Sudan and to ensure the delivery of humanitarian assistance." The announcement said that she would work closely with me and with leaders of Ethiopia, Kenya, Uganda, and Eritrea in the IGADD peace effort.

Since January, when the White House, for domestic political considerations, had overridden objections to appointing a special representative (the term "special envoy" had been dropped) for Sudan, the administration had been looking for a prominent person to take the job. At first the aim was to appoint someone well known to the public. One such person later told me he had refused an offer to become the special representative and he understood some others had done the same.

Former senator and candidate for the presidency George McGovern accepted the offer, then for health reasons had to decline it. For a time it seemed that former congressman Steven Solarz would be given the appointment, but problems had arisen from scrutiny of his use of official funds when he was in the House of Representatives, and he removed himself from consideration.

The administration then searched for an appointee within the State Department, and the White House selected Melissa Wells. A former ambassador to Guinea-Bissau, Zaire, and Mozambique and UN under secretary general for administration, she was prominent in diplomatic circles but not well known to the U.S. public. In appointing her, however, the administration had chosen a professional diplomat of great ability, whose intelligence, poise, prior experience in Africa, enthusiasm, and creativity would enable her to accomplish as much as anyone could accomplish in the job she had been given. I felt, though, that the job's potential for success was extremely limited.

From the time I first heard about a special envoy for Sudan when the matter was raised in Congress, I had strong doubts that the idea had much merit. I did not believe a special envoy could have any real impact on the search for peace in southern Sudan. The IGADD mediation attempt had shown that neither the Sudanese government nor the rebels were prepared to negotiate in good faith unless the other side virtually surrendered. There was no compelling reason for the president of the United States to embark on a negotiating effort that was bound to fail, unless circumstances changed radically—and there was no reason to believe they would in the foreseeable future.

I knew that despite whatever the administration might say, the arrival of a special representative from Washington would be perceived by some as undermining my authority as ambassador (Turabi said as much later on). That in itself was no big problem. No ambassador would have legitimate grounds for complaint if an outside negotiator could accomplish something that the ambassador could not get done. If I had believed a special representative for Sudan could really have made a significant difference, from the very beginning I would have enthusiastically supported the idea.

My doubts aside, I knew Ambassador Wells's work on the peace process would at least affirm that the United States promoted a negotiated end to the war and was not taking sides. And her negotiating skills, warm personality, and experience in relief operations in Uganda would enable her to make constructive suggestions about the humanitarian relief effort for Sudan and perhaps convince other donor governments to contribute more money.

# 14

# No Peace in Our Time

Melissa Wells's appointment added a new page to the chronicle of U.S.-Sudanese relations but left the basic points of friction between the two countries unchanged. Initially the Sudanese misread her appointment and her first visit to Khartoum as signals that relations with the United States were moving in a positive direction. After a time, they were disabused of that notion, and ineluctably—in the absence of any progress in overcoming our fundamental disagreements—the tension-ridden status quo continued.

Their incorrect view of Ambassador Wells's mission was another instance of the Bashir government's tendency to misinterpret events or believe erroneous information it received from its intelligence services or other sources. I saw this happen time and again, virtually from the day I arrived in Sudan. In August 1994, about a week before my arrival, Representative Melvin Dymally, chairman of the House Foreign Affairs Subcommittee on Africa, made approving comments about Sudan at the close of a short visit to Khartoum. This and a U.S. vote in favor of Sudan on an issue before the International Monetary Fund (IMF) had convinced Bashir and others that relations with the United States had improved. They had not, and it fell to the embassy and the State Department to make that clear.

For a time in 1994 it became an article of faith with the government and the NIF that on Sudan the White House was more objective and reasonable than the State Department. This apparently had its genesis in conversations that Sudanese diplomats had with midlevel National Security Council officials. The Sudanese derived from those conversations an impression of a White House that was at the very least less tendentious than the State Department.

Mahdi Ibrahim, a graduate of California State University–Chico and a staunch disciple of Hasan al-Turabi, had been sent to Washington several times to reach out to influential Americans and convince them of the rightness of the government's policies and the wrongness of what the Sudanese characterized as a State Department–inspired vendetta against Sudan.[1] On at least one occasion, Ibrahim bypassed the State Department and met with officials at the National Security Council.

I pointed out to Washington that Ibrahim's perceived entrée with the White House could reinforce the Sudanese misperception that the State Department and the White House had different opinions about Sudan. Shortly thereafter, with Washington's blessing, I informed the Foreign Ministry that Sudanese representations to the U.S. government should be made through the embassy and the State Department, who were as one with respect to U.S. policy on Sudan.

Nevertheless, the Sudanese persisted in seeing the White House as relatively friendly and the State Department as anti-Islam. And through no fault of Ambassador Wells, her visit to Khartoum in June contributed to that assumption.

●　　●　　●

On Saturday, June 13, I went to the airport to meet Melissa. Outgoing, likable, and well acquainted with Sudanese issues, she would live up to her fine reputation. Larry Benedict and Lucien Vandenbrouke joined us at lunch for an in-depth discussion. Later, UN officials came to the house for a meeting on problems of the relief program. That night, INGO representatives and some donor-country ambassadors came to eat and to talk about issues relevant to humanitarian assistance and peace talks.

Over the next two days Melissa, accompanied by either Larry Benedict or me, had a series of meetings with government officials and members of the NIF on the peace process and the relief program. Now and then the Sudanese alluded to the differences between the United States and Sudan on human rights and terrorism. Melissa, making it clear she had come to talk about the peace process and humanitarian aid, scrupulously avoided allowing them to draw her into discussion on other aspects of U.S. policy toward Sudan.

One of the meetings on Monday was with Ali al-Haj. I was annoyed when he said the U.S. government had wrecked the peace talks the previous year by letting Garang go to the United States. I said his accusation was totally untrue, as he should have known from what I had previously told him.

On Tuesday at 5:30 A.M. Melissa and I flew in her plane—a U.S. Air Force version of a Lear jet—to El Obeid, where we boarded a UN-chartered Twin Otter to fly to Wau and Kadugli, whose landing strips were too short for the jet. At Wau we were met by local dignitaries, people carrying posters with pro-government slogans, and a gathering of school children singing songs of welcome and encomiums to the government in Khartoum. After hearing speeches by various dignitaries, we had an unproductive and essentially uninformative meeting with the governor and other local officials. Neither at Wau nor at Kadugli were we able to get a feel for the problems of the people in displaced-persons camps. It was, however, important for Melissa to be able to say she had visited government-held towns as well as the SPLA-held towns she later visited farther south.

About a half-hour out of Kadugli on the way back to El Obeid, where Melissa would board her aircraft to fly on to Nairobi, we noticed the aircraft-to-ground visibility had begun to diminish. As the minutes passed, the air took on a decidedly reddish cast and the visibility decreased further. It became apparent we were flying over a full-fledged *haboob*. We were at about 12,000 feet and soon were just barely above the dense dust. I began to wonder whether we would be able to land at El Obeid and to hope the pilot would not chance going down through the dust. But we soon came to the edge of the storm, a clearly defined bank that looked like an ochre-colored line squall extending to the right and left of our flight path. The pilot began his descent, and in less than 15 minutes we were in El Obeid, where Melissa departed for Nairobi. By the time the Otter was refueled for the flight to Khartoum, the *haboob* was fast approaching. It arrived within minutes of our takeoff.

After Melissa left Sudan the Sudanese government began misrepresenting the meaning of her visit. This emerged in public statements by President Bashir, commentary in the press, and private remarks by a cabinet minister to some friends of mine. The theme was that the Sudanese government now had a direct line into the White House, enabling it to bypass the State Department, which was hostile to Sudan.

In mid-June Ghazi confided to two Western ambassadors that the U.S. State Department was hostile toward Sudan but that his government was pleased with its new link, as he put it, with the White House. (In addition, according to Ghazi, the Sudanese were gratified that they had made substantial progress in influencing African Americans to side with them.[2] Ghazi said closer cooperation between Sudan and the European Union countries would serve as an example to the U.S. government. Once relations with Europe were improved, the United States would fall into line, he contended.)

The Sudanese also said that because Ambassador Wells did not bring up issues like Sudan's human rights violations, Washington was setting aside any concern it might have about them. After I reported this and the rest of the misreading of the Wells visit, the State Department called in the Sudanese ambassador and instructed the U.S. Mission to the United Nations to meet with Sudan's permanent representative to the United Nations.

As laid out in talking points prepared for the two meetings, the Sudanese were told the United States government appreciated the cordial reception given to Ambassador Wells. However,

> there appear to have been some misimpressions in Khartoum about her mission. . . . While Ambassador Wells has been designated the President's special representative on Sudan, our ambassador in Khartoum, Donald Petterson, continues to represent the U.S. government in all aspects of the relations between our two countries, including the peace process and humanitarian assistance.
>
> Ambassador Wells has been charged by the President to focus on those two issues exclusively and on a full-time basis, travelling to the mediatory countries as well as to Sudan and elsewhere as appropriate. Her efforts are an adjunct of the normal diplomatic relations between our two governments. The fact that while in Khartoum she did not raise other issues that affect relations between the United States and Sudan, such as human rights and terrorism, should not be interpreted as a sign that these issues have diminished in importance to us. The United States remains deeply concerned about them.

As time passed, the Sudanese seemed to conclude that the White House was, in their eyes, as bad as the State Department. This did not happen right away. In September Turabi said to me that visiting African Americans had confirmed that the White House was relatively friendly toward Sudan and that the State Department was anti-Islam. However, at the end of the year Turabi told me President Clinton had insulted all Muslims when he met with Salman Rushdie. Later, not long before I ended my assignment to Sudan, Turabi declared to me that there would be no improvement in U.S.-Sudanese relations while Clinton was president.

Favorable references to Melissa Wells eventually disappeared, too. However, for weeks the message conveyed to the Sudanese ambassadors to the United States and the United Nations made no impact. The Sudanese seemed unable to accept that the reason she did not criticize Sudan for human rights violations or supporting terrorism was that her mission was confined to the peace process and humanitarian aid. The Sudanese also persisted in their belief that her visit in June indicated an improvement in relations between Sudan and the United States. Not until the end of the summer did they began to regard her in a different light.

• • •

On July 9 I was back in southern Sudan, at Chukudum in eastern Equatoria, site of John Garang's military headquarters. The fourth round of the IGADD peace talks was scheduled to begin July 18, and I urged Garang to send a delegation that would arrive on time (both rebel delegations had been late in getting to Nairobi for the previous rounds), would be empowered to negotiate, and would be prepared to negotiate seriously. He assured me he would do as I asked, even though he was pessimistic that the IGADD negotiations would produce a settlement. He referred to the "basic incompatibility of the North and the South" and said the North was bent on Arabizing and Islamizing the South and would never accept the condition that a united Sudan would have to be democratic and secular.

Commenting on this conversation to Washington, I said,

Garang's . . . view of the basic issue underlying the years of strife between northern and southern Sudan puts in clear relief the magnitude of the difficulty facing would-be peacemakers. If the establishment of a secular,

democratic state is the southerners' sine qua non of maintaining a united
Sudan, Garang is quite correct in assuming that a negotiated settlement
acceptable to the GOS/NIF is beyond reach.

I was unable to get Garang to admit that his troops had recently seized
and stolen all the cargo of two barges on the Nile carrying relief supplies
to Juba. He tried to put the blame on the United Nations for not getting
proper permission. I said I could not accept that and told him that, in any
event, his soldiers had no right to seize food destined for civilians.

The best I could get from him was an assurance that he would cooperate with the United Nations and others to establish new procedures to
improve the prospects that relief supplies would get to where they were
intended to go.

My party and I flew from Chukudum northwest into Bahr al-Ghazal
to have a look at what World Vision, an INGO, was doing to help the
people of the area, many of whom were displaced as a result of recent
fighting there. After landing at a dirt strip in the middle of nowhere,
we drove to World Vision's base camp at Ngap-Ngok, fifteen miles
away, and then on to Thiet, which I had visited more than a year earlier. It had been overrun by northern troops in May. After killing nine-
teen people who were unable to flee in time and burning and looting
the town, the soldiers went away. World Vision workers were distributing air-dropped food and setting up a clinic to replace the one they
had administered before it was destroyed by the northerners.

We spent the night at the base camp, then flew southeast to Lafon,
where I met with Riek Machar and his principal deputy, William
Nyuon. Like Garang, Riek made the right noises about participating in
the peace talks but said he doubted he could send a delegation unless
someone paid the hotel and other bills they had run up at the previous
sessions. Not surprisingly, Riek and William avoided answering when
I probed William's relationship with the northern government and
cited reports that he was getting arms from them to use in fighting
Garang. William made no comment on this and, in fact, said nothing
at all during the talk. Later that day he admitted to a friend of mine
that he had used the arms to attack the town of Nasir, which his force
razed, and said he would employ them to destroy Garang.

There were hundreds of newly arrived people at Lafon, displaced by
recent intratribal fighting, and many were emaciated, obviously se-

verely malnourished. As a result of our stop there, the United Nations undertook to air-drop food right away and send a team to assess relief needs.

On this trip, as on others, I had nothing but admiration for relief workers, who lived and worked in very difficult, sometimes dangerous, circumstances to help people who desperately needed assistance. Each time I spoke to journalists in Nairobi after returning from southern Sudan, I praised the NGO and UN field-workers for their selflessness and courage and their dedication to helping the hundreds of thousands of victims of the war. At times they were harassed by government or rebel soldiers who wanted to get their hands on relief-program food destined for needy southerners. The killing of three UN relief workers in late 1992 starkly illustrated the hazards relief workers could face in carrying out their work in southern Sudan.

These men and women endured privations that most people would find too tough to bear. They lived in huts or tents, had to make do with primitive bathing and toilet facilities, worked long days in often blistering heat and enervating high humidity, witnessed heartbreaking scenes of adults and children too wasted by disease or starvation to be kept alive, and often fell victim themselves to malaria or other diseases that were rampant among the people they assisted.

When I traveled into the South, NGO, UNICEF, and World Food Program relief workers shared their food with my companions and me and gave us a place to sleep overnight. They and Sudanese relief organization personnel representing either the government or the rebels escorted us to different locations in the area we were visiting and gave us information about their work and the local situation. We almost always brought them something they lacked—like food items, soft drinks, and beer—which they very much appreciated.

Some of my best moments in Sudan were spent at their encampments at night, sometimes sitting around a campfire, having a beer or two and talking with the young and not-so-young American, English, Irish, French, German, Nigerian, Norwegian, Australian, Ghanaian, Dutch, Belgian, Sudanese, or other-nationality relief workers. Their dedication and compassion never failed to restore my sometimes flagging faith in the basic goodness of most of humankind.

• • •

My travels had taken a toll on my back. The worst effect of this was that I had to stop running for a time. Sitting at a desk also aggravated the back problem, and, of course, I did a lot of that at my office in the embassy. But after a couple of weeks in Khartoum, I was fit again and ready to travel.

In mid-July I flew to Nairobi for a nine-day stay. I went there to take the place of Melissa Wells, who was ill in Washington and unable to travel. The negotiations, which opened on July 19, got off to a slow start. During most of the first several days the Sudanese government's delegation disagreed strongly with the draft declaration of principles that the IGADD mediators had submitted as a guide for the peace talks. The declaration's major points included attainment of a peaceful solution to the conflict; the South's right to self-determination, which would be expressed through a referendum; the preferability of unity; establishment of a secular and democratic state; and equitable sharing of the country's economic wealth. The references to secularism, democracy, and self-determination were completely unacceptable to Khartoum. In the years ahead, the Bashir government would continue to resist any effort to make the declaration of principles binding on the two sides, but eventually it would agree that the principles could form a basis for negotiations.

I met several times with the Ethiopians and Eritreans, mostly with the Ethiopian foreign minister, Seyoum Mesfin. From the beginning they were angered and frustrated by what they characterized as maneuvering by the Sudanese government's delegation. At one point they were about ready to end the negotiations.

The Ethiopian and Eritrean governments had had a foretaste of Sudanese inflexibility shortly before the IGADD conference began. Ethiopian president Meles Zenawi and Eritrean president Isaias Afwerki had met with President Bashir and other Sudanese, including Ali Osman Taha, in Ethiopia on July 16 and 17. Meles and Isaias had spoken of their concern about Sudan's policy that there should be no national borders separating Muslims of one country from those of another. This policy, combined with Sudan's nurturing of differences between Muslims and non-Muslims, was having a negative influence on the region. They had asked the Sudanese to confine their Islamic activities within Sudan. According to sources who were at the meeting, Bashir and Taha were both defensive and unrepentant.

Although the Ethiopians and Eritreans later began aiding the SPLA, at this time they were not. They were sharply critical of the Sudanese rebels for failing to treat civilians decently and for acting, instead, like armies of occupation. They emphasized that grassroots support during their own wars for independence was a major factor in their successes as guerrilla movements. They regarded the SPLA's depredations against southern Sudanese civilians as nothing short of idiocy.

I found that a U.S. special representative would spend a lot of time at the talks waiting for sessions to end and then trying to locate participants and get together with them to find out what had happened. There was only limited time for discussions, but in the time I had I tried to reassure the IGADD mediators and to emphasize to the warring parties that the United States fully supported the IGADD effort. I asked southerners to refrain from using terminology that would give the North an excuse to break off negotiations. And I joined others in urging the northerners to let the issues be brought to the table for discussion and to stop objecting to the form in which they were being framed.

According to participants, the talks were accomplishing little more than averting a total breakdown. After five days Melissa Wells arrived in Nairobi. She was now in good health and eager to go to work. The talks limped along for a bit longer. However, despite the best efforts of mediators and of Melissa and others in the wings advising the participants, this round of talks ended in failure. The two sides agreed to take part in another round in September.

Before leaving Nairobi for Khartoum I was able to spend the weekend with friends of mine, John and Angela Sutton. John, a white Kenyan, had been one of East Africa's best-known hunters. He now had a safari business and was a prominent conservationist. We had become friends in Tanzania in the 1980s. When I came to Nairobi from Khartoum, I stayed at their home whenever I could; they gave me a refuge and a reprieve from dealing with the issues of Sudan.

On the day before I left for Khartoum, the three of us drove south to the Rift Valley escarpment. About twenty-five miles out of town, we drove off the dirt road and over a rock-strewn slight incline to the edge of the escarpment. We had a spectacular view south to Lake Magadi and east toward the Masai Mara plain. The area through which we passed was Masai country, and we saw many herds of their cattle.

Even though this was not a game reserve, we also saw numerous ze-
bra, Thompson's and Grant's gazelles, and some ostriches. They
seemed to coexist quite well with the cattle.

No matter how many times I traveled in the African bush, there always was something new to learn. For example, when I remarked to
John that there were no acacia trees, just thorn bushes (a species of
acacia), he told me they were called whistling thorn bushes. They
have pods that I would guess average about an inch and a half in di-
ameter and around which the sharp thorns cluster. Ants drill one hole
in each pod, then enter, occupy the space inside, and lay their eggs.
When the wind blows, as it often does across the savanna, it pushes
air into the holes. The result, repeated countless times over the miles
and miles of savanna covered with the bushes, is a high-pitched
whistling sound.

• • •

In August the Nile rose considerably, to its highest level since the flood
of 1988. At places along the riverbank adjacent to Nile Road, near the
presidential palace, for example, the river was only a foot lower than
the street. Parts of Tuti Island, which is in the Blue Nile along a stretch
of the city, were flooded, as were low-lying areas south of town alongside the White Nile, which was backed up by the force of the turbulent
Blue. I thought the flow of water in the Blue Nile was impressive in
July, but now it was awe-inspiring—an unimaginable volume of water
rushing past town toward its merger with the White Nile.

Carlos the Jackal was a big topic of conversation that month. Now
that he had been taken to Paris, it seemed just about everyone had
seen him while he was in Khartoum, though only very few knew who
he was at the time. I heard that someone in town was doing a good
business selling T-shirts that proclaimed "I saw Carlos."

Pointing to their role in capturing Carlos and turning him over to
the French, Sudanese officials told us the United States should have
seen that action as proof that they did not harbor terrorists and should
therefore have taken Sudan off the list of state sponsors of terrorism.
But after we had made it clear to them that we knew the government
had facilitated Carlos's arrival in Sudan and kept him under their protection during his stay in the country, they backed off. Turabi, however, refused to accept our account and, as noted earlier, angrily in-

sisted that the CIA was behind Carlos's presence in Sudan. This was one of the topics of a discussion I had with him August 28.

He and I talked for almost three hours that day. We went round and round, sometimes angrily, sometimes with humor, on various topics. He told me the peace talks were destined to fail unless the IGADD countries changed their attitude toward the government of Sudan. He charged that largely because of the State Department, the U.S. government had become increasingly anti-Islamic. Sudan, he said, opposed the Population Conference in Cairo, which was then in session, because it would legitimize "immoral practices" and because it represented a Western effort "to reduce the number of black and brown people in the world." He further stated Sudan was of little importance to the United States, and in time Washington would lose interest in it and ease its anti-Sudan campaign; but in the Islamic world, Sudan was extremely important.

Needless to say, we disagreed a lot. From time to time, I had to tell him that what he was saying was either untrue or made no sense; he more or less said the same about my arguments. Turabi brought up the message I had delivered the previous September in which Washington had warned the Sudanese they would suffer dire consequences if they harmed Americans. He told me that if the United States ever tried to use force against Sudan, we would fail. We failed in Somalia, he said, and Sudan was tougher than Somalia ever could be. I told him we had no intention of invading Sudan but he should not write off U.S. resolve to oppose Sudan's actions. This led him to say that if we tried anything, Sudan would strike at U.S. interests in many places.

• • •

Melissa Wells came to Khartoum near the end of August. In meetings with Ali al-Haj and Mohamed el-Amin Khalifa, Khartoum's chief negotiators, we got an earful about the IGADD mediators' bias against Sudan and about the Sudanese government's determination to resist, during the next round of talks, any discussion of self-determination or religion and the state. Those were the two issues that in July the IGADD mediators thought the Sudanese government had finally agreed could be put on the agenda.

Al-Haj and Khalifa also told us their government probably would not attend the September 5–7 round of talks. I believed this to be an

idle threat, for the Bashir government did not want to be seen as uni-
laterally ending the peace talks, for they feared that such a perception
could lead to some action by the UN Security Council.

In both Nairobi and Khartoum, what I heard in conversations with
leading figures involved directly or indirectly in the peace talks indicated strongly that the talks would not succeed. The mutual distrust
that had grown between northern Sudanese negotiators and the
IGADD foreign ministers, most notably the Ethiopian and Eritrean
foreign ministers, not to mention the implacability of North-South
animosity, virtually guaranteed failure.

As I had anticipated, Khartoum did send a delegation to Nairobi for
the September round of peace talks. Nevertheless, the negotiations
failed to achieve anything at all. According to participants, Ghazi, the
new head of the government's delegation, was unbending with the
Ethiopian, Eritrean, Ugandan, and Kenyan negotiators. Participants
told us also that he refused to consider any additional discussion of either self-determination or religion and the state.[3] The IGADD foreign
ministers called off the talks and asked President Moi to convoke a
summit meeting between the presidents of the four IGADD mediation countries and Bashir of Sudan.

For reasons I failed to understand, after the September round of talks
failed our embassy in Nairobi cabled Washington that the government
of Sudan could be brought around to a reasonable position on the issue
of religion and the state. I sent a message stating that the country
team and I disagreed.

I pointed out that a prepared statement made by President Bashir
shortly before the Nairobi talks began had foreshadowed Khartoum's
adamancy on the issues of religion's role in the state and self-determination. Bashir had said Sudan absolutely rejected any discussion of
what he termed the "so-called right of self-determination" or of a return to secularism. Talk about abandoning Sudan's "civilizational
[that is, Islamic] project" and returning to a secular system was "an in-
sult to Sudan."

The application of *sharia* was another principle that Sudan's Islamists
were not about to abandon, I noted. A paper that Ghazi presented at the
talks asserted that "*sharia* and custom as they stand are irreplaceable"
and that "legislation inspired by other sources are gauged and ratified
according to the principles of *sharia* and custom."

The North's positions on the two main issues of the talks were clearly defined. And the South would never voluntarily accept either one of them. I told Washington that under existing circumstances the talks could not succeed.

Melissa Wells and I separately made some suggestions as to what the United States should do in reaction to the failure of the talks and the intransigence of the government of Sudan. She proposed that the United States should work for a Security Council presidential statement supportive of the IGADD effort. Achieving this would not be easy. Fearing an imposed settlement, Khartoum was opposed to any Security Council involvement in the peace process, however tangential. In a statement released September 1, the Sudanese had declared that "all issues relating to the war in southern Sudan are absolutely internal matters which Sudan will handle through its own means and processes." Because of "Sudan's respect of . . . neighborly and brotherly relations," they had not objected to the IGADD initiative. For the Sudanese government, an IGADD mediation attempt was acceptable, but even a Security Council statement that did no more than support it was not.

I endorsed Melissa's suggestion, adding that "firm support from the IGADD governments and willingness on their part to get out in front on the effort" would be required for it to succeed. But IGADD support did not materialize, and with help from friends, the Sudanese easily forestalled a Security Council statement.

Melissa also recommended that Washington proceed further to firm up a cooperative relationship with "the friends of IGADD"—countries, such as the Netherlands, that backed the IGADD undertaking. I thought that in addition we should see if the IGADD governments could explore ways to get Khartoum to be more flexible. I also suggested that we ask Ugandan president Museveni to try to keep Garang from making statements or taking actions that could undermine the peace initiative.

With peace talks going nowhere, the Sudanese military resumed preparations to launch another military offensive in the South once the rainy season ended. Melissa focused on trying to get the warring sides to agree on means to reduce the obstructions to delivery of relief supplies.

• • •

The director of the State Department's Office of East African Affairs, David Shinn, came to Khartoum in early September for two days to get a firsthand impression of the state of play in U.S.-Sudanese relations. He met with government officials, southerners, businessmen, academics, professional people, and NIF figures—an array of pro- and anti-regime people. David brought no new ideas from Washington on how to deal with the Sudanese situation, nor did anything new come out of his meetings. However, it was useful for him to hear directly from government and NIF leaders, including Turabi, their inflexibility on the divisive issues in U.S.-Sudanese relations.

I complained to David, and later sent a cable to the State Department, about its inability to fill consular and general services officer positions that had been vacant for months after having been restored. Vacancies in positions at unpopular posts like Khartoum occurred mainly because State's personnel system had no backbone. If no one bid on a job, the position went unfilled for months until Personnel finally wheedled somebody into taking the assignment. Or, unable to get a job he or she bid on and desperate to get an assignment, someone finally decided to accept Personnel's offer to go to Khartoum.

I believed the State Department should restore the system that was in place when I joined the Foreign Service: Essentially, individuals were notified of their assignments, and unless they had a compelling reason not to, they either accepted it or, if unable to get out of it, resigned. At the risk of sounding like a cranky old-timer, I said all this in my cable. But of course, I was running against the tide of the Department's desire to avoid controversy and potential lawsuits and to demonstrate that its personnel practices were democratic. For my pains, I got a somewhat peevish response from the deputy director of personnel, who disagreed with what I had written.

In the second week of September a heavy rain shower drenched Khartoum. The city, except for its relatively few paved streets, was full of deep puddles and covered in mud. Khartoum's drainage system was built during the Condominium but had been poorly maintained and was not designed for a city as large as Khartoum had become. The city's dense soil does not absorb water very well. However, after a few days the heat evaporates the water, the mud dries out, and Khartoum reverts to its usual dusty self. The streets are covered with sand so fine that it is really dust, and when cars pass the dust rises in the air.

One evening, about a half-hour before dusk, I was being driven back to the residence. The traffic had raised a mist of dust that in the fading orange light of the setting sun looked like a cloak of light fog hanging over some of the streets. For a moment, it made me feel pensive and even a little blue, as I faced another night in Khartoum without my wife and son, who now had been gone from Sudan for a year.

• • •

The State Department instructed me to meet with the foreign minister to deliver an oral message containing evidence of the Sudanese government's assistance to terrorist organizations. At long last, I had been given some factual information to pass on to the Sudanese. The evidence, which was from sensitive sources and very conclusive, concerned a camp north of Omdurman used now and then for training foreign terrorists. It also included some information on Carlos that made it clear he had been in Khartoum with the knowledge, consent, and protection of the government.

At a September 13 meeting with Abu Salih, slowly, so the note takers could get it down accurately, I read our presentation. When I finished, he hit the roof. The crux of his angry response was that none of this was evidence and that I was again dredging up an unsubstantiated allegation. I said we seemed to have different definitions of the word "evidence."

After further exchange on this, I told him that the United States wanted better relations but that Sudan appeared to be unwilling to change its policies so relations could improve. The United States continued to be deeply concerned that Sudan was doing nothing about its human rights abuses, supported terrorism, and had failed to begin to restore democracy.

He said he had agreed to meet me to talk only about terrorism. He insisted I had given no evidence at all and declared he saw no reason to continue talking.

I repeated that what I had presented was real evidence. I said his response made it clear to me that no matter what evidence the United States offered, the government of Sudan was not going to admit its involvement with terrorism. On that note, the meeting ended.

Although I knew that would not be the end of it, I did not expect Abu Salih to go public, which he did the same day. He told the Su-

danese media that I had seen him and had repeated the same old
charges. That was mild, but then came a blistering commentary by
the government's radio station. It not only blasted the U.S. government for false allegations and, incidentally, for trying to reduce the
Muslim population throughout the world, but it also upbraided me for
not venturing out of my "steel cage" (the embassy), for allowing others—including a woman!—to do my job, and for not resigning because
of it.

I thought the part about me was funny, but the State Department
was not amused. The next day the Department spokesman made a
statement criticizing the Sudanese for going public about a démarche
delivered in confidence, for distorting what we had said, and for in-
sulting me. We followed up the next day with a protest note that
Larry delivered at the Foreign Ministry. By then the ministry had
chided Washington for having made the statement. It added that the
Sudanese government had confidence in me and said more or less
what a fine fellow I was. The ways of diplomacy sometimes are indeed mysterious.

# 15

# The Reasons Why

President Omar al-Bashir, Hasan al-Turabi, Ali Osman Taha, Ghazi Salah Eddin, Mohamed el-Amin Khalifa—all of these men and others in the upper reaches of the power structure ruling Sudan insisted that the U.S. government was antagonistic toward Sudan primarily because of the particular Islamic orientation of the Bashir government. This concept, like many other ideas they came up with, was first articulated by Turabi, then picked up and repeated as dogma by people in the government and the NIF.

Their basic argument was that many other countries, such as Egypt, had worse human rights records than Sudan's but were not subjected to the kind of treatment the United States was inflicting on Sudan. Therefore, the United States was singling out Sudan because of the Islamic path its government had chosen and also because Sudan dared to take positions at odds with some of those championed by Washington.

It was true that the measures the Bush and Clinton administrations had taken against Sudan were more severe than actions taken against other governments whose abuses of the rights of their own people were on a par with or worse than the government of Sudan's. Why was this so? For one thing, Washington's Sudan policy was predicated on more than human rights considerations.

In all the policy-related materials I read and the briefings I received before I went to Sudan, and in the communications that came from

Washington after I got to Khartoum, none contained a consolidated, historical explanation accounting for the current U.S. policy toward Sudan.[1] In thinking it through, I saw that it was an aggregation of events and actions by the Bashir regime that, taken as a whole, put Sudan in such a bad light with the U.S. government. (I mentioned some of these in chapter 3.) I offered this explanation time and again in discussions in Sudan. And I spelled it out more than once in cables and in debriefings in Washington. As far as I could tell, it was accepted there as a valid interpretation.

My thesis was as follows: The cumulative combination of factors putting Sudan in such a bad light began with the military takeover in July 1989. This brought into play the act of Congress that stipulates that when a democratically elected government of a country is forcibly overthrown, all forms of U.S. government aid to that country, except humanitarian assistance, must cease.

A second factor quickly emerged as the government took repressive steps to neutralize its opponents or suspected opponents. Hundreds of people were detained and denied any legal recourse. Several months after coming to power, the government summarily executed twenty-eight military officers. As the years rolled by human rights organizations, Western governments, and the United Nations cited extensive human rights violations by Khartoum.

A third element was the absolute control the government exerted over the political process. Freedom of speech and assembly did not exist. Elections, when they did take place, were neither free nor fair.

Fourth, the war in the South was often prosecuted in a way that was an affront to the outside world. At one time or another both government and rebel military forces burned villages, killed civilians, and committed other excesses against the populace. For military reasons, both sides sometimes impeded the humanitarian relief program and took relief supplies for their own use.

Fifth, tens of thousands of displaced southerners living in Khartoum were forcibly moved to the fringes of the city, to areas that lacked the most basic of amenities, like potable water. Khartoum ignored protests by Western governments and the United Nations that this was inhumane and should stop.

Sixth, Sudan sided with Iraq during the Gulf War. Moreover, Khartoum's opposition to U.S. foreign policies was often expressed in shrill, sometimes extremist, terms.

And seventh, soon after it seized power the Bashir government embarked on a policy of giving refuge and help to terrorist organizations.

No single one of these factors by itself would account for the full array of steps Washington took to demonstrate its disapproval of the Sudanese government's behavior. But taken together, that government's words and deeds depicted, in Washington's opinion, an exceptionally bad actor on the international scene.

Even so, until late 1992 these factors had not been enough to cause the Bush administration to single out Sudan for special treatment. In terminating military and economic development aid to Sudan in 1989, the administration had not taken a sui generis step against Sudan; instead, it had merely acted in conformance with U.S. law. Washington condemned the Bashir regime's human rights violations yet stopped short of taking the matter to the United Nations for action. We publicly criticized the regime for its conduct of the war in the South, its treatment of the displaced people living in the Khartoum area, and other aspects of its behavior. We had not, however, gone beyond criticism on those issues.

Then, in September 1992, the Sudanese authorities executed USAID employees in Juba. This eighth factor, as it were, was a catalyst that propelled the Bush administration and the successor Clinton administration into taking tougher actions against Sudan. Arguably, at least some of those actions might have been taken anyway at some point. For example, Sudan would probably have been put on the terrorism list regardless of what happened to the USAID employees in Juba.

Be that as it may, after the killings in Juba the United States led efforts in the UN General Assembly and the Human Rights Commission to condemn Sudan's human rights abuses and to appoint a special human rights rapporteur for Sudan. We urged aid donor countries to reduce or end their economic assistance to Sudan. And later on, Secretary Christopher added Sudan to the terrorism list.

When I explained to Sudanese in the government and NIF why Sudan had come to be seen as it was by the U.S. government, I said it did them no good to point to other transgressors of human rights. If Sudan's relations with Washington were to improve, the Sudanese government had to look to its own behavior and begin to modify it. I stressed that Washington was not asking for total change overnight. What we wanted to see were beginnings: for example, an acknowledgment by the government that human rights violations were indeed a problem and a convincing affirmation that it intended to do something about that problem.

When government leaders protested that the United States was unconcerned about human rights abuses in many countries—Egypt, for example—I said they were mistaken and called their attention to the administration's annual report to Congress on human rights in all countries of the world. The latest report was quite critical of human rights violations by the Egyptian government. I told the Sudanese, however, that they should understand that Washington would handle its disagreements, including over human rights questions, with its friends and with countries very important to U.S. interests differently from the way it dealt with hostile countries and that although perhaps this was not fair, it was a political reality.

Once in a while someone within the leadership would acknowledge privately that some changes were in order. In general, though, embassy officers and I continued to hear that none of the accusations against Sudan were valid and that the U.S. government's policy vis-à-vis Sudan stemmed from an anti-Islam bias. However inaccurate this belief was, it became the principal ingredient in the Sudanese government's anti-American propaganda.

Another element in the Sudanese Islamists' animus against the United States was their deep anger at Washington's support for Israel and for Arab governments, such as Egypt and Saudi Arabia, that they said were repressive and not truly Islamic. Turabi, for one, often brought this up in our conversations. Furthermore, the United States had come to symbolize to radical Muslims in Sudan, as elsewhere, what they saw as decadent, irreligious materialism.

Beginning in 1994 the Sudanese said Washington should back away from its demands and start treating Sudan as an equal. It was up to the United States to demonstrate that it really wanted better relations with Sudan. Turabi and Ghazi, and subsequently others, also told us that U.S. policymakers needed to understand how important Sudan was becoming in the world; already it was the leader in the new Islamic movement that was taking hold throughout the Muslim world, they said. Once the U.S. government recognized Sudan's importance, it would back away from its current policy and work out an accommodation with the Sudanese government.

What all this indicated to us in the American embassy in Khartoum in the waning months of 1994 was that at the end of the tunnel was another tunnel, not light.

On September 22, in a message to the State Department, after outlining how Sudan had come to be regarded as it was by Washington, I said the various diplomatic and economic pressures the United States had applied to Sudan over the past two years had failed to get the Sudanese to change their ways. In considering what to do about this, I said, the U.S. government needed

> to bear in mind that the Islamists in charge have a firm grip on power and, barring the unexpected, are unlikely to be displaced in the foreseeable future. In furthering their aims to retain power, Islamize all of Sudan, aid radical Islamic groups in neighboring countries and elsewhere, and spread their brand of political Islam far and wide, they will not renounce their ties with terrorists, they will pursue a strategy of dividing and overcoming those Sudanese who oppose them, and they will work to gain support from groups and individuals in the U.S. and Western Europe in order to soften or end policies unfavorable to Sudan.

I said proposals to increase pressure on the regime in Khartoum had been examined but not applied for various reasons, including danger to the embassy and "the unlikelihood of getting sufficient international support for sanctions against Sudan." Knowing that Washington was in no mood to push for increased sanctions, I suggested as an alternative approach internationalizing the Sudan issue. I said this could include (1) closely coordinating and planning with some of Sudan's neighbors to get an agreed strategy on how to deal with the Sudan problem and (2) working for a consensus on Sudan among Security Council members and for a resolution calling for an end to the war, a UN-monitored cease-fire, and an internationally sanctioned conference that would bring together all legitimate elements having a direct stake in ending the war in Sudan.

Once again, however, the climate of relations soured. The most proximate cause was the killing of some people being forcibly moved from Khartoum to a displaced-persons camp at the edge of the city, and Washington's angry reaction to this. Serious consideration of anything other than greater pressures would have to be deferred.

• • •

For a time Sudan became increasingly isolated. In part this was a result of U.S. policy, in part an outcome of other factors. The antagonism of some of Sudan's neighbors, for example, came about because
of the Bashir government's actions affecting them, not because of
Washington's wishes.

Western countries, including Japan, that had not already ended economic aid to Sudan phased out existing projects beginning in late
1992. Among the countries with diplomatic representation in Sudan,
Britain, the Netherlands, and Germany joined the United States in
making strong approaches to the Sudanese about human rights and
the humanitarian aid program. The Office of the European Community did the same. On the other hand, the Swiss ambassador, based in
Cairo but accredited to Sudan as well as Egypt, privately railed against
the United States on human rights, arguing with me that Westerners
had no right to impose their standards on other peoples. I argued back
that she was ignoring the universality of the meaning of fundamental
human rights.

The French viewed Sudan largely through the optic of their interests
in French-speaking Africa. Paris did not want Sudanese Islamists interfering in francophone countries, such as nearby Djibouti, and
treated Sudan gently. The French also did not want French firms to be
at a disadvantage, as U.S. firms came to be, in possible commercial
deals. The French ambassador rarely brought up Sudan's human rights
record or other controversial matters. This encouraged the Sudanese,
who saw an opening they could exploit to try to wean the Europeans
away from the Americans.

Most Eastern European countries, once well represented in Khartoum, had closed their diplomatic missions after the end of the Cold
War. The Russians, who remained, were little involved except for
looking for commercial ventures. Viscerally opposed to outside exam-
ination of their internal affairs, the Russians, like the Chinese, could
be counted on to side with Sudan if the United States tried to bring a
Sudan issue before the UN Security Council.

China benefited from arms sales to Sudan and other commercial un-
dertakings. The Chinese knew they could cultivate their relationship
with Washington and at the same time ignore U.S. concerns about Sudan. Khartoum rightly regarded Chinese friendship as a valuable asset.

Moderate and conservative Arab countries continued to look upon Sudan with suspicion. Egypt, the Arab country of most importance to Sudan, remained at loggerheads with the Sudanese. In the space of about two years, Sudan closed the Khartoum branch of Cairo University and expelled its teachers, Egypt countered with its own expulsions of Sudanese, Sudan nationalized Egyptian property, and Egypt took control of the Haleib Triangle, a small disputed territory along Sudan's northeastern border. Khartoum and Cairo mistreated each other's diplomats and regularly traded insults.

Sudan enjoyed little support in sub-Saharan Africa. Some countries, Zambia and Namibia for example, gave assistance to the SPLA. By 1995 Sudan's relations with two of its neighbors, Eritrea and Uganda, had been severed. Uganda had long been aiding the SPLA, and Eritrea and Ethiopia, which also was unhappy with Khartoum, began to do so.

The Sudanese worked hard to better their international status. They launched a diplomatic offensive in 1994–1995 that had some success, must notably in the Muslim world. Malaysia, interested in economic investments, was one of a number of countries that responded favorably for Sudan. Working in Khartoum's favor was the U.S. stance toward Israel. As Washington showed no sign of taking a tougher stand against the hard-line Likud-led Israeli coalition government, whose policies were undermining the Israeli-Palestinian peace process, fewer Arab and other Muslim governments were willing to be associated with the United States against Sudan.

All in all, however, Sudan's international reputation remained poor. It had its friends, enough to avoid the label of pariah, but its detractors were numerous enough to ensure continued criticisms and condemnations in forums like the UN Human Rights Commission.

# 16

# More Events in Khartoum and Elsewhere

In October I made another trip to southern Sudan. I wanted to see how the people from the Triple-A camps were faring in their new camp to the east at Labone, a few miles north of the Ugandan border. I also wanted to find out how the people I had seen moving east through Bahr Olo were getting along in their new camp at Antugua, southeast of Maridi.

The notes I made during the trip describe what I saw and experienced and give a flavor of what it was like to travel in southern Sudan:

**Oct. 7, 0900:** We are at 8,000 feet flying through rain clouds on our way to Maridi in w. Equatoria from Labone in e. Equatoria. Yesterday morning I flew from Nairobi to Lokichokio in an Antonov twin-engine turbo-prop aircraft that is funded by the European Union for the UN relief. It takes passengers to and from Loki. It's a military cargo plane with benches running fore and aft along both sides of the fuselage. No windows. Enter and exit through the cargo door in the stern. From Loki my party [an AID/Washington staffer, a UN security officer, and Gordon Wagner, a USAID contract employee who knew southern Sudan and its people better than anyone else in the U.S. government] and I flew to Labone in the same Cessna Caravan single-engine aircraft we are traveling in this morning.

In Labone the head of the Norwegian People's Aid contingent took us to the hospital, which we toured with the Ethiopian doctor in charge. 100 to 150 patients per day. Camp population is 60,000—Bor Dinka who fled from the Nimule Triple-A camps several months ago as the Sudanese army approached from Juba. All things considered, they are doing fairly well, thanks to their own efforts (growing food) and the NPA's help. Food is trucked in from Uganda—a dangerous business given the attacks by the Lord's Resistance Army [extremist Ugandan rebels] on convoys. Catholic Relief deserves much praise for continuing to deliver supplies (mainly sorghum).

Labone camp's main problem is water. All water there comes from two streams, both of which are very polluted. Another source must be found. Conventional means of putting in bore holes have failed, for the water table is too deep and there's a layer of rock that can be penetrated only with a good drilling rig.[1]

Spent part of the afternoon bouncing around on a bumpy, muddy road that is being bulldozed over surrounding mountains south to Uganda. Last night was cool, even chilly. Sat around a roaring campfire, had some beer and stew, talked with NGO folks. Felt good about being there. Arose at dawn to a stillness interrupted only by a rooster's crowing, and breathed cool pure fresh air of a kind unknown in Khartoum, and gazed out on the beauty of the mountains.

1745: Logi-Serv compound, Maridi. Dark inside my hut; I'm writing by candlelight. After landing at the Maridi airstrip this morning, went to the office of John Garang's area commissioner, Edward Bakulo, a man who often has been overbearing in dealing with NGO personnel. Listened to his warning of the threat to world peace posed by the Islamic fundamentalists in Khartoum, and how the US, since it has no serious problems elsewhere in the world, must intervene militarily in Sudan. I explained why US intervention was not in the cards and told him we will continue to provide humanitarian aid and try to further the peace process, moribund though it is. At noon walked for over an hour through shoulder-high grass and around the fields of a cooperative farm that is doing very well—a model for others.

Later drove down the USAID-funded all-weather dirt road being constructed. Runs SSE toward the Zaire and Uganda borders. We turned off at a junction and drove through part of the Antugua displaced camp, where 25,000 Bor Dinka trekked in February after fleeing from their previous camp at Kotobi when the northern army attacked nearby Mundri. A Médecins sans Frontières–Belgium doctor, who looked to me to be in her 20s, told me there is now very little severe malnutrition present in the camp. The people look much better than when I saw them at Bahr Olo in February as they were walking toward Antugua. Anxiety is growing that the northern offensive will be renewed soon and will come this way, forcing the Dinka to flee again—but where can they go?

**Oct. 8:** 0920: We are passing over the GOS-held town of Torit at 11,500 feet. The pilot, Richard Herman, who is from Bellingham, Washington, and once was a bush pilot in Alaska, says the UN-chartered relief program airplanes are supposed to keep ten miles away from the garrison towns unless they are going to one and have prior clearance from the GOS. But at 11,500 feet there is no danger that they can hit us. That's comforting. Nice clear day, can see for miles. Flew over the Nile 20 minutes ago and could see Juba, 14 miles to the north. Richard says the UN has given us a green light to fly to Kapoeta [a government-held town] after we get to Loki. The UN's chief security officer, Trevor Harvey, told me two days ago that because an SPLA attack on Kapoeta was expected at any time, we couldn't go there today. I assume he's heard from the SPLA that it's now o.k. I had told government officials in Khartoum before I left there that I wanted to fly to Kapoeta.

Last night Bakulo and the SPLA military commander for Maridi dropped by the compound for a talk. I told them their idea that the SPLA will tell the NGOs where and how to distribute relief food is unacceptable to the donors. Bakulo seemed to get the message and offered a lame excuse that there must have been a misunderstanding. Anyway, Gordon will follow up on this with SPLA officials in Nairobi.

**Oct. 9:** It was cool again when I woke up this morning in Maridi, the sky dotted with just a few clumps of altocumulus.

1135: Got into Lokichokio at 1100, out at 1130 and off to Kapoeta.

1155: We are approaching Kapoeta, which is said to be surrounded by SPLA soldiers. We'll pass over the northern edge of town at our present altitude of 11,500 feet, then double back and drop down pretty fast to the airstrip, clearances by both sides notwithstanding. Down we go at 3,000 feet per minute.

1405: On our way back to Lokichokio. Impressions of Kapoeta: Went with the wali to his office for discussion with him and other officials. Appointed by Khartoum, he is the governor of all of East Equatoria State, but in fact the GOS has effective control of only the garrison towns, like Kapoeta. They said the town has 4,500 people, with a population of 30–40,000 in nearby villages, which is probably a highly exaggerated figure. Place is full of soldiers—regular Sudanese army, People's Defense Force [PDF] militia, and Taposa tribesmen militia. The civilians are mainly Taposa, many or most of the women and a lot of the men wearing next to no clothing. Another hospital to be toured, this one run by a doctor from Khartoum who's been in Kapoeta since the GOS took it almost three years ago. 40 beds in two wards, one [ward] reserved for military. 430 cases of malaria last week, almost no chloroquine or quinine. A child of about 5 years was brought in while I was there. Convulsions due to malaria.

Kapoeta is a squalid town of mud-brick houses and shops that were damaged or destroyed during the fighting in '89 when the SPLA took the town and '92 when the GOS recaptured it. It sits on a semi-desert plain that must be hot and dry most of the year.

1600: Back on the Antonov cattle car[2] and returning to Nairobi. Full load of relief workers—Brits, Kenyans, Ethiopians, Americans, French—headed for R&R in Nairobi.

• • •

In June I had sent a message to the State Department stating I saw no reason why U.S. Mission dependents should continue to be kept away from Khartoum. Senior members of my staff disagreed with me, and I noted this in my message. The Department replied that the time had not come for dependents to return.

On October 13 I recommended, for the second time, that dependents be allowed to return. And again I told Washington that my staff did not share my view. Opinion in Washington on this issue was also divided, with some State Department offices and some other government agencies supporting, and others opposing, a return to a more normal footing in Khartoum. A few days later, I received word from the State Department that dependents could now return.

Because of broken assignments and transfers over the past fourteen months, only a handful of people would be affected by the decision. The wife of one of our communicators would come back, but only for a few weeks, since they were leaving Sudan for an assignment to Egypt at the end of November. An assistant regional security officer's wife would return unless his hoped-for assignment to another African country materialized. He did get the assignment, so she did not return to Khartoum. That left only two others—Julie and Brian. We were elated. I anticipated they would come back to Sudan in January, after the end of the first semester of Brian's sophomore year in high school. However, it would be another half year before they returned.

Many of my days in Khartoum were taken up with routine events. In two days in mid-October, for example, in addition to holding meetings with the DCM and other mission officers, I received the new South Korean ambassador, who was making his official calls. I paid a return call on the recently arrived Ethiopian ambassador and discussed the abortive peace negotiations. Two representatives of Norwegian Church Aid came to the embassy to talk about the religious conference in town sponsored by the Sudanese government and about the situation in southern Sudan. A Reuters correspondent interviewed me; he wanted to hear the U.S. side of the foreign minister's denial that Sudan abetted terrorism. I went to a luncheon the Foreign Ministry gave for the departing French ambassador. I composed a message asking the State Department to approve my recommendation for additional embassy positions and attended an outdoor ceremony (mostly speeches) honoring United Nations Day.

Not exactly routine, but not unusual, the next day the acting director of the Foreign Ministry's Office of Political Affairs called me to the ministry to hear the government's latest complaint about U.S. policy toward Sudan. Definitely not routine was a visit a couple of days later to a Sufi religious ceremony at the invitation of Sheikh Hassan, the leader of the Sammaniyya sect. The Sammaniyya was established about 300 years ago in Saudi Arabia by an ancestor of Hassan. Hassan succeeded his father as sheikh when the father died. The invitation was a welcome change and a chance to see an important spiritual and ceremonial side of Sudanese life.

According to *Understanding Islam*,[3] Sufis "are Muslim mystics espousing a personal relationship with God based on love, in contrast to the submission based on fear and prohibition that characterizes the official religion." They seek God through mystical contemplation. Organized into brotherhoods (there is no role for women), the Sufis turned away from formalistic approaches to Islam. Conventional religious authorities regarded Sufis with suspicion and antagonism. Far from attracting just eccentrics, Sufism drew the best thinkers is Islam.

In Sudan some Sufis became politicized after the early nineteenth-century invasion by the Ottomans from Egypt. Years later, Sudan's two largest Sufi sects, the Mahdiyya and Khatmiyya, set up political organizations, the Umma Party and the People's Democratic Party. But most Sudanese Sufis, like the Sammaniyya, are apolitical. They differ, I was told, not so much in the substance of their religious beliefs as in the rites in which they observe their faith. These rites can include music and dancing (like that of Sudan's Dervishes, for example), which are a means of communing with Allah.

After being greeted by the sheikh and conducted to a room inside the Sammaniyya mosque, Larry and Gloria Benedict, Lucien Vandenbrouke, my secretary Shirley Dickman, and I talked for a while with leading members of the brotherhood—educators, lawyers, and doctors. Then we went outside to observe the ceremony, which had been going on for almost three hours. Women were not allowed at the ceremony, so Gloria and Shirley stayed inside talking with Sufi members.

I stood directly behind Sheikh Hassan, who was facing three lines, each of more than 100 men. Other men taking part in the ceremony extended in lines to my right and left. All told, about 500 men were participating. Each was dressed in a white *jellabiya* girded by a wide leather belt that had a strap going diagonally over one shoulder, and each wore either a white turban or a skullcap. To the beat of a drum, they were chanting and bowing in unison up and down deeply from the waist. At the direction of the sheikh the beat was speeded up or slowed and the chant varied. At times the chant gave way to a deep-throated rumble. Their movements also varied. The bowing changed to pivoting at the waist to right and left, for example, and once they leaped straight up and down about ten times.

We watched for an hour. Two or three times, the participants stood still for a few minutes while one of several men recited from the Koran. After sunset it was time for prayers, following which Sheikh Hassan preached. During this we went back inside to talk with others until he finished and we could visit with him and make our farewells.

It had been a fascinating affair, thoroughly apolitical. Nevertheless, as we would learn later, the Iranian embassy and apparently some in the NIF were unhappy that I had attended it.

• • •

Ten men came to the embassy on October 15 to tell us there had been a shooting in Omdurman. The people of an area called Khuddeir had been told they were going to be moved to a camp out on the edge of the city. The people, squatters most of whom had lived in Khuddeir for more than ten years, demonstrated against the move, and in the ensuing melee the police killed several of them and wounded or beat others. After we had verified from more on-the-scene witnesses that this account was accurate, we reported it to the State Department and sent a draft statement that we asked the Department to make.

The opening of the statement, made on October 18 by State Department spokesman Michael McCurry, hit at the Sudanese government:

> The U.S. Government strongly condemns the slaying and wounding of several demonstrators who were protesting the razing of their squatter settlements in the Khuddeir neighborhood of Omdurman on October 15.
>
> The incident, in which armed riot police shot into a crowd of unarmed protesters, which included women and children, is unjustifiable and a clear abuse of force by the Government of Sudan.
>
> The incident underscores the brutality and callousness of the policy of forcible resettlement of squatters in the Khartoum area, which has been proceeding off and on for years.

By early November I seemed to be back in the good graces of the government, even though the embassy was being vilified in the press for the U.S. condemnation of the Khuddeir shootings. A foreign journalist who came to the embassy told me that officials he had seen in

Khartoum spoke well of me. So it went—appreciated one week, out of favor the next.

At the foreign minister's request, I went to see him. Our last meeting had been contentious. This time we both went out of our way to be pleasant. We succeeded, in part because the topic of our conversation was the peace process, and issues such as terrorism and human rights did not come up. I seemed now to have an opening to resume meeting with other government officials, something that I had been unable to do for several weeks.

The Kenyans were making an attempt to breathe new life into the IGADD peace effort. Zackary Onyenka, the Kenyan chairman of the previous negotiating sessions in Nairobi, came to Khartoum to talk with government officials, southerners, and nongovernment northerners. Shortly before he returned to Kenya, he told me he believed there was sufficient basis for the mediation to continue.

I hoped he was right but remained doubtful that IGADD could succeed, since the warring parties were not disposed to compromise on important issues. Government officials whom I talked to admitted privately that they doubted the mediation would produce a settlement. However, fearing that the UN Security Council might take up the Sudan problem if the IGADD effort collapsed, Khartoum would go through the motions of cooperating to keep the mediation going.

The government's Islamists had become convinced that neither a military solution nor a negotiated settlement was essential to their objective of achieving a unitary state in which Islam would be the unifying factor and governing principle. Under the label of "peace and development," the government initiated various projects, such as a road to Malakal, aimed at winning the hearts and minds of southerners. In July 1994 Ghazi told me "not most, but many" southerners supported the Bashir government. This, he said, was partly attributable to the government's peace and development projects. Ghazi claimed census figures showed that Muslims outnumbered Christians in the South.

A month later an influential and prominent member of the NIF told Lucien Vandenbroucke the government faced no serious internal opposition. He said the regime was giving the Sudanese people what they wanted, an Islamic state. In September, Ali Osman Taha, who several months later would succeed Hussein Abu Salih as foreign minister, stated to me that the movement for an internal settlement to the war was gathering momentum. He said that in the final analysis peace from Sudan had to come from within. Later he told an African ambassador the internal peace process was having great success.

● ● ●

An ambassador generally needs to spend most of his or her time in the capital of the host country. But it is well worth the effort to seize every opportunity to travel outside the capital to learn as much as possible about what is happening in other parts of the country and what people there are thinking. Because I went to the South so often, I realized I had to make an effort to go to places in the North more frequently than I had been doing.

On November 6, with Abu Ouf, other Sudanese officials, a visiting USAID officer from Nairobi, and the head of an INGO, I flew about 300 miles northwest of Khartoum to Dongola and then to Merowe to donate some microscopes and other laboratory equipment and antimalaria drugs to local authorities in the two towns. As we gained altitude and headed for Dongola, I was struck by how different Khartoum looked from the air at the end of the rains, compared to most of the rest of the year. All along the river, but also in some other parts of town, the scene was surprisingly green instead of the ochre and brown I was used to seeing when I flew in or out of the city. Soon, though, as we proceeded north, the sandy wastes took over.

The terrain was as arid as could be, except for the narrow band of lush vegetation along the river and stunted trees lying in the dry beds of shallow wadis. After about twenty minutes we crossed the Nile and passed over miles of sand relieved by black rocky outcrops and pockmarked by many sandy knolls. The outcrops become small jagged hills and then faded away, becoming flat, black stains on the desert expanse of beige sand.

North of Khartoum the Nile swings east. It disappeared from sight as we flew to the northwest. Farther on in its course, the river turns to the north and then southwest in a great bend, and we came upon it again about seventy miles south of Dongola. There we saw the first sign of human habitation in over an hour and a half of flying over the desert, which now was pure sand.

At Dongola, Abu Ouf, the others in our party, and I were met by the wali of Northern State and other officials. We went to the wali's office and talked about the increase in malaria and other effects of the recent flood. In a ceremony afterward, I handed over the lab materials and the medicines. Because of the upsurge in malaria, the donation would have an immediate beneficial effect on the people of Dongola and Merowe.

At Merowe, about seventy miles to the east of Dongola, there was a similar welcome and presentation ceremony. After that we drove around the town to look at the flood damage, then crossed the river on a ferry and drove north for a few miles to Karima, the site of an archeological treasure that to my mind rivaled ancient wonders of Egypt. In a sandstone hill looming over the desert was a tomb on whose walls were marvelous, well-preserved carved figures depicting men and women and religious symbols, such as snakes. The tomb and nearby pyramids and ruins of temples and other structures dated back 5,000 years and were similar in style, to my untrained eye, to the works of ancient Egyptians.

The people I met were pleased I had come and warmly received me. Despite the anti-American propaganda being broadcast on the radio, government officials and civilians alike expressed pro-American sentiments. Although I knew that some of this could be attributed to the courtesy traditionally extended to a guest, most of what I heard seemed genuine. There was no doubt about how much the medical equipment and antimalarial drugs were needed and how much they were appreciated.

Back in Khartoum, the political climate was not so friendly. In mid-November the press was attacking me on a variety of counts. My visit to the Sufi mosque a month earlier was portrayed as something sinister. One newspaper asked why the U.S. ambassador, "who is known to be anti-Islamic," went to the mosque. We learned that the Iranians suspected the visit was an effort by the United States to infiltrate Islamic institutions and undercut Iranian efforts to forge ties to them. They probably had a hand in the belated denunciation of the visit.

Another media attack referred to the last time I was in Nimule, some months earlier. I was accused of having gone there to oversee the distribution of Israeli arms and ammunition to the rebels.

The government, through the media, continued to excoriate the embassy, Washington, and me for the State Department's statement on the killing of squatters in Khuddeir. Had it not been for our reporting and our repeated request that the Department make a statement on the incident, very few Sudanese and virtually nobody outside Sudan would ever have heard about it. The public disclosure infuriated the government.

I made plans to go to Washington for consultations in mid-December, and then on to New Hampshire, where I would meet Julie, Brian, and others of our family for Christmas. After that Julie and Brian would return to Mexico, where they had gone from Oregon early in 1994 to be with her family.

After the State Department had granted my request that dependents be allowed to return to Khartoum, Julie and I thought she and Brian would leave Mexico and return to Khartoum in January, at the end of the semester at the American School in Mexico City. However, the school counselor strongly advised us not to move Brian again. He told Julie that Brian was happy there, had made friends, and was doing well in his schoolwork. In the less than five years since we left Tanzania at the beginning of 1990, Brian had been moved six times and another move now, followed by still another when we left Sudan, would not be a good idea. Almost all his friends in Khartoum had gone, and his only reason for wanting to return was to be with me. So we decided he and Julie would remain in Mexico until the end of the school year.

I had another Thanksgiving without family. I gave a dinner for fifty people—all the Americans, some of our Sudanese employees and their spouses, a few diplomats and several Sudanese government officials with their wives, and some people opposed to the government.

About a week later, with two embassy officers, I drove south to Kosti and then off the main road for about ten miles to Kenana, the site of Sudan's largest and only privately owned sugar plantation and factory. We passed large tracts of mechanized farms, which used to grow cotton but now were for the most part devoted to sorghum. It was nice to get away from the current acrimony in Khartoum and to see a good side of Sudan, in this case at Kenana, an agricultural enterprise that treated its workers in exemplary fashion and, overcoming production problems, was enjoying a successful year.

The war ground on in the South, with the main action still at Kapoeta. Khartoum's newspapers carried no war news at all. Throughout the more than two years I had been in Sudan, the government had heavily censored information about the war. On rare occasions the media mentioned that someone relatively well known had been "martyred" in the jihad in the South. When northern troops took Kajo Keji, near the Ugandan border, earlier in the year, the government trumpeted it as a great victory. But other than these rare exceptions, there was not a word in the media, certainly nothing about reverses or casualties among the government forces.

The most interesting development at this time had nothing to do with the war. Instead, it was an announcement in Asmara that the Eritrean government had broken relations with Sudan. Fed up with what he claimed was active assistance by Sudan to the Eritrean Islamic Jihad, which aimed to overthrow his government, Eritrea's President Isaias Afwerki decided he had had enough. On December 5 the Sudanese embassy staff in Asmara was given twenty-four hours to pack up and leave the country. This action—and the fact that two of the four IGADD countries, Uganda and Eritrea, were now openly hostile toward the Islamist government in Sudan—was another nail in the coffin of the IGADD effort to mediate a settlement to Sudan's civil war.

I sent word to Turabi that I thought it would be useful for us to have a talk before I had consultations in Washington. Our subsequent meeting reaffirmed that for now rapprochement between Washington and Khartoum was unattainable. Turabi held tenaciously to his mistaken notions about our motives. Interestingly, he tacitly acknowledged he was the de facto leader of the NIF-dominated government of Sudan, something he often publicly disavowed.

Turabi was now categorical in stating that he believed the CIA had tried to do him in. He speculated that the United States had had a hand in Eritrea's decision to break relations with Sudan and in the SPLA attack on Kapoeta. He said he refused to accept that the United States cared about human rights in Sudan. He reiterated his insistence that because of Zionist influence, U.S. foreign policymakers were anti-Islamic and that this was the real reason Washington was antagonistic toward Sudan. He said it was up to Washington to do something to show it really wanted better relations with Sudan.

With no end in sight to the impasse in U.S.-Sudanese relations, I left for Washington and New Hampshire.

# 17

# Working with the United Nations

My association with United Nations agencies and aid donor–country representatives required a lot of my time and energy. In addition to the weekly meetings with them, which I chaired about one-fourth of the time, I had many ad hoc meetings with individual UN agency heads, donor-country and INGO representatives, and Sudanese officials. Not only were the many and varied problems associated with the humanitarian relief program time-consuming, but coping with them—especially with the government and rebel acts that hindered the delivery of food and other supplies—was often frustrating.

There were times when disagreements cropped up between the donors and UN officials in Khartoum. This was to be expected, but too often they grew out of what we donors regarded as indefensible operational deficiencies on the part of some UN agencies. The UN's fragmented structure of separate, independent agencies was mirrored in Sudan, where a UN official having ambassadorial status headed each agency. The inefficiencies and financial costs spawned by this separation into bureaucratic baronies were, to put it mildly, unfortunate.

As ambassador I had authority over all the U.S. Mission personnel, regardless of which agency they belonged to. That authority, which stems from a presidential directive, was essential for the proper management of the mission. There was never any question as to who was the boss; thus my dismay, which was shared by other donor-country ambassadors, at the weaknesses of the UN system. The top UN official in Khartoum had the title of UN coordinator. As far as we could tell, the coordinator was not empowered to direct agency heads to do this or that; instead, he or she had to rely on powers of persuasion. Sometimes this simply did not work.

My colleagues and I also believed that the United Nations could have been more aggressive in dealing with the Sudanese government. Arbitrary decisions by government officials, most frequently military or security personnel, that hampered relief operations were commonplace. In our opinion, the United Nations should have been prepared to express to the Sudanese government in much stronger terms than it did the anger we all felt when this happened. UN officials—not all, but many—did not agree. This, they indicated, was not their function.

One high-level UN official told me a more aggressive approach would make it even more difficult for UN agencies in Khartoum to accomplish their mission. It occurred to me that, in addition, some UN officials wanted to avoid a repetition of what had happened to an earlier UN coordinator. The Sudanese government had not liked his way of doing business and expelled him from Sudan.

The organizational and policy deficiencies of the United Nations did not obscure the fact that there were many superb, dedicated UN people working in the relief effort in Khartoum, in Nairobi, and in the field, where they encountered difficult and sometimes dangerous conditions. And despite our problems, the coordination between donors and the United Nations in Sudan was the best I had observed in my experience in Africa.

Our weekly meetings and numerous other interactions were useful mechanisms to inform ourselves about problems and develop strategies for dealing with them. I believe they also helped improve the coordination within the UN family itself.

Excerpts from some of my cabled reports on the weekly meetings give a flavor of the kinds of things we dealt with and of the scope of the disaster in southern Sudan:

[February 24, 1994]

WFP [World Food Program] and ICRC [International Committee of the Red Cross] reported that there is an acute food shortage in Juba. Children, especially, are suffering. Relief workers in Juba informed WFP that 65 children died during the past two weeks. Food stocks are almost exhausted. . . . WFP is attempting to airlift 3,000 metric tons of maize from Entebbe, but it has not yet obtained donor funding for the local purchase.

The UN Emergency Unit Officer verified an earlier report that over 50 mud-brick houses were demolished at Wad Al Bashir, an official displaced camp in Khartoum. This . . . may have been carried out by security officials angered at the refusal of camp residents to participate in a GOS-organized demonstration against the report on Sudan by the UN Human Rights Special Rapporteur. As for the Khartoum displaced in general, as much as a third of the people in camps received none of the donated food distributed in 1993, and the percentage of people getting other services was small. Malnutrition rates are terribly high. In short, the situation of the Khartoum displaced continues to be deplorable.

[March 3, 1994]

I opened the meeting by passing along what we have heard about the bombings at Nimule and Aswa camp. Referring to my previous visit there, I said there could be no military justification whatsoever for dumping bombs on the displaced at Aswa.

UN Coordinator Per Janvid[1] said that in addition to the Nimule and Aswa raids, the Sudanese airforce had bombed a location some 40 kilometers southwest of Torit.

WFP Director Khalid Adly said the effort to supply towns along the Sobat [River], from Malakal to Nasir, has been scrubbed. Ten trucks loaded with supplies had been taken from Kosti to Malakal on barges and driven southeast along the bank of the Sobat. For two weeks they were held up at Nagdir because of mines on the road. . . . Now, because of the threat of military action at Nasir, WFP is canceling the operation and sending the trucks back to Kosti.

Janvid reported that the Ame and Atepi displaced who had gone to Parajok are now at Labone. . . . CRS [Catholic Relief Services] had pre-positioned 8,000 bags of grain at Parajok prior to the arrival of the displaced there, but because of poor road access to Labone, replenishment of food and other supplies is not going well. The UN is considering air-dropping food, medicines and blankets.

The UN remains deeply concerned about its four employees who remain in the custody of the SPLA at Arrat. As of this morning, the UN had received no reply from the SPLA to its request for clearance for an aircraft to fly UN officials to Arrat for direct talks with the SPLA military commander there.[2]

Before heavy-handed GOS inspection of the cargo at the required interim stop in Juba closed down the Maridi airdrop, 86 metric tons of grain had been delivered there by OLS aircraft.

[March 24, 1994]

The growing concern . . . about the inadequacy of food deliveries to those in Sudan who are in great need was underlined at today's meeting. WFP Director Khalid Adly told the gathered donor chiefs of mission and UN agency heads that WFP Khartoum has on hand only four days' supply of food for delivery to all served by its aircraft and barge operations.

Adly also pointed out that donors have not been forthcoming with sufficient funding for the delivery system. Most immediately this affects the airlift and airdrop operations on which, given the failure to expand road deliveries, so many people are totally dependent. . . . Information in from the field shows an alarming increase in malnutrition levels.

Comment and action request: On the basis of what we are hearing, extremely serious food shortages could occur at many locations throughout Sudan in the coming months. Already there are signs that urgent action is needed to turn around unacceptably high rates of malnutrition. Shortfalls in food aid and funding for relief operations are beginning to be felt and could have further, dire, consequences. Because of our staffing constraints, this mission does not have the expertise necessary to properly evaluate the various factors I have described and make appropriate recommendations. I believe that the magnitude of the problem requires an immediate evaluation. Accordingly, I ask that AID send someone here as soon as possible to assess the situation.

[June 2,1994]

Per Janvid said all NGO and UN personnel have been evacuated from Nimule, with most going to Gulu, Uganda. GOS troops are now just north of Aswa, and Nimule is believed to be within range of the Sudanese army's artillery.

UN and NGO personnel are making daytime visits to the Nasir area. They report that all the huts in both Nasir and Ulang have been burned to the ground. . . . The UN continues to get reports of fighting in various places in Bahr al Ghazal, e.g., near Awiel and Tonj.

Khalid Adly reported that the relief train to Wau arrived at Awiel June 1 with no food left following repeated looting at various places. Only about 300 of the train's load of 1500 metric tons of grain were delivered to intended targets. . . .

I said that even if the SPLA leadership in the South intended to honor its agreement to protect the train, it could not control its local commanders. The growing serious malnutrition in Bahr al Ghazal virtually ensures that trainloads of food are going to be looted. It did not, therefore, seem to make any sense to continue sending food by train. Adly said the WFP wanted to continue to try to make use of the railroad [because of the high cost of air transportation]. It would investigate what has occurred, make representations to the SPLA and probably try again. I reiterated my skepticism that train deliveries make any sense in today's increasingly insecure environment in Bahr al Ghazal.

[ICRC representative] Armin Kobel told the meeting that a recent trip into the South by an ICRC nutritionist adds to the evidence that southern Sudan "is on the edge of a major humanitarian crisis." An ICRC report based on the nutritionist's survey states, "Only an urgent and massive food assistance programme is able (sic) to stop the rapid deterioration of the situation."

[October 27, 1994]

I asked [the new] UN Coordinator Christoph Jaeger whether the UN would be making a statement about the shooting of Khuddeir squatters last week. (FYI: The U.S. government has been the sole entity to condemn the GOS for this latest outcome of its policy of forcible removals of squatters and displaced people from Khartoum to ill-prepared locations in the far reaches of the city. The Department's statement about the Khuddeir incident has resulted in a flood of invective in the GOS-controlled media. End FYI.) Jaeger replied that UN headquarters in New York had "no intention of making a statement."

Fighting between the SPLA-Mainstream and the force led by Kerubino Kwanyan Bol is still going on at Mayen Abun. The SPLA-M persists in refusing to allow the ICRC to evacuate wounded from Mayen Abun. ICRC Representative Armin Kobel asked that countries with diplomatic representation in Nairobi intercede with Garang's people to get them to agree to permit the ICRC to carry out the evacuation.

[January 26, 1995]

The Department will recall that UN agency heads and the chief of mission occupying the chair of the donor group meet with Relief and Rehabilitation Commission [RRC] officials a day before the weekly meeting [of the UN and donors]. At the January 25 meeting, UN Coordinator Jaeger brought up allegations in the Sudanese press that Operation Lifeline Sudan is using relief-program aircraft to supply arms and ammunition to the SPLA.

In stating that the charges are blatantly false, Jaeger said subsequent statements by GOS officials have been unhelpful. The acting RRC commissioner said he had no information from his government. Noting that Minister of State Dr. Ghazi Salah Eddin had said that if the information about the OLS proved to be correct, it raised suspicions about the UN program, Jaeger said statements of that kind give weight to the allegations, which he repeated were totally false.

I said it was outrageous that GOS officials are lending weight to the allegations instead of refuting them. In response, the acting commissioner merely repeated that he had not been given any information on this from the government.

Fighting is continuing at Kapoeta, near Torit and at or near Morobo, Akon and Alek. Nimule has been heavily shelled by government forces these past few days, and all UN and NGO personnel have been evacuated from the town. [Nimule never did fall to the government forces, despite the strong effort to take it.]

The GOS has told the WFP that because of the insecurity at Torit, it cannot allow a food monitor to go there. At the same time, the government is asking that food be sent to Torit. WFP has turned down the request, telling the GOS that it will not deliver food to locations that cannot be monitored.

The battle by UN relief agencies, donors, and NGOs to overcome obstacles to the relief program was constant. Successes were hard to come by, requiring a judicious mixture of tact and belligerence. Considering that my colleagues and I were doing our best to save lives, for that, in the final analysis, is what we were doing, our efforts were time well spent.

# 18

# New Year,
# Same Old Problems

At the beginning of 1995 I had a series of talks with Foreign Minister Abu Salih and other cabinet ministers about the latest erosion of both the IGADD mediation and Sudan's relations with Eritrea. Bashir was not invited to a January 4 summit in Nairobi at which the IGADD presidents asked the United Nations to send an observer to the next round of peace talks. They should have known this would anger the Sudanese, who continued to be adamantly opposed to any form of UN involvement in the peace process. In addition to denouncing this action, the Sudanese said they would not participate in any IGADD talks as long as Eritrea remained a participant. They argued that having broken diplomatic relations with Sudan, Eritrea could not be regarded as a neutral party.

U.S. policy continued to be one of full support for the IGADD initiative, and I said as much to reporters who sought interviews with me. But in my debriefings in Washington in December I said the peace talks were virtually dead and buried.[1] Sudan's angry reaction to the IGADD call for a UN observer at the talks and the Sudanese denunciation of Eritrea were further signs that the talks would not succeed. The reality was that, as things were now, in the absence of some form of forceful international pressure, the war in Sudan would not end.

And there was no prospect at all that the outside world was going to do anything at all in that regard.

Before I left Khartoum on leave a month earlier, my staff and I were getting the impression that the human rights picture was getting better—fewer detentions and reports of torture. That, in its limited sense, may have been true, but in mid-January the government continued to add to its record of human rights abuses. Another atrocity took place along the railroad line between Babanusa and Wau in Bahr al-Ghazal. For at least the third time in the past couple of years, militia accompanying the troop train burned villages along the way, killing people and taking others captive. The United Nations knew of this. Yet as often happened in these kinds of human rights violations in Sudan, UN officials in Khartoum adhered to instructions from New York and did not make an issue out of it.

On January 14 I met with Ghazi at the palace. I went to hear what he had to say about the IGADD talks but got more than I expected. He told me the United States had instructed the IGADD presidents to seek UN observance of the peace talks, we had engineered Eritrea's break in relations with Sudan, and we were manipulating the IGADD leaders, who he said were not very capable and, furthermore, were dependent on U.S. aid. He also charged that the United States was providing military assistance to the SPLA. My telling him that all this was untrue made no impression on him.

As for relations between the United States and Sudan, he said Washington had ignored Sudan's efforts to improve them. Repeating a Turabi theme, Ghazi said that in doing this the U.S. government was following the dictates of Israel and its U.S. Zionist backers.

I was going to go to southern Sudan at this time, but decided not to. Two weeks earlier I had talked on the phone with Philip O'Brien in Nairobi. I asked him whether it would be useful for me to go to the South again. He enthusiastically endorsed the idea, but later, after I had begun making arrangements to go, he and I agreed that I should hold off for a while. With Garang at least momentarily on the offensive and receiving new infusions of arms and ammunition and with Khartoum accusing both the OLS and the Americans of aiding Garang, a trip by me into rebel-held territory would probably do more harm than good, especially if, as I had planned, I saw Garang and Riek Machar.

One night I went to a Sudanese friend's house in Khartoum to have a talk with Nafi Ali Nafi, now the head of external security and still considered one of the most powerful men in the country. He had jumped at the chance for a private meeting when my friend had proposed it to him. We talked mainly about the peace process, Sudan's relations with its neighbors, the war, and allegations that the United States was aiding Garang and that the United Nations and United States had recently delivered arms to him. Although Nafi was more flexible than others whom I had been seeing in recent months, even conceding some of the points I made, I had little reason to expect that anything significant would come of our meeting.

My pessimism was based in part on the public utterances of Sudanese leaders. On February 12 a Jordanian newspaper, *Al-Dustur*, reported the remarks President Bashir had made in an interview filmed by Baghdad Youth Television. The U.S. government's Foreign Broadcast Intelligence Service translated the *Al-Dustur* report. An account of the interview also was printed in the Sudanese press:

> Sudanese President 'Umar Ahmad al-Bashir has accused the United States of practicing international terrorism and described it as the number one terrorist state.
>
> Al-Bashir . . . said Israel is the country with the worst human rights record, and it receives Washington's care in spite of its repressive practices against the Palestinians, its tightening siege on them, its demolishing of their houses, and its restrictions on their movements.
>
> The Sudanese president criticized Washington's position on incidents in his country and for attacking the unarmed Somali people by airplanes.
>
> He revealed a U.S. plan to invade Sudan, similar to the U.S. occupation of Haiti. He emphasized that the Sudanese people are prepared to confront the invaders, and said the Sudanese Government will enlist 5,000,000 Sudanese volunteers, in addition to the regular forces and the local police force, saying: "All these are mujahidin who are waiting for those who will come on board barges and tanks to invade Sudan."
>
> Bashir expressed opposition to the peace efforts between the Arabs and Israel and said: "The Arabs will not accept the existence of Israel, and what is going on does not represent their will." He described the

Middle East peace plan as a plan designed to give Israel a free hand in
the region.

President Bashir's bombast about confronting a U.S. invasion force
echoed similar militancy voiced by Hasan al-Turabi in a conversation
we had had a few months earlier. The distance between the Sudanese
and U.S. governments' viewpoints was also shown by a statement that
Turabi made a week after Bashir's remarks to Iranian youth. In an address he gave at the University of Khartoum, Turabi declared Sudan
had nothing to fear at being placed on the list of state sponsors of terrorism. That list, he said, "is a list of honor."

To say that publicly indicated he was either ignorant of or indifferent to Americans' strong negative feelings about terrorism in all its
forms—particularly in the aftermath of the New York City and Okla-
homa City bombings. In view of Turabi's good access to news of the
world outside Sudan, it is logical to conclude that he was indifferent
rather than ignorant.

The Sudanese intensified their publicly stated allegations that the U.S.
government was providing military assistance to the SPLA. Foreign correspondents began picking up on this, and prominent newspapers and
newsletters (like *Africa Confidential*) carried articles about the possibility that the United States was supporting the rebels in southern Sudan,
some indicating that the allegations might well be true. They were not.

Even before I came to Sudan, the idea of giving support to the rebels
had been raised in policy discussions. This had also come up during
my tenure. In every instance, both before and while I was in Sudan,
the idea was rejected. The rebels, like the Sudanese government, had
committed atrocities against southern civilians. Because of this, military aid to them would have drawn fire both domestically and internationally. In addition, there was considerable opposition in the executive branch to taking any steps that could in time lead to deeper, more
direct involvement in Sudan's civil war. And finally, it was clear that
the U.S. Congress and the public at large would not favor U.S. military
involvement of any kind in southern Sudan.

•  •  •

The fasting of the month of Ramadan began with the sighting of the
moon on the first of February. Because most of my Sudanese body-

guards were Muslims, I was even more reluctant than usual to make them work any more than absolutely necessary over the weekends. So I knew that in the coming month I would have a lot of quiet time cooped up in my palatial jail. At sunset that evening I wandered outside, said hello to the cats, watched as hundreds of birds flew in to roost in a large tree in the yard, talked to the gate guards, and came back inside to write a letter to Julie and Brian.

On February 6 CNN reported that Siddiq Ali, one of the six Sudanese among the twelve defendants in the terrorism-conspiracy trial in New York had pled guilty and was expected to testify against some of his codefendants, including Sheikh Omar Abdulrahman, the "blind Sheikh." The twelve were accused of conspiring to bomb in July 1993 the UN building in New York, a federal office building, and two Hudson River automobile tunnels and of planning other terrorist acts.

Siddiq Ali's guilty plea came on the heels of a statement that we had released in Khartoum denying allegations by the Sudanese government that the accused were being grossly mistreated. Our statement provided information in response to some of the specific charges that had been leveled.

In the next day's Khartoum newspapers, commentary about the statement was critical but relatively restrained. Not so, however, the reaction to the news from New York. The government's position on this appeared the following morning in an editorial in *Al Engaz al Watani*. The editorial charged that the authorities in the United States had deluded the poor young Sudanese man into falsely confessing. It denounced the U.S. system of justice.

The indictment and trial of Sheikh Abdulrahman and the other eleven men raised concern in Washington that if they were convicted, terrorists in Khartoum might retaliate by committing an act of violence against official Americans in Khartoum.

Responding to a message from the State Department that February, I cabled that "the terrorist organizations here would, I believe, be constrained not to act against us if the GOS did not sanction it." It was, I noted, impossible to say categorically that the Sudanese would not condone violence against us. But I said it would be illogical for them "to do something that would lead to some form of serious retaliation" against themselves. I indicated that on balance I believed Americans in Khartoum would come to no harm if the conspirators were convicted. As it turned out, when the twelve were convicted in late 1995 nothing untoward happened to Americans in Sudan.

There was another element in the conspiracy trial that could have had ramifications for the embassy. The Justice Department and the FBI knew early on that two officials of the Sudanese mission to the United Nations had assisted the conspirators. Yet because of fear that revealing this might adversely affect the prosecution's case against Abdulrahman and the others, knowledge of the officials' involvement was kept under wraps for months. Before the trial was over the Sudanese government transferred one of the two officials back to Khartoum. To avoid possibly increasing the danger facing our embassy, Washington decided not to take action against the other Sudanese official, who remained in New York.[2]

• • •

I went to Port Sudan in mid-February, with a bodyguard and two drivers. We left one morning at six and drove for twelve hours. It was a long but not a difficult trip because the road was paved all the way, except for about eighteen miles. For most of the way to Kassala, a large town about halfway to Port Sudan, we passed through Sudan's most productive agricultural land. This rich alluvial plain to the south of Khartoum lies between the two Niles, which accounts for its name, El Gezira, "the island." Although it is semiarid, its fertile soil and river-fed irrigation give the Gezira a great potential for agricultural output.

There was no look of prosperity to the land and towns, however. During the 1970s and into the 1980s Sudan was touted as the future breadbasket of the Arab world. The Gezira's potential was squandered, however, largely because of mismanagement (heavy reliance on marginal land, for example) and too much government involvement. As has happened so often in government-directed large-scale agricultural schemes, the farmers on whose labor success in the scheme depended lacked sufficient incentives. Not one of the major agricultural projects started between 1975 and 1985 succeeded. In that decade Sudan's "farm productivity stagnated and its export earnings actually declined."[3]

Turning northeast after Kassala, we drove mainly through grazing country and semidesert, where we saw few humans but many camels, sheep, and goats. The people of that part of Sudan are Beja, pastoralists who were known as fierce warriors. After passing through the barren, rocky Red Sea Hills, we got to Port Sudan just after nightfall. We spent the night at the state government's guest house—by far the most comfortable accommodations I had anywhere in my travels in Sudan.

The next day I called on the wali, met with port officials, toured the port, then drove about thirty miles to the old port town of Suakin. There I was taken across a causeway to a small island that had been the headquarters of the British colonial administration for the area. After the British moved to Port Sudan in the 1920s, Suakin was gradually deserted by its other inhabitants, and the buildings, made of crushed coral, succumbed to the elements.

Back in Port Sudan that evening, I dined with the wali and other officials at an *iftar* (it was still the month of Ramadan) at the guest house. I had been favorably impressed by what I had seen and heard from the Sudanese I met, and I thought Red Sea State might, unlike many or most of the newly created states, do reasonably well economically and perhaps in time even politically. However, I learned soon afterward from unimpeachable sources that the government there was just as oppressive as the one in Khartoum. There were no democratic freedoms, and, fearful of the security police, people did not dare speak out.

Several days before going to Port Sudan I paid a call on officials of the Election Corporation, which the government had created to conduct the elections scheduled to begin in March. I asked and they answered some questions about their powers and the procedures for the elections. The officials seemed to be sincere, and even though I knew that the complicated electoral system the government had devised was far from democratic, I did not take issue with what they said to me.

A Sudanese journalist holding a tape recorder asked me some questions as I left the corporation's offices. Choosing my words carefully, I told him I had sought information about how candidates would be nominated, said something to the effect that free and fair elections are essential to democracy, and said my embassy, like all embassies in Khartoum, would be following the election process.

Later I was a bit apprehensive that my words would be interpreted in such a way as to make it seem I was endorsing the electoral system. I needn't have worried. The reaction in the media to what I had said was one of outrage. I was accused of prejudging the elections and interfering in Sudan's affairs.

The elections represented a major effort by the government to burnish its image and counter accusations that it was undemocratic and a gross violator of human rights. Sudan's rulers had interpreted my remarks as criticism, and their angry reaction, expressed in extensive press commentary criticizing me, indicated I had inadvertently hit a raw nerve.

It had been about a year since I met with the two women of the Martyrs' Association, which continued to try to get information about the members' sons and husbands whom the Bashir government had executed in early 1990. The two women were still being hounded by security police. In early March I saw them for the second time. They told me that in January, on the fifth anniversary of the executions, women of the Martyrs' Association blocked traffic on a street in Khartoum and were handing out leaflets when security police picked them up. They were detained, beaten, reviled, and made to stand on a rooftop out in the hot sun for some hours. One was threatened with death before they were released. Some ambassadors and other diplomats who believed that the United States was too tough on the Sudanese government tended to pay little heed to that kind of occurrence.

I met with Turabi the morning of March 11. In the course of our conversation I cited what had happened to the women of the Martyrs' Association as evidence that serious human rights violations really continued to occur here. His response? What happened was "normal." Furthermore, he said, police everywhere in the world sometimes used excessive force. Besides, the women had "probably provoked the policemen," and in any event they undoubtedly exaggerated what had actually taken place.

About this time I met with the new foreign minister, Ali Osman Taha. I entertained a faint hope that a discussion with him in his new role as foreign minister might possibly lead to at least a modicum of progress in reducing the tension between Khartoum and Washington. My talk with Taha was amicable; so, too, was the one with Turabi, for that matter. Like Turabi, Taha said he accepted my explanation refuting allegations that the United States was providing arms and ammunition to the SPLA. But that was the extent of anything positive. Our conversations revealed again that the basic differences between Khartoum and Washington on human rights, terrorism, and the absence of democracy, along with other issues, remained firmly entrenched.

# 19

# Farewell

An ambassador's life has its share of dull moments. In Sudan, however, they were few and far between and of short duration. The last four months of my assignment were as eventful as any period in my three years in Sudan. Among other things, we had to deal with yet another imbroglio with the government of Sudan, one that caused U.S.-Sudanese relations to deteriorate even further.

During those four months former president Jimmy Carter came to Sudan twice. He was no stranger to Sudan, having visited the country a number of times previously. In March he was successful in getting the warring parties to agree to a cease-fire. His timing was good: The rainy season, which in parts of the South begins about January and lasts for several months, was in full swing. It renders some areas impassable by motor vehicle and generally causes a sharp drop in military operations. In addition to being slowed down by the rains, both the government and the rebel forces were having serious logistical problems and needed some time to regroup.

President Carter's success in getting the cease-fire, however, was mainly a result of his negotiating skills and prestige. He is highly esteemed in Sudan, as he is throughout Africa, because of his tireless efforts to combat disease and hunger. Before coming to Khartoum, he convinced John Garang and Riek Machar to agree to a pause in the fighting so that the Carter Center, in conjunction with UNICEF, could initiate a badly needed health project in southern Sudan. The Carter Center had helped to greatly reduce or to end the prevalence of guinea worm, an awful parasitic disease, in other countries. Sudan now had the highest incidence of guinea worm in the world, and Carter was determined to launch an effort there to eradicate both guinea worm and river blindness, another terrible malady that could also be totally eliminated by a simple procedure.

Guinea worm, found in Africa and Asia, is a parasite that enters the body through drinking water. The tiny filarial nematode grows in the body, reaching a length of as much as several feet. It causes blisters, boils, and tumors and can destroy tissue as it emerges from the body. An inexpensive filter placed over the openings through which water is poured into containers is all that is needed to prevent the disease. River blindness, or onchocerciasis, is also transmitted by a filarial worm; it can be prevented by periodic ingestion of a pill.

In Khartoum President Carter played his cards with great skill. With the government having indicated to him that it was not in favor of a cease-fire, he gave a speech at the opening session of a conference on guinea worm. Pointing out that he had gotten the rebels to agree to a cease-fire, he said that all that was needed was the government's agreement. The cease-fire would enable teams to enter areas closed to them by the war and carry out their work. In graphically describing the terrible effects of the disease, he emphasized how imperative it was that the fighting stop and the eradication campaign begin. He said he had brought with him from Nairobi a CNN correspondent to record the historic moment when the government of Sudan agreed to his cease-fire proposal.

After some hemming and hawing, Bashir and his advisers, who must have realized they had nothing to gain and perhaps a lot to lose by refusing to accede to Carter's request, agreed to go along with the cease-fire.

With the cease-fire he sought in place and with assurances from the government and the rebels that they would cooperate in the program to eradicate guinea worm and river blindness and provide children with essential vaccinations as well, President Carter had achieved his immediate objective.

He found, however, no opening to pursue his longer-term goal of helping end the war in the South. He regarded the Sudan war as the worst ongoing man-made disaster in the world, and he hoped that circumstances might permit him to play a role in bringing it to a negotiated end. He would do nothing, however, without the blessing of the IGADD presidents and a demonstrated readiness by the government of Sudan and the rebels to negotiate in good faith. Unfortunately, neither of those two conditions existed at that time.

It was nice to have people in the house for a change—President and Mrs. Carter, one of their aides, and a couple of Secret Service agents. The Carters are genuinely nice, engaging, and generous people, as well as fascinating individuals, and I very much enjoyed the time we had together.

I briefed them on the causes of the abysmal state of relations between the United States and Sudan. A year and a half earlier the former president had been quoted as saying the U.S. government lacked enough evidence to put Sudan on the list of state sponsors of terrorism. Therefore I was glad for the opportunity to inform him, drawing on some recent additional and convincing information, why Sudan was on the list. He took this with equanimity, taking no issue with any of the points that I had made.

• • •

As the end of my tour of duty in Sudan approached, I had more discussions with President Bashir, Hasan al-Turabi, Foreign Minister Ali Osman Taha, Minister of State Ghazi Salih Eddin, and others in the upper reaches of the power structure. I had no illusions about making some sort of breakthrough in the wall of antagonism and misunderstandings that stood in the way of any improvement in relations between our two countries. I thought, however, that perhaps I could at least disabuse them of some of their worst misconceptions about U.S. motives and actions.

Because my wife and son would be returning to Sudan, if I had had a choice I would have opted to remain there for another year. Julie, Brian, and I liked living in Khartoum. As far as I was concerned, the negative aspects of my job were outweighed by the sheer interest of what was taking place in Sudan, the personal satisfaction that came from working to help alleviate the conditions of the Sudanese who suffered from the effects of the war, and the challenge inherent in being the American ambassador to a country whose government is on

distinctly unfriendly terms with Washington. Despite the poor relations between the United States and Sudan, in general I continued to
have good personal rapport with leaders of the government and the
NIF. The same held true for my relationship with the government's
opponents, both in Khartoum and in southern Sudan.

But I could not remain in Sudan. For some years the State Department had been adhering tightly to an unwritten rule limiting ambassadorial assignments to three years. It was time to say farewell to Sudan, and also to the Foreign Service. I would soon reach mandatory
retirement age. Unlike other FSOs, ambassadors, as presidential appointees, are not affected by the age requirement as long as they hold
their appointment. However, there were no ambassadorships of any
attraction or relevance to me coming up in the near future, and I
would revert to regular FSO status. In addition, Under Secretary Dick
Moose rightly told me that with mandatory retirement for age being
almost universally applied, he could not keep me on the payroll in a
temporary job for many months until a suitable ambassadorship became available and then for more time until the lengthy appointment
confirmation process was completed.

No matter how difficult an assignment has been, departure from a
post, I have found, is always tinged with sadness. Two or three or more
years of one's life have been invested in living and working in a country and being absorbed with the political and societal drama taking
place there. Saying good-bye to friends, knowing one will probably not
see most of them ever again, is not easy. I found it especially hard to
take my leave of the Americans and Sudanese who worked with me in
the embassy. We had been through tough times together, and I deeply
appreciated their courage, their skills, and their dedication.

●   ●   ●

After the Carters left Sudan, I made my second-to-last trip to the
South, arriving there March 31. At the first stop, Panthou, a village in
Bahr al-Ghazal, it was humid and hot—112 degrees Fahrenheit that afternoon. We had a look at the area where an airdrop of food would take
place the next day. We talked with the Sudanese we met there and at
other nearby places we drove to and got a thorough briefing from
INGO and UN relief workers on why the airdrop was needed: crop
failure and effects of the warfare in the region.

At the moment it was quiet militarily, but a force led by Kerubino Kwanyan Bol was at the village of Gogrial, not far away. Karabino had broken away from Garang, who had imprisoned him some years back, and had joined forces with Riek Machar. Karabino now was operating independently and was said to be receiving arms from the Sudanese government. (This was subsequently verified.) Kerubino had attacked villages in the area, and there were fears he would do so again before long.

We spent that night and the next at the relief workers' camp. It was in a clearing, forty yards by thirty yards, surrounded by a six-foot fence of bamboo, reeds, and grass. No one slept in the camp's three mud-walled, thatch-roofed huts—it was too hot inside.

The following morning we watched a C-130 drop fourteen metric tons of sorghum and beans from an altitude of 800 feet. Only a few of the 280 plastic sacks, which were double-bagged, broke open. They hit the ground with such great force that it was easy to understand the extreme precautions that were taken to ensure that no one was anywhere near the drop zone. After a few dozen men toted the bags to where they were stacked for later distribution, a horde of women and children came onto the drop zone and cleared the area of virtually every grain of the scattered contents of the broken bags. The previous evening we had watched food being distributed efficiently and fairly by a relief committee composed of women from the surrounding villages.

After the airdrop we flew to Mayen Abun, a village that Kerubino's men had occupied and partially destroyed the preceding year. We talked to the UN personnel who were overseeing distribution of the food being dropped there, and we heard a lot about the destitution caused by Karabino's raids. At Mayen Abun and our next stop, a place called Malwal Kon, I explained how the cease-fire came about and why it was so important that everyone observe it. It would benefit the Carter program and also enable the OLS relief program to get back to a more normal footing.

At Malwal Kon, the SPLA military commander for northern Bahr al-Ghazal came to see me. He accused the northern government of already breaking the cease-fire. I counseled patience, noting that violations were bound to occur, particularly in the early stages of the cease-fire.

On April 2 we got an early start for Thiet, about an hour's flight to the southeast. At Thiet I met with the rebel governor of Bahr al-

Ghazal. I repeated my explanation of what the Carter Center intended to do with its health program, why the cease-fire was needed, what its weaknesses were, and how important it was that it not be violated.

After getting back to Nairobi I met first with Philip O'Brien and then separately with John Garang and Riek Machar. I urged the rebel leaders to honor the cease-fire, for cogent humanitarian reasons if nothing else. Although Garang complained that the northern military was violating the cease-fire and Riek accused Garang of doing the same thing, both men said they would adhere to it.

•   •   •

A new development in May made it uncertain that Julie and Brian would return to Sudan. A security problem arose involving what seemed to be surveillance of one of our apartments by nationals of a country hostile toward the United States. If this took a bad turn, it could have led me to decide that the ban on dependents would have to be reimposed. On May 15 I went to the Foreign Ministry to give Omar Berido some details about the men who were surveilling us. Berido said the cooperation I sought would be given. It did not become necessary, however, inasmuch as the apparent surveillance turned out to be of no danger to Americans.

A long talk with Minister of State for Security Fatih Irwah, whom Bashir had chosen to be his next ambassador to the United States, was the first of a series of conversations I planned to have in the weeks ahead with major figures in the government and NIF. I intended to stress that terrorism as an issue was going to loom larger and larger in the consciousness of Americans and that any country identified with terrorism, as Sudan was, was likely to come under ever closer scrutiny.

I went to the presidential palace on the morning of May 11 for the president's *Id al Adha* reception for heads of diplomatic missions. Bashir told me he wanted to have a one-on-one meeting with me soon. After the reception I joined about fifteen other ambassadors at Turabi's house for the now customary call on him on feast days. The speaker of the National Assembly's reception at Friendship Hall the next morning would be the last of my official attendance at functions of this kind.

As the waning days of my assignment to Khartoum and of my career in the Foreign Service wore on, there were a number of other final occasions. I felt less a sense of regret or sadness than a sense of impatience to get them over and done with so my wife and son and I could begin the next chapter in our lives. The reality that I was leaving Sudan was brought home in the second week in May, when I got a telegram from the State Department telling me that because my successor had been named, I should write a letter of resignation and send it to President Clinton. On May 17 I received orders and fiscal data for my departure and travel to the United States.

That spring, power outages became the norm in Khartoum. They were so bad in some parts of town that people demonstrated in the streets in April. Many were arrested, but all were released shortly afterward. The government reduced power to some industrial users and spread the outages more evenly to lessen the potential for even more serious demonstrations. Frequent power problems continued into the summer, until the Blue Nile rose enough to fill the area behind the Rossires Dam, a major source of Khartoum's electrical power.

In mid-May Jan Pronk, the Dutch cabinet minister who chaired the Friends of IGADD, went to Nairobi to talk to President Moi about extending, broadening, and monitoring the cease-fire and getting the Friends of IGADD more directly involved in the peace process. I met with Pronk when he came to Khartoum the day after he met with Moi. He said Moi had agreed to work to keep the cease-fire alive and to accept a larger role for the Friends of IGADD. Moi was noncommittal when Pronk asked him if he was open to inviting Jimmy Carter to participate in mediation aimed at ending the Sudan war. I believed that Moi saw himself in the role of peacemaker and would not want to share this with Carter or anyone else.

I continued to consider the IGADD effort as over and done with. In a cable to Washington I said that nevertheless it could provide a framework for someone like Carter to use for mediation. I added, however, that whoever tried to mediate would face an almost impossible task as long as the warring parties remained bent on prosecuting the war.

I told Pronk and Washington that an extension of the cease-fire was likely. The Sudanese army was in no shape to mount another offensive, the rains would hamper operations in some areas, and the international attention that President Carter had drawn to the humanitarian need for continuing the cease-fire made it difficult for either side to say no to a request for an extension.

Moi came to Khartoum near the end of May to meet with Bashir. As was the custom when a foreign head of state came to Khartoum, the chiefs of diplomatic missions were trotted out to join Sudanese government officials and Bashir in greeting Moi when he arrived at the airport. Luckily, he did not arrive until after 5 P.M., by which time the sun was pretty low to the horizon. But it had been a hot day, as usual, about 110 degrees, and the tarmac we were standing on seemed close to boiling. My feet got hotter and hotter as we waited for Moi and Bashir to walk down the receiving line and shake our hands. I swear I could see steam rising from my shoes. All this waiting and suffering just to shake the hand of Moi, a man generally considered to be one of Africa's most corrupt politicians.

At the conclusion of Moi's short visit, an extension of the cease-fire was announced.

• • •

Two nights earlier I had met with Bashir—just the two of us and Fatih Irwah, who was a close friend of Bashir. The meeting was very friendly yet essentially unproductive. Our differences on human rights and terrorism remained as strong as ever. For example, at one point I listed for Bashir the several terrorist organizations that had offices in town. He replied that only Hamas did. Either he was poorly informed or he was being disingenuous.

I tried out on Bashir an idea that I had unsuccessfully run by the State Department about a year earlier. I had brought it up again with George Moose a month or so before my meeting with Bashir. Moose was open to considering it, depending on how things were going in Sudan whenever I decided to propose it formally. The concept's central point was that a small delegation of carefully selected people from the regime would be received at an appropriately high level in Washington for talks aimed at letting them hear in detail, directly from important U.S. officials, the bases of our policy toward Sudan. Despite what we had been telling the Sudanese for so long, they continued to put their own incorrect spin on the reasons behind U.S. policy. I reasoned that if prominent members of the regime went to Washington, at the very least what they heard there should dispel any misconceptions the Sudanese had about our motives and our resolve.

Bashir seemed to be taken with the idea of talks in Washington, and I planned to follow up on it. However, unfavorable circumstances led to another turn for the worse in U.S.-Sudanese relations and put the idea on ice indefinitely.

• • •

In June the government had imprisoned Sadiq al-Mahdi once again, this time along with many of his followers. On June 9 the State Department issued a statement criticizing the government for his imprisonment. The statement angered the government. It came on the heels of an International Monetary Fund action inimical to Sudan. Ghazi told me the United States had been responsible for the IMF action; he was right, I soon learned.

Those two events—the U.S. statement and the IMF's actions—were pretty much standard fare in our dealings with the Sudanese and by themselves did not lead to anything more than the scolding from Ghazi, the usual spate of denunciations in the media, and some hard words from the Foreign Ministry. But another event, stemming from Bashir's choice of Fatih Irwah to be the next Sudanese ambassador to the United States, would be regarded by the Sudanese as far more tendentious than the statement and the IMF action. From what Ghazi told me later, the Sudanese government concluded that all three items provided more proof of what Ghazi said was a U.S. design to make relations even worse than they had been.

As a rule, a request by one government to another for acceptance of the person it intends to send as ambassador is a routine matter. The receiving government will expect to hear from its embassy an opinion about the suitability of the proposed ambassador. It will also examine any other information it might have available concerning the individual in question. Formal acceptance is known in diplomatic parlance as *"agrément."* It is standard practice that the *agrément* process is kept confidential; otherwise, if the nominee is not acceptable to the receiving government, the ensuing refusal to grant *agrément* would be embarrassing, or worse, to the proposing government and to the nominee in question. Again, the *agrément* process is usually pro forma and quietly handled by the two governments.

But as seemed to happen so often in U.S.-Sudanese relations, Murphy's Law applied. The U.S. government received information alleging that General Fatih Irwah had been personally involved in some of the executions in Juba in the summer of 1992. If true, this would mean that Washington could not, and would not, accept him as Sudan's next ambassador to the United States. When I had met with Bashir and Irwah in May, I said then that it was possible the request would be denied (even at that time, some information had come our way raising a question about Irwah's acceptability as ambassador). Bashir told me, "This appointment is my appointment," not the foreign minister's or any one else's. He would be personally offended, he said, if Washington rejected Irwah. Making matters worse, the Sudanese let word out, which reached the press, that Irwah was President Bashir's choice to replace the incumbent ambassador in Washington.

In a meeting on June 7 Ghazi asked me, "What about our ambassador-designate?" After telling him the details of the problem, I said that although Washington had not yet made a decision, it could be negative and that I had said as much to Bashir and Irwah. Ghazi said rejection "would have grave consequences" for U.S.-Sudanese relations. He also said rejection of Irwah would be a deliberate act to worsen relations. I replied that he was wrong; far from trying to make an already bad situation worse, the United States had been attempting to find ways to begin to bridge our differences. Ghazi disagreed and repeated that turning down the request for *agrément* would have serious repercussions.

Not unexpectedly, I took the brunt of the Sudanese ire over the issue. I was the messenger bringing them bad tidings, and in addition they no doubt knew I had played a role in providing Washington with some of the information on which it would make its decision.

On the morning of June 12 I received a cable from Washington instructing me to tell the foreign minister the United States could not grant the request for *agrément*. Before doing that, I was to deliver a letter to Fatih Irwah. The letter came in another cable. Later that morning I went to the palace to see Irwah. It was not a pleasant occasion. He reacted bitterly to the letter from Washington. He repeatedly denied he had been involved in the Juba killings and said he had been betrayed, for in the past he had performed a number of services for the U.S. government. He said the government of Sudan was absolutely certain that I was "totally responsible" for the rejection and warned that there would be a strong negative response by Sudan.

Irwah appealed to me not to see the foreign minister, as I had told him I was going to do, and to ask Washington to reconsider. He said we were being unfair to the government of Sudan, to Bashir, and to himself. He assured me the government's reaction would not include any violence directed at me. He did not rule out a request for my removal or a withdrawal of the *agrément* that had been granted to my successor, Timothy Carney. And he hinted that we might be told to reduce our American staff significantly. I told Irwah that the chances of a reversal of the decision were remote, but I said I would go along with his request. After all, a short delay would not hurt us, and I saw no point in adding to his, and no doubt Bashir's, anger.

In a telephone conversation with the State Department's Office of East African Affairs, I was told that the Department had no problem with the delay. Later that day, after postponing my meeting with the foreign minister, I got a cable from our embassy in Addis Ababa recounting a plea the Sudanese ambassador there had made to Ambassador Mark Baas that we grant the request for *agrément*. His pitch contained the same warning I had heard from Irwah and likewise blamed me for the whole affair. This was the beginning of an orchestrated effort to try to convince Washington to change the decision.

The White House wanted to look at all the information on the *agrément* request and consider it in light of what I had reported by cable. Two days passed before a decision was sent to me. In the meantime, I learned that Irwah had gotten in touch, as he told me he would, with Americans he used to work with and asked them to weigh in on his behalf. In addition, Bashir sent a message to Jimmy Carter asking him to intervene, which the former president chose not to do.

On the evening of June 13 a friend came to see me at the residence to tell me he had spoken with Bashir after my meeting with Irwah. What Bashir had told him was very similar to what I had heard from Irwah. My friend said Bashir would regard a negative decision as an action intended to weaken his government and one for which I would bear full responsibility.

I told Washington I was unsure what to make of the threats implicit in what Irwah, Ghazi, and Bashir had said. They might have been no more than bluster aimed at getting a favorable decision for Irwah. And although there was no denying that the Sudanese could take some kind of retaliatory action, we knew that inside the government there were many who did not like Irwah and opposed his nomination. They might recommend that the best course would be to do nothing.

On the fourteenth the State Department cabled me to proceed as instructed earlier and tell the Sudanese government that the request for *agrément* could not be granted. I met with Foreign Minister Ali Osman Taha that morning and conveyed this to him. I explained why the decision had been made. In asking that the nomination be withdrawn, I said Washington had no intention of making the matter public and suggested that the government of Sudan follow suit. I said the decision was not aimed, as some in Khartoum were saying, at worsening relations between our two countries. I said it would be a mistake for his government to withdraw the *agrément* it had given for Timothy Carney.

Taha replied that it was Washington's right not to accept Sudan's nominee, but he rejected the reasons we gave for our decision. What happened in Juba was a domestic affair and was carried out with due process of law, he said. It appeared that in turning down Fatih Irwah the United States was deliberately creating another problem. He said Washington's decision "adds to the dark clouds" hanging over U.S.-Sudanese relations.

As for me, he said, "your personal part is not important." It was a U.S. government decision, and "we won't personalize the issue." Nevertheless, the failure to get *agrément*, he said, reflected badly on my ability to improve relations. He said he was not in a position to tell me what the reaction would be, but the U.S. decision would "not be well received." He would let me know next week.

That week and two more passed before we learned that the Sudanese intended to do nothing much at all. David Shinn, who was in Khartoum for a three-day stay, and I met with Ghazi on July 8. Ghazi told us that Tim Carney would be received politely. He implied, though, that Carney would not find the government in a mood to be cooperative. I never heard any more from Taha, and what Ghazi said was the last word we got on the Fatih Irwah matter.[1]

During that meeting, Ghazi expressed his government's bitterness over what he said was a pattern of hostile U.S. actions against Sudan. He accused us of actively supporting the government's enemies and conspiring with the Eritreans and others against Sudan. Shinn's response, which included a summary of our concerns about human rights and terrorism, drew an angry rebuttal from Ghazi.

· · ·

The failure of U.S. policy toward Sudan to achieve its primary objectives was virtually foreordained, in view of the kind and extent of the differences between the U.S. and Sudanese governments. During my three years in Sudan, and also later on, obstacles to accommodation grew rather than diminished. The nature of some of the measures the Bashir government employed to keep itself in power and to prosecute the war in southern Sudan were bound to be repugnant to any administration in Washington. The Sudanese actions constrained the ability of policymakers to come up with any new approaches to ameliorate the sorry state of relations between the United States and Sudan.

As time went on, there were ever fewer pressures the Clinton administration could apply against the regime in Khartoum. With the end of U.S. economic and military assistance in 1989, the United States could do little else of lasting material damage against Sudan, beyond encouraging other aid donors to follow the U.S. lead. Putting Sudan on the list of state sponsors of terrorism in 1993 was essentially symbolic, having no significant economic impact; the steps called for in the action had already been taken.

Powerful sanctions were not possible. There would be neither domestic nor international support for a measure like imposing and enforcing a total trade embargo, which would have required involvement of the U.S. Navy. Ultimately it was not the administration but the U.S. public that narrowed the range of actions the United States might have taken against Sudan. Following the debacle in Mogadishu in 1994, Americans were not keen to see their soldiers going into possible harm's way in the absence of a clear threat to major U.S. interests. Certainly Congress would be in no mood to endorse direct U.S. intervention either to put great pressure on the Sudanese government or to end the war in southern Sudan.

· · ·

My last *haboob* in Khartoum was not, as I wrote to family and friends, the mother of all *haboob*s, but it was the most formidable of all that I had experienced. I was in the house when, at about 5 P.M., I noticed that the light outside was fast fading. And then I smelled the dust. When I went out the front door, the leading edge of a dust cloud was rushing past, driven by a wind that was gusting at near-gale force and bending the tall palm trees in the yard almost horizontal. Within seconds, I could feel grit on my teeth. After a couple of minutes, the cloud thickened, reducing the visibility to yards. It quickly changed from orange to brown, and soon daytime gave way to night an hour before its time. What a mess the next day! A thick layer of dust on all outside surfaces—verandah, shutters, sills, plants—everywhere. And inside, although the house was pretty tightly sealed, everything within a few yards of the windows was coated.

Julie and Brian arrived on June 20, almost two years since they were evacuated. Needless to say, it was a joyous reunion. Julie immediately got back into the swing of things, organizing a dinner party for about thirty people, in part to pay back some of those who had entertained me during her absence. Brian, now approaching his sixteenth birthday, made some new friends, including the Marines, my bodyguards, some Sudanese, and an Italian family. He got a job with the recreation association, inventorying their equipment, furnishings, and supplies and taking care of the recreation site's swimming pool.

In our final weeks in Sudan there was no letup in the Sudanese media of denunciations of the United States and occasional swipes at me. In June the Sudanese were infuriated when Eritrea sanctioned a conference in Asmara involving groups opposed to the Bashir government; they promptly accused the United States of masterminding the conference.

During both times Sadiq al-Mahdi was imprisoned while I was in Sudan, I made a point of calling on his wife, Sara. This angered some in the government and predictably drew media criticism. The State Department's June 9 press release concerning Sadiq's latest imprisonment produced a furious reaction from the regime's leading propagandist, Lt. Col. Mahmoud Younis. In part, the Department's press release said, "Sadiq was arrested by the government of Sudan on May 16, shortly after he delivered a sermon at a mosque which was sharply critical of the regime and its de facto leader, Hasan al-Turabi." As soon as we in the embassy saw the wording "its de facto leader, Hasan al-Turabi," we knew the Sudanese would be irate.

Commenting in a broadcast on radio Omdurman, Younis said, "As for the insolent American statement, which discussed who the real president of Sudan is, we say that this is a purely Sudanese affair. So, let us ask: Who is really ruling America—the saxophone player or Hillary or the Jews? Khartoum will remain unstained by the Jews." Younis also took aim at me: "The American ambassador ... has achieved nothing but paying condolences to detainees' families, visiting rebels behind closed doors, and attending the birthday parties of leaders of Sufi sects."

In July in Addis Ababa assassins failed in an attempt to kill Egyptian president Hosni Mubarak. They had entered Ethiopia from Sudan, and the Egyptian and Ethiopian governments accused the Sudanese government of involvement in the assassination attempt. No doubt feeling beleaguered, the Sudanese tended to react defensively in their media, continuing to lash out at the Americans while saving some of their best shots for the Egyptians.

Foolishly, Turabi praised the authors of the assassination plot. He said, "When Mubarak dared to go to Addis Ababa to attend the OAU summit, the sons of the Prophet Moses, the Muslims, rose up against him, confounded his plans, and sent him back to his country." Recalling past talks he had had with Mubarak, Turabi said, "I found the man to be very far below my level of thinking and my views, and too stupid to understand my pronouncements."[2]

• • •

President and Mrs. Carter again stayed with us after they arrived in Sudan on July 19. The next day I went with them and their entourage to southern Sudan. We toured treatment centers in remote villages where guinea worm and river blindness were widespread. We returned to Khartoum on the twenty-second, and the Carters left for the United States the following day.

As my assignment to Sudan was drawing to a close, I began to sense more than intellectually that I would actually be leaving both Sudan and the Foreign Service behind me in only a matter of days. However, I had neither the time nor the inclination to dwell on this. There was too much to do and, I felt, nothing to be gained from an exercise in introspection. Perhaps another day.

After the Carters had gone Julie and I finished getting our effects ready for shipping and resumed going to the farewell dinners in our honor that we had been attending for the previous two or three weeks. On the twenty-fifth we gave a farewell reception, which was the custom in Khartoum for departing diplomats. On the twenty-sixth the Americans and Sudanese of the embassy had a party for us. At 2:30 in the morning of July 28, we left our house for the last time and drove to the airport.

Thirty years earlier, Julie and I had been melancholy when we left our first post in Africa—Zanzibar. Two of our children were born there, we had witnessed some momentous events, and we had had to say farewell to close friends. But we knew that some day we would return to work again in Africa and possibly could come back to that beautiful tropical island. Once again, taking leave of our last post in the Foreign Service, we experienced the sadness of saying good-bye to friends, most of whom we would never see again, and departing from a house and a city that had been our home for a significant part of our lives.

But this time we did not have the solace of knowing we would be coming back again to live and work in Africa. We might visit, but visiting a country and living there are two distinctly different experiences. In all likelihood, our farewell to Khartoum and Sudan and to the Foreign Service was also a farewell to Africa.

# 20

# Afterward

Our place in Brentwood in southeastern New Hampshire is as different as can be from Khartoum. In Khartoum, although our house was secluded by the high wall surrounding the property, it was adjoined on one side by a busy thoroughfare and was close to the University of Khartoum. The noise of traffic and passersby was not noticeable inside the house, but when we were out on the verandah or in the yard, the sounds reminded us that we were living in a city. Khartoum and its mostly arid environs stretched for miles in all directions from the house, and on its outskirts the city gave way to desert.

Here our nearest neighbors are 200 yards away. In the winter we can glimpse their house through leafless trees. During the rest of the year even it is lost to sight. The outskirts of Exeter, the nearest town of any size, are about three miles away. Woods border our house on three sides. Most of our land is covered with trees—white pine, cedar, spruce, oak, ash, wild cherry, birch, and quaking aspen—and in the spring and summer it is a riot of green.

The cultural and societal differences between New Hampshire and Sudan are as great as, or greater than, the differences in their physical surroundings. There are some similarities, though, in the nature of the people of the two places. One similarity is the friendliness, openness, and warmth of most Sudanese and of the people we have met in the three years we have lived in New Hampshire.

We moved into our house in September 1995 and began our new life. By the end of that school year, we faced another disruption. It had became clear to us that Brian's many moves from place to place and school to school had taken a toll on him and that it was in his best interest to finish high school in Mexico City, where he had been happy and where his best friends were. So at the end of August 1996 Julie and he went there and remained for the nine months he was in school. I stayed in New Hampshire waiting for a United Nations job that never materialized. We did not want another separation, but given Brian's needs, Julie and I had no other choice.

We were reunited in June 1997. A week later Brian left for Israel, where he worked as a volunteer in a kibbutz for almost six months. He came back to New Hampshire in time for Christmas and left a month later to enter college in Boston.

As for Sudan and the Sudanese, by the summer of 1997, with the war still going on and the economy in sore straits, the misery of the people had not been alleviated.

There had been no improvement in relations between Sudan and the United States. If anything, they were worse than they were when I left Khartoum. On several occasions during my tenure in Sudan, I had asked Washington to weigh the value of having an embassy in Sudan against the danger to the lives of the Americans manning it. Each time this was done, those who made the assessment concluded that the value outweighed the risk, a conclusion I agreed with. By February of 1996, half a year after I had departed from Khartoum, the administration apparently decided that the risk was no longer bearable, and all the American staff, including the ambassador, were ordered to leave Sudan. According to a report in the *New York Times* on September 21, 1998,[1] the information on which the decision was made was probably fabricated.

•   •   •

In June 1997 C. William Kontos, who was U.S. ambassador to Sudan from 1980 to 1983, telephoned me from Washington, D.C. He said Anis G. Haggar, a Sudanese businessman, wanted us to explore whether, by going back to Sudan, we might be able to help find ways to end the impasse in U.S.-Sudanese relations and open the road to a peaceful settlement of the war. Anis would pay our expenses.

We had both known Anis during our respective assignments to Sudan. His father had been a well-known philanthropist who had engaged in charitable works in Sudan and was revered by many southerners and northerners alike. Not long before his death in 1996 he had tried to help mediate an end to the war. When we met with Anis three months after Bill called me, he said that, of course, ending the war would be good for his business, but he was primarily motivated to carry on his father's generosity toward the Sudanese people and to emulate his effort to be a peacemaker. Bill and I were convinced of his honesty and compassion and had no doubts about the altruism of his motivation.

During a visit to Washington Julie and I had dinner with Tom and Alice Pickering, old friends from our days in Zanzibar. Tom, the best of the brightest in the Foreign Service, had recently retired after his last assignment, ambassador to Russia. Within a short time, however, Secretary of State Albright asked him to become the under secretary of state for political affairs, the third-highest position in the State Department. After I told him of Anis Haggar's proposal and noted that Bill and I had no illusions about our prospects for success, Tom said the idea was intriguing, and he encouraged us to look into it further.

The time was in no way propitious for an improvement in U.S.-Sudanese relations. With significant public support, some senators and House members were decrying persecution of Christians in certain countries of the world, Sudan included. Legislation to apply sanctions against those countries was making its way through the Congress. Anti-Sudan sentiment was also strong in the National Security Council. When in September the State Department announced that several Americans, not including an ambassador, would be assigned to the embassy in Khartoum, officials in the NSC, picking up on an outcry from a few congressmen and senators, were able to get the announcement retracted.

In early September Bill and I met with Anis in Washington. At an Institute of Peace conference on conflict and religion in Sudan, we talked to Sudanese officials, southern Sudanese strongly opposed to the government, academics, and others knowledgeable about Sudan. All were in favor of what we proposed. As private citizens, Bill and I did not need U.S. government approval, but we did not want to do anything inimical to U.S. interests. From the State Department we got the assurances we wanted, and on October 22 the two of us flew to Khartoum.

We spent six days there talking with President Bashir, Hasan al-Turabi (now the speaker of the National Assembly), other government officials, southern and northern opponents of the regime, former rebel faction leaders who had given their allegiance to Khartoum, and religious leaders. We were also able to have private chats with friends.

I was not sure what kind of a reception I would get from government leaders. After all, on many occasions I had not exactly endeared myself to them, and my last days in Khartoum had been tainted, in the eyes of some, by the Fatih Irwah affair. I needn't have been concerned; I was welcomed and received with great cordiality.

From Khartoum, Bill and I flew to Nairobi, where the long-stalled IGAD (once IGADD[2]) peace talks were about to resume. We met with Kenyan president Moi; deputy chairman of the Sudan People's Liberation Movement Salva Kiir; members of the Sudanese, Ethiopian, and Ugandan delegations to the talks; and a private group that was giving advice to the Sudanese government and the rebel delegations. We also talked at length with the American ambassador to Sudan, Timothy Carney.[3] After a week in Nairobi we returned to Khartoum to see two religious leaders we had not been able to meet with earlier, foreign diplomats, the heads of several INGOs based in Khartoum, and a UN official.

Khartoum looked much the same as it did when I left two years earlier. Unfortunately, political and economic conditions were also much the same, despite some marginal improvements. In the report we wrote at the end of our trip, Bill and I observed that the economy, notwithstanding some recent substantial investments by China, Malaysia, and Germany, among others, remained in great difficulties. The average Sudanese, at least in urban areas, was suffering a great deal. War weariness was pervasive among all segments of society, yet the war continued with no end in sight. Conscription of teenage boys was having a strongly negative impact on northern families.

The government, nevertheless, seemed to remain firmly in control in Khartoum. We found no indications of any organized resistance in the greater Khartoum area that would constitute a credible threat to the Islamists in power.

We judged the military situation to be essentially a standoff. The SPLA had made some gains in the South, thanks in part to the assistance Garang was getting from Ethiopia, Eritrea, and Uganda. However, it had been unable to take Juba, a major military objective.

Northern opponents of the government, together with the SPLA, were conducting military operations near Sudan's borders with Eritrea and Ethiopia. After escaping from Sudan in December 1996, Sadiq al-Mahdi had helped energize the National Democratic Alliance (NDA), an ineffectual coalition of northern exiles opposed to the government. The NDA put a military force in the field in 1997. Another northern military force opposing Khartoum was the Sudan Alliance Forces (SAF), led by a respected Sudanese soldier, Brig. Gen. Abdul Aziz Khalifa. The NDA, SAF, and SPLA operations in eastern Sudan put an added burden on the Sudanese army. These military activities may have been worrisome to Khartoum but, we were told, had yet to become a serious threat.

President Bashir and other government leaders denied to us that human rights abuses were taking place. Government opponents, however, maintained that frequent gross violations of human rights remained an unhappy fact of life in Sudan. In our report Bill and I concluded that "although there may have been some decline in the frequency of abuses," the government bore responsibility for the serious human rights violations that continued to take place. Evidence of arbitrary arrests and torture was compelling.

There were indications that differences of opinion within the ruling establishment were more pronounced than during my time in Sudan. Perhaps reflecting this, public criticism of the government was occasionally appearing in the press and being heard in the National Assembly. Government opponents said the criticism was nothing but a sham. In any event, true freedom of speech and of the press did not exist, for newspapers were still not free to publish anything the government did not want to appear in print for public consumption. Moreover, Sudan radio and television stations remained a government monopoly.

Bashir, Turabi, and their colleagues told us that although Sudan had taken measures to meet U.S. concerns about terrorism, democratization, and human rights, Washington had failed adequately to acknowledge this and act accordingly. (In Washington we were told that what the Sudanese had done fell far short of being significant changes.) They complained that by its military support to Ethiopia, Eritrea, and Uganda, the United States was contributing to the continuation of the war. They said it appeared to them that Washington was bent on the overthrow of the government of Sudan.

Khartoum had signed an agreement on April 21, 1997, with rebel factions opposed to John Garang and long suspected of accepting military aid from the government. Riek Machar and other former rebel leaders were now high-level government officials. At the November peace talks in Nairobi, the government delegation presented a position paper advocating that the April 21 agreement be the basis for a negotiated settlement of the war. The SPLM rejected the position paper, stating that the April 21 agreement left unresolved key issues dividing the two sides and would leave the government in control of the country after the war, ensuring that Khartoum would determine the future political shape of Sudan. The SPLM's counterproposals were unacceptable to the government, and the talks ended in failure.

• • •

When we saw Moi in Nairobi, Bill and I asked him whether, within the IGAD framework, he would be agreeable to someone of international stature assuming a leading role in the negotiations. He said he could agree to that. The Sudanese government and its opponents, in both Nairobi and Khartoum, told us that they would welcome a direct role by the U.S. government in the peace process.

In our report, which we finished writing a day or so after we got back to Washington, Bill and I said, "Given their deep mutual distrust and antagonism, the government of Sudan and the SPLM are no closer to peace now than they were at the beginning of the year." It seemed to us that "if IGAD is to overcome the current dismal prospects for peace, it needs to look for a new approach to the negotiating methodology." Accordingly, we recommended that Washington propose that a respected international figure experienced in negotiating become the lead negotiator in the IGAD peace effort. Under the leadership of that person, experts would examine the positions of the two sides to see whether there was a realistic possibility for useful negotiations and, if that was the case, would help develop a strategy for negotiation.

Looking at U.S.-Sudanese relations, we concluded that whether or not one agreed with U.S. policy, it had failed to achieve its objectives, and the latest sanctions were unlikely to make any appreciable difference. Consequently, the United States should try a different approach. We suggested that, while keeping pressure on the Sudanese government, Washington should provide a means for direct engagement with Khartoum in order to more effectively put to the test Sudanese assertions about terrorism, human rights, democratization, and the relief program. If, and only if, this produced some useful results, we said, the United States should consider taking a more active part in seeking an end to the mutually destabilizing actions involving Sudan, Ethiopia, Eritrea, and Uganda.

We believed that the U.S. government was handicapped in not having a permanent embassy presence in Khartoum to observe what was happening there and elsewhere in Sudan, interact with government leaders and others, and gather information from diverse sources and assess it. We recommended that Washington once again assign some American personnel to the embassy in Khartoum.

Our report got a mixed reception in Washington. Some who saw the Sudanese government as beyond the pale believed that no overtures whatsoever should be made to Khartoum. Others saw merit in our conclusions and some of our suggestions. However, they thought serious consideration of them would have to wait until more time had passed following the administration's imposition in November of new sanctions against Sudan. To help forestall legislation pending in Congress that would have applied sanctions against Sudan and other countries in a way that would have limited the executive branch's options in dealing with those countries, the administration issued an executive order curtailing U.S.-Sudanese commerce and trade. President Bashir condemned the new sanctions. He described the United States as a thief plundering and robbing Sudan's wealth and said Sudan would reply with further holy war.

In December Secretary of State Albright made a trip to Africa. In Uganda she met with John Garang and leading figures of the National Democratic Alliance. She said publicly that the United States wanted to isolate the Sudanese government and contain its capacity to support terrorist activities.

Khartoum responded angrily to the secretary's statements and her meeting with Garang and the others. The Ministry of Foreign Affairs said her words manifested "America's interference in other countries' affairs" and "do not target Sudan alone but are aimed against the national and free leanings of all Arab, Islamic and African nations." This latest downturn in U.S.-Sudanese relations at the end of 1997 made it clear that for the time being there would be no receptivity in Washington and Khartoum for the kind of ideas that Bill Kontos, Anis Haggar, and I were advocating.

• • •

In February 1998 Vice President al-Zubeir Muhamed Salih died in a plane crash. President Bashir appointed Ali Osman Taha to succeed him. Taha's place as foreign minister went to junior minister Mustafa Osman Ismail. The political import of Taha's appointment would become apparent later when Bashir clashed with Hasan al-Turabi in a struggle for power. Rumors that some of Turabi's disciples were unhappy with his leadership and wanted to see an end to his prominence had surfaced from time to time for years. But nothing came of them. When I heard the rumors again in 1997, I discounted them. But I was wrong. My assumption that Turabi's power base was secure stemmed from outdated information. Not only were Taha, Ghazi, and others of their generation fed up with Turabi, but also Bashir was tired of being viewed as second fiddle to Turabi. He wanted to be Sudan's leader in his own right, free and clear of Turabi's influence. There was no reason to doubt that Bashir was fully aware that Turabi, for his part, was intent on taking his place as president.

Turabi had been biding his time. Since 1996 he had been speaker of the parliament, but his real power continued to be exerted behind the scenes. By early 1999 he had given up the speakership to concentrate on running the National Congress, a coalition party composed mainly of members of Turabi's National Islamic Front, which, in name at least, no longer existed. The National Congress was the instrument by which he intended to rise to undisputed power as the leader of Sudan's government. Perhaps blinded by his not inconsiderable ego, Turabi underestimated Bashir. Over the years, the president had become increasingly self-assured as head of state and had no intention of ceding power to Turabi or anyone else. His base of power in the military was, he knew, secure, and he had gained the loyalty of key individuals in the security services, police, and government, including Taha and Ghazi.

In October 1999 Turabi was elected secretary-general of the National Congress. He soon moved against Bashir. In November, he was able to get the parliament to agree to debate amending the constitution to reduce the power of the president by creating a strong parliamentary system with a prime minister. It seemed that Turabi's opening public salvo was a victory for him. But he had overreached. In December Bashir struck back, declaring a three-month national emergency and dissolving the parliament. Efforts that were made to reconcile the two leaders failed. At the end of January 2000 Bashir appointed a new cabinet, shorn of Turabi loyalists. Turabi countered in March by installing some of his supporters in key posts in the National Congress. In May, Bashir, Taha, Ghazi, and other senior members of the government were expelled from the party's ranks.[4] Two days later Bashir announced that the party's leadership was suspended, and security forces closed down party offices throughout the country.

During the rest of the year, the two sides maneuvered for advantage. In April Bashir announced that presidential and parliamentary elections would be held in October. In June he expelled Turabi from the National Congress. In response, Turabi created a new political party, the Popular National Congress (PNC). In September, after some anti-government demonstrations, dozens of PNC members were detained. In October Turabi announced that the PNC would boycott the elections, now slated for December. With all major parties, except Bashir's National Congress, boycotting, Bashir was re-elected.

In 2000 and on into 2001 Turabi kept up a steady barrage of public criticism of Bashir. At one point he said that if his party's endeavors to expose the government's shortcomings and corruption were blocked, there would be an uprising. Turabi and his followers orchestrated protests by university students and others. Throughout all this, Bashir and his advisors had stopped short of jailing Turabi. They knew that he had substantial support within the country and they did not want to run the risk of triggering instability by incarcerating him.

But in February 2001 Turabi once again went too far. On the 18th of that month the PNC and the SPLM signed a joint memorandum in

Geneva. In it they agreed on self-determination for southern Sudan
and on an escalation of popular resistance to force the Bashir government to allow the people to choose a democratically elected government. It was ironic that of all people Turabi, whose opposition to
Sadiq al-Mahdi's attempt in 1989 to reach a negotiated settlement
with the southern rebels was a factor in Sadiq's overthrow and who
was for years afterward a hard-liner on continuing the war, was allying
himself with John Garang.

Outraged, the Bashir government arrested Turabi and many PNC
members. Turabi was charged with undermining the constitution and
waging war against the state. In time all the detainees except Turabi
were released, although some were detained again. Turabi was held in
Kober Prison in Khartoum North until May 2001 then transferred to a
government house. In August 2002 a court ordered his release, only to
deny it had done so later the same day. The next day President Bashir
extended Turabi's detention for another year. At this writing, Turabi
remains in custody.

Although the struggle for power and its outcome significantly altered the political makeup of the ruling establishment in Sudan,
events would show that the Bashir government's domestic and foreign
policies would remain essentially unchanged, at least for many
months. The government continued to hold onto to power by force, it
pursued its Islamist agenda, and the war went on.

• • •

When he eliminated Turabi as a force in the political structure, Bashir
opened the door wider to better relations with Egypt. The two countries had been at odds since soon after the Bashir/NIF government
came to power. The state of their bilateral relations reached a low
point following the attempted assassination of Hosni Mubarak in
Ethiopia in 1995 and Cairo's accusation that the Sudanese government
was involved in the attempt. But in December 1997, after a meeting
between the Egyptian and Sudanese foreign ministers, movement toward normalization of relations began. They steadily, if slowly, improved. Turabi's continued influence was distasteful to the Egyptians,
and Bashir's break with him in December 1999 could not have been
but well received in Cairo. Within a few months the two countries

once again had ambassadors back in place in both capitals. Relations became even better after the Egyptians took a firm public position against separation of the South from the rest of Sudan.

Of the four IGAD countries associated in the effort to negotiate an end to Sudan's war, only Kenya maintained good relations with Khartoum throughout the 1990s and into the twenty-first century.

By the spring of 1999 Ethiopia and Eritrea had been at war for a year. In this lies the explanation of why both were seeking to end their disputatious relations with Sudan. In January 2000 Eritrea and Sudan resumed diplomatic ties, broken in 1994. By then Sudan's relations were also normal again with Ethiopia, which, like Eritrea, had been providing support to the SPLA for several years. The newfound warmth between Ethiopia and Sudan would continue, but in time Eritrea and Sudan would have a falling out again. Relations between them improved until October 2002, when Khartoum accused Eritrea of involvement in an attack in eastern Sudan by forces of the National Democratic Alliance (in December 1996 the NDA and SPLA had formed a joint military command). The border was closed and tension between the two countries grew.

Uganda, like Eritrea, had broken relations with Sudan in the mid 1990s. Charging Uganda with supporting the SPLA, the Sudanese government gave backing to the Lord's Resistance Army (LRA), including refuge inside Sudan's border with Uganda. Cross-border incursions by Sudanese and Ugandan military units occurred from time to time. Finally, in December 1999 negotiations under the auspices of the Carter Center led to a peace agreement signed by presidents Bashir and Museveni. It broke down almost immediately, however, with both sides claiming violations by the other. In the summer of 2000 another agreement was reached at talks held at the Carter Center in Atlanta. In March 2002 the two countries signed a protocol allowing the Ugandan army to deploy inside Sudan to attack the LRA.

Complementing its bid to improve its relations with the IGAD-partner countries, the Bashir government worked hard in the 1990s to counter the Clinton administration's efforts to isolate it. It largely succeeded in doing that. It mended its frayed ties with conservative Arab states, angered when Sudan backed Iraq in the Gulf War, put off by Turabi's hostility toward Arab monarchies, and apprehensive about

Sudan's harboring of radical Islamic terrorist organizations. Relations with Saudi Arabia improved to the point that the Saudis offered a $375 million grant to Sudan in 1999.

The Sudanese also had success in wooing European governments. Most of them, while continuing to criticize Khartoum for its human rights violations, came to regard the U.S. policy toward Sudan as too inflexible. Their desire for possible commercial benefits that would materialize from closer ties with Khartoum was also a factor. This became more apparent after Sudan began to export oil in 1999.

In 1975, Chevron had signed a production-sharing agreement with the Sudanese government to explore for oil and gas. After carrying out extensive geological and geophysical work, Chevron started drilling operations. In 1979 it struck oil at Abu Gabra, in southern Kordofan. Later discoveries would take place on a line running southeast of Abu Gabra and falling on both sides of the 1956 boundary between northern and southern Sudan. Because of the war in the South, Chevron began curtailing its operations in the mid-1980s, finally abandoning its concessions altogether. The Sudanese government divided the concessions into smaller blocks. A Canadian oil firm, Arakis, obtained a concession north of the town of Bentiu and started production in 1996. Arakis then entered into a consortium with the China National Petroleum Corporation, Petronas of Malaysia, and the Sudanese government's Sudapet. In 1998 Arakis was purchased by another Canadian company, Talisman Energy. The consortium, the Greater Nile Petroleum Operating Company, increased oil production and contracted for the construction of a pipeline from the oilfields to Port Sudan. The pipeline, build by the Chinese, was completed in 1999, and in September of that year the first cargo of Sudanese oil left Sudan for Singapore. By October 2002, production had risen to 240,000 barrels a day.

A substantial portion of Sudan's oil revenues was used to buy war materiel. By the government's own admission, defense spending increased 96 percent from 1998 to 2000. Some of the newly purchased defense items, including helicopter gunships, were put to use in protecting the oil field operations. From time to time the SPLA blew up the pipeline, but the damage was quickly repaired. Attacks on the pipeline and the proximity of rebel forces in the area of oil production did little to lessen the desire of foreign oil companies to participate in exploiting Sudan's oil reserves.

By 2002 the national origins of companies either having shown interest or actually operating in Sudan's oil fields included—in addition to China, Malaysia, and Canada—Sweden, Russia, Belarus, Algeria, India, the Netherlands, Britain, France, Iran, and various Gulf states. The involvement of China, Russia, and France was particularly important to Sudan's foreign relations. It meant that the Bashir government had little reason to fear possible UN Security Council action against Sudan; either one or all three could be counted on to cast a veto if a call for action against Sudan ever came to a vote in the Council.

• • •

Although the U.S. failed to isolate Sudan, the Bashir government's violations of human rights routinely earned Sudan denunciations in the UN General Assembly and UN Commission for Human Rights. In addition to dealing with the threat posed by Turabi and his followers, in the four years from 1998 through 2002, Bashir and his supporters in the upper reaches of the government resorted to whatever means they deemed prudent or necessary to retain political power. Confident of their ability to do that, they relaxed restrictions on political activity, allowing the formation of "political associations" in early 1999.

Following a meeting between Bashir and Sadiq al-Mahdi in Djibouti later that year, Sadiq's Umma Party broke away from the opposition National Democratic Alliance and reached a modus vivendi with the government. Bashir also reached an accommodation with Mohammed Osman al-Mirghani, the leader of Sudan's other main political party of the days of parliamentary democracy. Sadiq returned to Sudan in 2000, Mirghani in 2001. But there was no return of democracy. Citing a lack of true political freedom, the former major political parties and the PNC of Hasan al-Turabi (who was temporarily not in custody) boycotted the December 2000 presidential and parliamentary elections. As expected, in a low voter turnout President Bashir and his ruling National Congress party pulled off a landslide victory.

Each year the United Nations special rapporteur for Sudan issued a report strongly critical of both Khartoum and the SPLA. Even stronger condemnations were made by Amnesty International and Human Rights Watch Africa. The Sudanese government continued arbitrarily to detain people who opposed its policies—members of Turabi's PNC, supporters of the NDA, human rights activists, and others whom the government decided had excessively gotten out of line. President Bashir annually extended the state of emergency, which gave the government broad powers to act against individuals and organizations. There was little if any perceptible relaxation of controls over the press. Newspapers that went too far in expressing criticisms of the government were suspended and fined; some newsmen were brought to trial. Floggings and other punishments for *sharia* violations were imposed. Restrictions on freedom of assembly remained in place. Discriminatory actions against Christian churches were carried out.

In a report released in October 2002, Gerhart Baum, the UN's Special Rapporteur for Sudan, declared that there had been no overall improvement in the human rights situation in Sudan. He cited continued abuses by both the government and rebels. With reference to the government, among the main issues of concern in Baum's report were those related to the continued state of emergency, the "virtual impunity" enjoyed by the security services, the persistence of press censorship, and the limited room for the political activities of opposition parties.[5]

But it was the war that accounted for the worst occurrences of human rights violations, and until 2002 there seemed to be no end in sight to it. Both sides could claim victories but neither could inflict a decisive defeat on the other. Khartoum's stratagems to divide its southern opponents and to draw some of them to its side bought only temporary successes. Kerubino Kwanyin Bol, a real thorn in Garang's side, surprised many in 1998 by defecting from his alliance with the government and apparently rejoining the SPLA. But shortly before the end of that year he switched sides again. Whatever side he was on, Kerubino led military operations in Bahr al Ghazal that had devastating effects on thousands of people in the area until he was killed in September 1999.

Riek Machar's dalliance with Khartoum lasted longer than Kerubino's but also came to an end. Dissatisfied with his place in the government and with certain of its policies, he broke with Khartoum in February 2001 and returned to his home area in the South. He and Garang rejoined forces in January 2002.

The war remained stalemated but the human cost went up and up. Government and rebel forces alike continued to raid and burn villages, killing men, raping women, and sometimes abducting women and children. The disrupting effects of warfare on food production, along with adverse weather at times, led to periodic UN and NGO appeals for increased aid to avert catastrophic famines. Khartoum maintained its policy of placing restrictions on where relief flights could go, adding to the difficulty of providing adequate supplies to the victims of the war. Despite drawing severe international criticism, this practice persisted. Still stronger condemnation came about as a result of Khartoum's indefensible policy of bombing civilian targets. Year after year, Sudanese military aircraft dropped bombs on villages, hospitals, and NGO compounds. One of the worst instances of this came on February 20, 2002, when a helicopter gunship attacked the village of Bieh, where World Food Program food was being distributed. At least seventeen people waiting to receive food were killed and many others wounded. It was the second attack of that kind in less than two weeks.

The methods the government employed to protect the oil fields and pipeline were also condemned. There was considerable evidence that whole villages were emptied of people, sometimes brutally, to create a cordon sanitaire around the oil operations. In October 1999 Leonardo Franco, who succeeded Gaspar Biro and preceded Gerhart Baum as the UN special rapporteur for Sudan cited accounts of "a policy of forcible population displacement in order to clear oil-producing areas and transportation routes of southern civilians, who were suspected of supporting sabotage actions by the SPLA."[6] Two years later, Gerhard Baum told delegates to the General Assembly in New York, "Oil exploitation has continued to have a negative impact on the human rights situation." He added, "There is no concrete evidence of oil revenues being spent for the development of the south, in spite of the fact that 40 percent of the national budget comes from oil."[7]

Human rights activists urged the oil companies to suspend their operations until there was a lasting peace that could provide conditions for a fair distribution of oil revenues. For the most part, this fell on deaf ears. The Chinese government's China National Petroleum Corporation, for example, which placed increasing importance on its Sudan production, was not about to be swayed by human rights considerations. However, the Canadian partner in the Greater Nile Petroleum

Operating Company, Talisman Energy, was not immune from the growing criticism of the oil companies operating in Sudan, nor was the Canadian government.

In 1999 Ottawa commissioned an assessment to study the impact of Talisman on the conflict in Sudan. The ensuing report, issued in January 2000, stated: "The underlying reality is that there has been, and probably still is, major displacement of civilian populations related to oil extraction. Furthermore, oil has become a major focus of the fighting. Worse, the oil operations in GOS [Government of Sudan]-controlled territory are used, even if to a limited extent, and possibly without the knowledge or approval of the oil companies, to directly support [Sudanese Government] military operations." The report declared that "the oil operations in which a Canadian company is involved add more suffering."[8]

Responding to growing criticism of its involvement in Sudan, Talisman insisted that that far from harming residents in the oil producing area, it was helping them by providing basic amenities and monitoring human rights abuses. Talisman President and CEO Jim Buckee stated that Talisman workers had not seen any evidence of forced displacement or relocation in Talisman's area of operations. Talisman's efforts to defend itself had no impact on its critics. An international campaign was launched urging pension funds and mutual fund companies to sell their Talisman holdings. Some Talisman shareholders joined in the criticism of the company. Finally, in October 2002, despite its repeated insistence that it would remain in Sudan, Talisman announced the sale of  its Sudan holdings to a subsidiary of India's national oil company, Oil and Natural Gas Corporation Ltd.

The Talisman controversy was one of a number factors that, beginning in the late 1990s, substantially increased public awareness in the United States of issues relating to Sudan. As noted earlier (page 81), in 1993 Congressman Frank Wolf made public a report written by the embassy in Khartoum describing crimes against southern Sudanese civilians, including abductions and forced labor. But the issue of slavery, while not exactly lying dormant, for several years attracted relatively little attention in the United States. This changed, and dramatically so, by the end of the 1990s, when organizations like Christian Solidarity International (CSI) became directly involved in southern Sudan in efforts to redeem slaves, i.e., buy their freedom.

The amount of good that was done by the redemptions was questionable. UNICEF and some humanitarian relief and human rights organizations criticized the practice, charging that buying the freedom of slaves encouraged more slave taking, since there was lots of hard cash involved. There was evidence, too, that many of the transactions were fraudulent. The accusations were denied by pro-redeemers, such as Charles Jacobs, President of the Boston-based American Anti-Slavery Group, who insisted that they were saving thousands of people from the dangers and degradations of human bondage.

Both the redemptions and the criticisms of them added to the prominence of the slavery issue. Awareness in the United States of slave taking in Sudan grew when some well-known Americans got directly involved in redemptions. The former chairman of the Congressional Black Caucus, Rev. Walter Fauntroy; African-American politician and activist Rev. Al Sharpton; radio and television broadcaster Joe Madison; and Republican Senator Sam Brownback of Kansas were among those who witnessed CSI redemptions in Bahr al-Ghazal. Pop star Michael Jackson announced he would go to Sudan to rescue children from slavery (as it turned out, he did not make the trip).

Protesting slavery in Sudan, Fauntroy, Madison, and the Hudson Institute's Michael Horowitz chained themselves to the fence in front of the Sudanese embassy in Washington. When they appeared in court their lawyers were Johnnie Cochran, of the O.J. Simpson trial fame, and the Monica Lewinsky scandal independent counsel, Kenneth W. Starr.

Lending credibility to the allegations of slavery, in an address to the UN Human Rights Commission in Geneva in April 1999, Special Rapporteur Franco said civilian targets, including hospitals, had been bombed, child soldiers conscripted, and women and children abducted into slavery. He said the Sudanese government bore the "largest share of responsibility" for the slave trade.[9] Khartoum rejected this and all other allegations of slavery in Sudan. It would admit only that there was a problem of some tribal militias abducting civilians.

Christian organizations were among the most active in the anti-slavery campaign. And Christians, particularly evangelicals, grew increasingly insistent that the United States had to do something to stop what they said was a jihad being conducted by the Sudanese government against southern Sudanese Christians. As the twentieth century ended, a strong coalition opposed to Khartoum had emerged in the United States. It was an odd mixture that included Christian groups, human rights activists, right-wing Republicans, Republican moderates, Democratic moderates and liberals, and African-Americans. All were urging new sanctions to punish the Bashir government.

Others took a different approach to the Sudan problem, centering in particular on the need to achieve a negotiated end to the war. Bill Kontos and I were among those who felt this way. Using various forums in Washington, we lobbied for the point of view we had expressed in our 1997 report following our talks in Khartoum and Nairobi. We pressed our case with members of Congress, State Department officials, NGO representatives, academics, Sudanese exiles, Sudanese diplomats, and others interested in Sudan.

Various organizations held meetings in Washington, D.C., on Sudan, but their outcomes had no perceptible effect on U.S. policy. Still, they provided an outlet for exchanges of ideas on the Sudan question. In March 2000 Bill and I attended a meeting on food aid to Sudan which was held under the auspices of the World Peace Foundation. Bill was not feeling well at the time and in June he died. I had lost a good friend and colleague; Sudan had lost a staunch advocate for peace and reconciliation in that troubled land.

In July 2000 the Center for Strategic and International Studies, with a grant from the U.S. Institute of Peace, began an initiative—the CSIS Task Force on U.S.-Sudan Policy—to revitalize debate on Sudan and generate recommendations for the administration that would take office after the November U.S. elections. I was one of the fifty-two participants, of whom an average of twenty-five attended each of the Task Force's half dozen or so sessions over the next several months. Among us were congressional staff members, foreign diplomats, U.S. government officials, human rights advocates, representatives of humanitarian aid organizations, academics, and retired senior-level American diplomats.

Most participants believed that something new had to be done to breathe life into the moribund peace process. IGAD-sponsored talks in May and August of 1998 had gone nowhere. The IGAD effort lacked verve and imagination, and nothing new of consequence was being injected into it. Additional rounds of IGAD talks in 1999, 2000, and 2001 failed to make any progress. A joint initiative by Egypt and Libya and interventions by Nigeria, South Africa, and other countries went nowhere.

CSIS Task Force participants also believed that U.S. policy toward Sudan needed a new approach. For the most part Washington continued to hold the Sudanese government at arm's length. The August 1998 cruise missile attack by the United States on a pharmaceutical plant in Khartoum brought U.S.-Sudanese relations to a new low. Even though, less than a year later, the Sudanese signaled that they wanted to enter into a new dialogue with Washington, relations continued to be strained throughout the remainder of the Clinton presidency.

In October 1999 Secretary of State Albright met with John Garang again, this time in Kenya. She praised him and condemned the Sudanese government. In June 2000, the State Department expressed opposition to lifting the UN sanctions against Sudan that had been imposed in 1996 after Sudan had refused to turn over to Egypt the men who had attempted to assassinate Hosni Mubarak in Addis Ababa. The sanctions remained in place. In October the United States successfully opposed Sudan's candidacy for a UN Security Council seat. A month later, speaking from Kenya after a trip into southern Sudan, Assistant Secretary of State for African Affairs Susan Rice pledged diplomatic, humanitarian, and moral support for the people of southern Sudan and spoke out against Khartoum's air raids in the South and against slavery in Sudan. Sudanese Foreign Minister Mustafa Mustafa Osman Ismail wrote to UN Secretary-General Kofi Annan protesting that Rice had violated Sudan's sovereignty by visiting the south without permission from the Sudanese government.

The Clinton administration's last word on Sudan came in remarks the outgoing president made on December 6, 2000, in commemoration of Human Rights Day when he sharply criticized the Sudanese government's human rights violations.

Despite the foregoing and other instances of mutual acrimony, the two sides never totally disengaged. Diplomatic relations were never severed, even after the cruise missile attack. In September 1999, responding to congressional pressure, President Clinton named former congressman Harry Johnson special envoy for Sudan. Johnson, however, lacked a clear mandate and did not have the active backing of the president. His subsequent trips to Sudan did little more than provide another means of continuing a dialogue between the two governments. But that dialogue did, finally, produce a useful result. In early 2000 Washington and Khartoum began discussions about sending a counter-terrorism team to Khartoum. The team arrived there in May of that year and remained in place. More than anything else, this demonstrated that the Bashir government continued to want to improve relations with the United States. The Sudanese failure to achieve that lay primarily in the fact that Khartoum did not see its way clear to go nearly as far as Washington wanted in the areas of differences between American and Sudanese policymakers.

The CSIS Task Force completed its deliberations in late 2000 and in February 2001 issued a report written by Task Force co-chairs Frances Deng and J. Steven Morrison. The report recommended that, inter alia, the Bush administration concentrate U.S. policy on the single overriding objective of ending Sudan's war; join with the United Kingdom, Norway, and IGAD states in pressing for serious and sustained talks between Khartoum and the southern opposition; assign priority in the talks to confidence-building measures; and resume full operations of the American embassy in Khartoum.[10]

One of the Task Force participants was Walter H. Kansteiner III. A founding partner of the Scowcroft Group, a high-powered Washington-based consultancy, Kansteiner had more than twenty years experience with African and emerging market business issues. In addition to his business background, during the first Bush administration he was director of African affairs on the National Security Council staff. He also served as the Africa specialist on the secretary of state's policy planning staff. In 2001, President George W. Bush nominated him to be assistant secretary of state for African affairs. Because of Kansteiner's participation on the Task Force, it is not a stretch to conclude it was no coincidence that the Task Force's salient recommendations found expression in the Bush administration's Sudan policy.

This had not been a foregone conclusion. Before taking office, president-elect Bush had heard about Sudan from Rev. Franklin Graham, son and successor of Billy Graham, Republican senators Bill Frist of Tennessee and Sam Brownback of Kansas, and Republican congressman Frank Wolf, all of whom had been to southern Sudan and no doubt expressed to Bush their horror over the human cost of the war in Sudan and their antipathy toward the Sudanese government.

In February 2001 a group of leading conservatives, including former Bush campaign adviser Marvin Olasky, urged the president to relegate Sudan to pariah status. In May the president announced that USAID Administrator Andrew Natsios would be his special humanitarian co-ordinator for Sudan. Bush said Natsios would "provide the leadership necessary to ensure that our aid goes to the needy, without manipulation by those ravaging that troubled land." The president declared: "Sudan is a disaster area for all human rights. But the right of conscience has been singled out for special abuse by the Sudanese authorities. Aid agencies report that food assistance is sometimes distributed only to those willing to undergo conversion to Islam."[11]

The stage seemed to be set for a policy of punitive measures against Khartoum. But it didn't turn out that way. The incoming secretary of state, Colin Powell, put an early and high priority on the Sudan issue. On March 7, testifying before the House International Relations Committee, he said, "There is perhaps no greater tragedy on the face of the earth today than the tragedy that is unfolding in the Sudan." He added, in words that adumbrated the core of his Sudan policy, "The only way to deal with that tragedy is to end the conflict."[12] That same week Powell participated in a brainstorming session on Sudan in the State Department, kicking off a review of Sudan policy.

Powell and Kansteiner, who had a personal relationship with the president, convinced Bush that the best course would be for the United States to become directly involved in an international effort to end the Sudan war. This would perforce mean dealing with Khartoum as well as with the SPLM. It would also mean taking some heat from the Bush supporters who were calling for harsh new measures against the Bashir government.

A more extensive interaction with Khartoum began, as the administration felt out the Sudanese on ways to ease tensions between the two governments and on energizing the peace process. The new relationship with Khartoum was far from problem free. In May the Sudanese expressed outrage when the administration completed arrangements to provide $3 million for logistical support to the National Democratic Alliance. In June Washington criticized Khartoum for not ending air raids against civilian targets in southern Sudan. Nevertheless, talks continued. In July Khartoum lifted a ban it had imposed on

travel to Sudan by U.S. diplomats after the cruise missile attack of
1998. By late August the Bush administration had concluded that the
United States would not oppose a resolution in the Security Council
to lift the UN ban on international travel by Sudanese government officials that had been imposed after Khartoum refused to extradite
three Egyptian suspects who Cairo believe had been involved in the
attempt to kill Mubarak and were still in Sudan.

In early September came the appointment of former Senator John
Danforth to be President Bush's special envoy for Sudan. Unlike Harry
Johnson, who lacked a direct relationship with President Clinton,
Danforth enjoyed the personal backing of President Bush, who main-
tained his interest in the Sudan issue. And Danforth had an action
plan, which circumstances had never allowed Johnson to develop.

Before Danforth went to Sudan, 9/11 had placed a new stamp on
U.S.-Sudanese relations. Wanting to avoid any possibility that Sudan
would be tagged as supporting Al Qaeda and be subjected to U.S. retaliation as a result, the Bashir government was quick to condemn terrorism and cooperate with the Americans in measures aimed against Al
Qaeda and other terrorist organizations. The White House and the
State Department acknowledged the increased cooperation. Guarding
his Islamist flank at home, President Bashir organized an anti-Israel
march, dropped sabotage and treason charges against Hasan al-Turabi,
and released some of Turabi's followers from jail. This aside, the tenor
of Sudan's relations with the United States changed dramatically and
in such a way as to improve the prospects for Danforth's mission.

After visiting Sudan in November and talking to leaders on both
sides of the conflict, Danforth proposed that they adhere to four confidence-building measures: transformation of an existing one-month
cease-fire in the Nuba Mountains into a renewable, internationally
monitored cease-fire to allow total access for humanitarian relief operations there; creation of zones of tranquility, enabling aid workers
to carry out immunization and other health programs; appointment
of an international commission to investigate charges of slavery; and
cessation of air raids and other military attacks on southern Sudanese
civilians.

Stopping in Cairo on his way back to Washington, Danforth commented that if either the government of Sudan or the SPLM indicated
by its actions that it was not really interested in peace, the United

States would back away from its involvement in the search for peace. At first, the signs coming from Sudan were not good. Although the government indicated that three of the four measures were negotiable, Bashir flatly rejected a cessation of aerial bombing. Khartoum and the rebels exchanged accusations of cease-fire violations in the Nuba Mountains and fighting occurred in other areas.

In January 2002 Senator Danforth returned to Sudan for more discussions with the two sides. At a press conference January 16, he said the government and SPLM had agreed on a proposal for negotiating a truce in the Nuba Mountains, on establishing zones of tranquility for immunization purposes, and on proposals regarding slavery and abductions. However, he was unable to get agreement on the "key to all proposals we have made," the issue of immunity of civilians from military attacks.[13] Speaking in Cairo a day later, he said that some progress had been made but that it was not yet clear whether the government and rebels had a sufficient will for peace. Neither side, he added, had done enough to cooperate with his mission.[14]

The February 20 helicopter gunship attack on the World Food Program feeding center at Bieh, which had been preceded by other attacks on civilian targets that month, drew outraged reactions from the State Department, UN organizations, Norway, Britain, and elsewhere. The United States suspended talks with the Sudanese pending an apology from Khartoum. But despite the negative events and Danforth's less than optimistic comments, a succession of positive developments kept the United States in the game.

On January 19, after several weeks of talks in Switzerland mediated by American and Swiss negotiators, the Sudanese government and the SPLM signed an agreement for a six-month renewable internationally monitored cease-fire in the Nuba Mountains. The agreement provided for the immediate dispatch of a relief and rehabilitation assessment mission to the Nuba Mountains. The two sides accused each other of cease-fire violations, but the truce held and soon monitors were on the scene and the area was opened to relief operations.

After the international reaction to the gunship attacks in February, Khartoum got the message and issued an apology. In March it accepted a revised proposal to "protect civilians," and its air attacks came to an end, for the time being at least. Progress continued on the other confidence-building measures. The areas designated as zones of tranquility were free of military operations, enabling polio vaccination teams to reach tens of thousands of children in south-central Sudan. An international commission—the "Eminent Persons Group"—to investigate slavery allegations arrived and carried out its study. Led by an American and composed of members from Britain, France, Italy, the Netherlands, and Norway, the commission released a report in May that stated: "We found evidence of exploitative and abusive relationships that, in some cases, do meet the definition of slavery."[15] The State Department welcomed the release of the report and called on Khartoum to take appropriate action to prevent the practice.

On April 23 Senator Danforth submitted his report to President Bush. After reviewing the status of each of his four confidence-building measures, he concluded that a peace settlement in Sudan was possible in the near term. Danforth recommended that that the United States not develop its own peace plan but continue to serve as an intermediary between the parties and to support the IGAD initiative. He also recommended that the administration continue to urge other countries interested in peace in Sudan to participate in measures such as monitoring the cease-fire in the Nuba Mountains. An energetic and effective U.S. role, he said, required an enhanced American diplomatic presence in Sudan.[16]

The British government, which had appointed its own special envoy for Sudan, and the Norwegian government were working closely with the Americans. The British and Norwegian efforts were enhanced by the personal commitment of Britain's Secretary of State for International Development, Clare Short, and Norway's Minister for International Development and Human Rights, Hilde Frafjord Johnson. The United States, Britain, and Norway each had a team of observers at IGAD peace talks in Kenya, which, after years of futility, seemed to be leading somewhere. There were two reasons for IGAD's new look. First, in late 2001 President Moi named Kenya Army Commander Major General Lazaro K. Sumbeiywo Kenya's special envoy for the IGAD talks. Sumbeiywo gave the IGAD negotiators the strong leadership they had sorely lacked and he conducted the talks (at Machakos, a sleepy town not far from Nairobi) on a sustained basis for a change, gave it a timetable, and stuck to a strict agenda. The second factor accounting for progress in the talks was the useful presence and advice of the Americans, British, and Norwegians. Working both together and independently, they exerted a positive influence on the proceedings.

U.S. observers at the Machakos talks included personnel sent from Washington or drawn from the embassy staff in Khartoum. American diplomats had resumed working at the embassy in the spring of 2000. As before, none were permanently stationed there, but those who rotated in and out stayed for longer periods of time than previously. In May 2002, shortly after the Danforth report was submitted, the Bush administration appointed a resident chargé d'affaires, career diplomat Jeffrey Millington. Before long, some twenty Americans were working in the embassy and living in Khartoum.

An important breakthrough at the Machakos negotiations took place in July. The Sudanese government and the SPLM signed a protocol that, while agreeing that the unity of Sudan would be the priority of both parties, accorded the right of self-determination to the South. After a six-year interim period that would begin once a final peace settlement was signed, the southern people would choose in a referendum whether to remain in a united Sudan. The protocol laid out the structure of a national government during the interim period and cited certain basic goals, such as a democratic system of governance. Though not a comprehensive peace accord, the Machakos Protocol was a major step toward achieving one, and the two parties agreed to continue to negotiate.

An international contingent, headed by a Norwegian brigadier general, was inserted to monitor the cease-fire in the Nuba Mountains. Its success was manifested by the continued cessation of hostilities and the ability of relief workers to carry out their work in the area, where they had been denied access for years. Although only a few Americans were in the contingent, the United States was the largest contributor of funding, providing $5 million. A smaller team, about twenty persons, to investigate any reports of attacks on civilians in the rest of the country was stationed in Khartoum and Rumbek. All members of this team were Americans, their leader also a brigadier general.

In the absence of a countrywide cease-fire, the Sudanese army and the SPLA continued to battle in parts of the South. After the SPLA took the town of Torit, on September 2 the government broke off participating in negotiations at Machakos, which had resumed in August.

In late September Khartoum banned all relief flights into Eastern and Western Equatoria. Air raids once again claimed civilian lives and elicited a condemnation from Washington and elsewhere. The army mounted a campaign to retake Torit, which it succeeded in doing in early October. With prospects for peace not looking good at all, international pressure was exerted on both sides to stop fighting and resume talking. The pressure had the desired effect, and on October 4 the government announced that its negotiators would return to Machakos.

October saw other favorable developments. On the sixth, UN deliveries of relief supplies resumed after Khartoum lifted its ban on flights into Equatoria. Talks at Machakos resumed on the fourteenth. The next day the two sides signed an agreement for a countrywide cease-fire to be in effect as long as peace negotiations continued. On the twenty-sixth, the government, SPLM, and the UN reached an agreement giving aid organizations unimpeded access to all areas of the country. This was the first time in the history of Operation Lifeline Sudan that no restrictions would be placed on the areas to which deliveries of food and other relief supplies could be made.

Talks continued at Machakos, centering on arrangements for power sharing between North and South. According to State Department officials, the question of sharing political and administrative power was the most difficult of what they termed were the "four baskets", i.e., the four major topics of the negotiations: power sharing, wealth sharing, a formal cease-fire, and the future status of disputed areas (Abyei, Upper Blue Nile, and the Nuba Mountains).[17] Thus it came as no surprise when, on November 18, negotiations were recessed with no agreement on power sharing. Nevertheless, it was encouraging that the two sides did agree on at least on the outlines of power sharing. More important, they reaffirmed a commitment to a comprehensive peace settlement and signed a memorandum of understanding to extend the cease-fire until the end of March and to resume talks in January.

The U.S. government had good reason to be pleased by the way things were going. At long last, an end to the war in Sudan seemed possible, and American involvement had been a critical element of the progress that had been made. Realists in the administration were fully aware that it could all fall apart. The Americans did not hesitate to let both sides to the Sudanese conflict know that less than full cooperation would not be tolerated. Senator Danforth made it clear to President Bashir when they met in Khartoum in August and to Garang that continued progress was imperative. He told Bashir that if Sudan were to have better relations with the United States and to avoid more sanctions, the Sudanese government would have to not only achieve a comprehensive peace settlement but also implement it.[18]

Whether to keep the heat on Khartoum or simply to bow to political realities in the United States, on October 21 President Bush signed the Sudan Peace Act. It was first introduced in the Senate in 1999. The proposed legislation's sponsors were unable to reconcile Senate and House versions in 2000. The major sticking point was language in the House version that stipulated that oil companies doing business in Sudan would be barred from being listed or trading on U.S. stock exchanges. The administration strongly opposed this language, stating that it could set a damaging precedent for political interference in U.S. capital markets. Passed in both houses again in 2001, when the bill went to conference committee for reconciliation the administration made known that the president would cast a veto if the House version, which still included the penalty against the oil companies, was adopted. Once again the bill failed to make it out of the conference committee.

Reintroduced in 2002, the Peace Act was again passed by large margins in both houses of Congress. Its proponents appeared to be impatient with the pace of the peace negotiations and skeptical of the Bashir government's intentions. This time there was no need for a conference committee, for the language of both bills was the same. Nor was there fear of a veto, for the offending language about oil companies had been dropped.

Stripped of its rhetoric, the essential element of the legislation was a proviso that if, after six months, the president certified that the Sudanese government was not negotiating in good faith or was unreasonably interfering with humanitarian relief efforts, he would, after consultation with the Congress, take certain steps. These would include seeking a UN Security Council resolution for an arms embargo against the Sudanese government; opposing loans, credits, and guarantees to Sudan by international financial institutions; taking steps to deny the Sudanese government access to oil revenues; and downgrading or suspending diplomatic relations with Sudan. None of the provisions would apply to the Sudanese government if the SPLM were deemed not to be negotiating in good faith. The Act also called upon the secretary of state to begin collecting information about possible war crimes "and other violations of international humanitarian law by all parties to the conflict."

Ten days after signing the Peace Act, President Bush extended for another year the bilateral sanctions against Sudan that had been imposed by the Clinton administration in 1997 and kept in force since then. The president cited continued concern over the activities of terrorist groups in Sudan. Sudan's most vociferous critics in the United States were still clamoring for new punitive measures against the Bashir government. If Bush had not signed the Peace Act and failed to extend the sanctions, he would have affronted, among others, some of his most ardent supporters. At the same time, the president's actions underlined to the Sudanese the possible consequences of a failure to end the war and to cooperate fully with Washington on the terrorism issue.

By the spring of 2003, the talks at Machakos had produced no final agreement. The two parties to the conflict were still far apart on some issues. But on others, substantial progress had been made. Important, too, was the fact that negotiations were continuing. President Bashir, Foreign Minister Minister Mustafa Osman, and the Sudanese parliament denounced the Peace Act. But, as we have seen, the U.S. actions had no adverse effect on the Machakos negotiations. It was clear that the Sudanese wanted to continue to cooperate with the Americans. As for the Bush administration, its willingness to remain engaged with the Bashir government, as well as with the SPLM, was shown once again when, in April, in his first report to the Congress as required by the Peace Act, President Bush said the Sudanese government and the SPLM were negotiating in good faith. Citing this and "significant progress in negotiating a just and comprehensive peace," he said negotiations should continue.

•   •   •

In taking the course it has chosen for its Sudan policy, the Bush administration made a wise decision. The estrangement of the United States from Sudan beginning in 1989 was inevitable and understandable. The forcible ousting of Sudan's democratically elected government, the ensuing gross violations of human rights, the harboring of terrorists in Sudan, Sudan's backing of Iraq during the Gulf war, the summary execution of the four USAID employees in Juba in 1992, and government-imposed obstacles to the delivery of urgently needed food and other relief supplies made an antagonistic relationship between Washington and Khartoum unavoidable. Through various pressures aimed at isolating Sudan, the first Bush administration and the Clinton administration, with the backing of the Congress, sought to convince Sudan's leaders to change their ways. For some years, Washington had strong support from other Western countries. But as time went on and it became increasingly clear that the policy was not producing the hoped-for results, that support largely evaporated. The Clinton administration, however, could not see its way clear to take a different approach in its interaction with a government it regarded as brutal and totally untrustworthy.

Ideas for a different policy found their way into the highest reaches of the new administration. Ending the war became the policy's leitmotif. In early 2003 it seemed that the long-awaited end of the war could come about in the not too distant future. Peace would not be a cure-all for Sudan but it would have an enormous positive impact on the lives of the Sudanese people and on Sudan's relationship with the rest of the world.

If peace does come, the United States will have to re-examine its relations with Sudan. The terrorism issue seems close to becoming moot. With an end to the war, some of the worst of Sudan's human rights problems will disappear. Both the government and the SPLM have endorsed a democratic system of government. But it would be naïve to believe that Sudan will soon become a full-blown democracy or that all will be sweetness and light between Washington and Khartoum.

Nevertheless, if a negotiated end to the war does come about, our differences with Sudan's government should be put into perspective. No longer should the United States view Sudan as sui generis. That is, we have normal, even cordial, relations with countries whose governments have poor human rights records and whose rule is undeniably undemocratic—Egypt and Saudi Arabia, for example. The way we deal with the Sudan that emerges after the end of the war should not be inconsistent with how we deal with other governments in northeastern Africa and the Middle East.

Which is not to say that the United States should go easy on using its influence to encourage movement toward a system of government in Sudan that is transparent, based on the free choice of its citizens, and responsive to their needs. To the contrary, the United States should be assiduous in this regard. Having normal relations with Khartoum should enhance Washington's effectiveness in getting its message across.

Who can say what a post-war Sudan will be like? There are too many imponderables for anything more than an educated guess. A new constitution will be written. Will it fundamentally alter the political makeup of the country, scrapping the previous form of elections and parliamentary government that produced sectarian parties and unstable coalition governments? Will southern factions be able to coalesce into an effective political instrument? How will the strain between the religious tolerance of Sufism and the rigidity of orthodox Islam play out in the North? Will the secularist tendencies of millions of Sudanese and the Islamic ambitions of millions of others permit coexistence in one state? Will the interim period result in the kind of relationship that would overcome southerners distrust of northerners and convince them that remaining in a united Sudan would be in their best interests?

At this writing, perhaps it is premature to be asking these questions, for a comprehensive settlement by means of which the outstanding issues of power sharing, resource (especially oil revenues) sharing, and the status of Abeyi, Upper Blue Nile, and the Nuba Mountains have been resolved is not yet a reality. But, according to Americans involved in the current deliberations, there is ample reason to believe that at long last Sudan's awful, immensely destructive war is about to end and a new chapter in Sudan's modern history about to begin.

# Notes

## Chapter 2

1. In this book, I have chosen to use the term "political Islam" instead of "Islamic fundamentalism." The latter has a legitimate meaning, referring specifically to the practice of going back to the old ways of Islam, but too often it is used generically to describe the Islamic revival in the Muslim world today. With regard to Sudan, "political Islam" more aptly denotes the force that has brought significant political and societal changes to the lives of the Sudanese since 1989. Neither political Islam nor Islamic fundamentalism should be equated with extremism, for although some Islamists are extremists, most of course are not.

## Chapter 3

1. Peter K. Bechtold, "More Turbulence in Sudan," in *Sudan*, ed. John O. Voll (Bloomington: Indiana University Press, 1991), 5.

2. Former American ambassador to Sudan G. Norman Anderson gives a full account of U.S. relations with the government of Sadiq al-Mahdi in his book *Sudan in Crisis: The Failure of Democracy* (Gainesville: University Press of Florida, 1999).

3. *Intervening in Africa: Superpower Peacemaking in a Troubled Continent* (London: Macmillan, 2000). See pp. 65–67.

4. Ibid., 68–75.

## Chapter 4

1. Although ambassadors are the president's personal representatives, they communicate to Washington through the State Department. Copies of reporting cables are distributed electronically to the National Security Council, intelligence agencies, and other U.S. government departments and agencies. The extent of the distribution depends on the subject of the cable.

2. Nongovernmental organizations are also called private voluntary organizations (PVOs). In Sudan, international NGOs—CARE International, Save the Children, Oxfam, Concern, World Vision, Catholic Relief Service, and many others—were participating in the humanitarian assistance program aimed at alleviating the suffering of victims of the war and recurrent droughts.

3. Alan Moorehead, *The Blue Nile* (London: Hamish Hamilton, 1962), 188.

4. Ibid., 278.

## Chapter 5

1. Although there is a distinction between the SPLA and the SPLM, SPLA is commonly used to denote both the movement and the army. Because of this and to make it easier for the reader, only SPLA is used throughout most of the book.

2. In U.S. embassies, the deputy chief of mission (DCM) is the second- highest-ranking official. When the ambassador is out of the host country, the DCM becomes chargé d'affaires and takes command of the embassy until the ambassador returns.

## Chapter 6

1. J. Millard Burr and Robert O. Collins, *Requiem for Sudan* (Boulder, Colo.: Westview Press, 1995), 5.

## Chapter 7

1. The accusation that the U.S. government was anti-Islamic became a Sudanese leitmotif in my discussions with government and NIF leaders. Turabi, in particular, became increasingly adamant that the United States was guilty as charged on this score.

## Chapter 8

1. "War-Torn Southern Sudan Called Another Somalia," *Washington Post*, February 12, 1993, A29.

2. For the sake of clarity, I use these names in the rest of this book.

3. An Irishman with UNICEF, Philip was one of the most talented and able UN officials I had the pleasure of working with in the many years I spent in Africa.

4. Operation Lifeline Sudan, inaugurated by the United Nations in 1989 and financed in large part by the United States, was headquartered in the UN agencies' office compound in Nairobi. The UN program for the transition zone and northern Sudan operated out of Khartoum.

5. Some sixteen years earlier, when I was with the embassy in South Africa, we decided to stop asking the host government for permission to go to the African townships. We embassy officers felt we had the right, as accredited diplomats, to go to the townships, and we thought that seeking prior permission, as the South African government required, was tacit acceptance of the apartheid system. Similarly, in Sudan I believed that my writ as ambassador covered the entire country. Furthermore, I knew that if I sought prior permission my trip could be blocked, delayed, or otherwise interfered with by the Sudanese government.

6. "Leaders of Bankrupt, Ostracized Sudan Blame West for Making It a Scapegoat," *Baltimore Sun,* April 21, 1993.

7. "A Silent Famine Spreads Death in Southern Sudan," *Los Angeles Times,* April 10, 1993.

8. Calling attention to the enormity of the disaster in southern Sudan, on April 7 the UN World Food Program issued a statement declaring, "While there is competition for emergency relief funds in many parts of the world, we believe that the needs for emergency assistance in southern Sudan should have the highest priority because nowhere else in the world are people in such dire straits."

9. Because of disagreements between Garang and the Sudanese government over the routing of the convoy, it was not sent.

10. For a full exegesis of the Abuja I and II talks, see Ann Lesch and Steven Wondu, *Battle for Peace in Sudan: An Analysis of the Abuja Conferences 1992–1993* (Oxford: University Press of America, 2000).

11. Many relief workers became emotionally attached to the people they were trying to help and came to hate the enemy force, of whatever side, that committed atrocities against those people. No doubt some workers acted individually in ways favorable to one or the other SPLA faction. However, I never saw any proof that an INGO, as an organization, aided a military force in Sudan.

12. Respected though these influential southerners were, their attempts to make Garang and Riek see reason had little effect then or later.

13. At that time the embassy had no evidence that would substantiate Salva Kiir's claim. Later, however, we learned that the Sudanese government had supplied arms to Riek Machar's principal deputy, William Nyuon. See chapter 10.

14. The issue of slavery in Sudan became more and more prominent in the ensuing months and years.

15. What coverage there was generally portrayed the Sudanese leadership in a bad light. For example, a feature article in the August 30–September 6, 1993,

issue of *U.S. News and World Report* was entitled "Maestros of Mayhem: Sudan's Colonels and Clerics Wage War on Their Own People and the West."

## Chapter 9

1. "Mission" is the term for the embassy and all other U.S. government agencies in the country, whether located inside or outside the embassy building (chancery).

## Chapter 10

1. "Remnants of jobless sectarianism," as translated, was a snide reference to members of the former government.
2. Gloria, an FSO, was the embassy's administrative officer.

## Chapter 11

1. Rohan Gunaratna, *Inside Al Qaeda: Global Network of Terror* (New York: Columbia University Press, 2002), 21. In addition to Gunaratna, other sources I have used for the passages on bin Laden are: Peter Berger, *Holy War Inc.: Inside the Secret World of Osama bin Laden* (New York: Simon and Schuster, 2001) and the testimony of Jamal Ahmed al-Fadl in the trial of Osama bin Laden and others for the August 7, 1998 bombings of the U.S. embassies in Nairobi, Kenya, and Dar al-Salaam, Tanzania: *United States of America v. Osama bin Laden, et al.*, Southern District of New York, February, 2001.
2. James Astill, "Osama: The Sudan Years," *Manchester Guardian*, October 17, 2001.

## Chapter 12

1. USAID put the number of dead at 1.3 million at the time this article was published. Within a year or so, 1.5 million was the accepted number. In view of the continued toll of war-related deaths, the figure would have to be close to 2 million by 1998.
2. Literally, the "path" or "way." A fuller definition is "[the] comprehensive system of personal and public behavior which constitutes the Islamic religious law." Noel J. Coulson, *Conflicts and Tensions in Islamic Jurisprudence* (Chicago: University of Chicago Press, 1969), 86.
3. Because the SPLA-Mainstream was in this instance and all future battles the only rebel force fighting the northern army, for simplicity's sake I refer to it as the SPLA rather than the SPLA-Mainstream.

4. This paper, which had only recently begun publication, occasionally criticized the government. We figured it got away with this most unusual practice because the publisher was a man with very good National Islamic Front credentials. But his NIF ties proved to be not enough when, not long afterward, his paper carried a piece criticizing members of Hasan al-Turabi's family for corrupt business deals. The paper was promptly closed down and the publisher imprisoned.

5. All countries celebrate their national day. For the United States it is the Fourth of July, for the French Bastille Day, for the British the queen's birthday, and so on. Embassies generally host a large reception on their national day.

6. The North's PDF was composed of conscripts and volunteers. Poorly trained and led, they often took heavy casualties in battles with the rebels.

7. The government had redrawn the political map of Sudan, replacing the provinces with more numerous states. I believe this was done to strengthen Khartoum's control over the administration of the country. One long-term objective of this would be to facilitate Islamization of the South.

## Chapter 13

1. In another conversation, Turabi intimated that Assistant Secretary of State Herman Cohen was prejudiced against Sudan because he was Jewish. Once when I mentioned then Acting Secretary of State Lawrence Eagleburger, Turabi said, "Eagleburger, that's a Jewish name, isn't it?"

2. Each paragraph of State Department telegrams is numbered.

## Chapter 14

1. In 1996 Mahdi Ibrahim was named Sudanese ambassador to the United States.

2. The Sudanese were deluding themselves. Their diplomats in the United States and a public relations firm they had hired in Washington cultivated African American groups and individuals, particularly Muslims, who seemed to be amenable to the Sudanese arguments against U.S. policy toward Sudan and in favor of the Sudanese position on the issues underlying the bad relations between Sudan and the United States. Some of these Americans were offered an all-expenses-paid round-trip to Sudan, where they were given VIP treatment, including meetings with the president and other high-level personages. Many became spokespersons for the government's views. But what the Sudanese never seemed to understand was that the influence of these men and women was primarily local and had little effect on the Congress or the administration.

3. Ghazi later denied he had said this. He maintained that his remarks had been distorted by opponents of the government and said Sudanese press reports that the government had ruled out any further discussion of religion and

the state in the peace talks were inaccurate. The IGADD negotiators insisted, however, that Ghazi closed the door on consideration of this issue.

## Chapter 15

1. Nor, I should note, did any of these make negative references to the Islamic orientation of the Sudanese government.

## Chapter 16

1. As a result of our trip, USAID brought a rig to Labone from northern Uganda.
2. The United Nations contracted with a private Russian company to fly UN personnel and other relief workers to and from Lokichokio in the company's aging former Soviet military transport aircraft.
3. Thomas Lippman, *Understanding Islam* (New York: New American Library, 1982), 146.

## Chapter 17

1. Janvid, a Swede, was a talented, very congenial man, for whom I had great respect, as I did for WFP director Khalid Adly.
2. The four employees were released unharmed.

## Chapter 18

1. Francis Deng, a resident scholar at the Brookings Institution and former minister of foreign affairs of the government of Sudan during the Numeiry days, told me in December 1995 that the IGADD presidents saw their peace initiative as dormant rather than dead. Indicating that he agreed with them, Deng said the IGADD effort would recommence whenever the parties to the war decided to seek a negotiated settlement.
2. In April 1996 he was declared persona non grata. By then, because of a perceived security threat, no Americans were any longer working in the embassy in Khartoum.
3. Steven Kontos, "Farmers and the Failure of Agribusiness," in *Sudan*, ed. John O. Voll (Bloomington: Indiana University Press, 1991), 137.

# Chapter 19

1. Months later Irwah became the Sudanese ambassador to the United Nations.

2. Interview with *Alliance Franç-ais Presse*, July 5, 1995.

# Chapter 20

1. Tim Weiner and James Risen, "Decision to Strike Factory in Sudan Based on Surmise from Inferred Evidence," *New York Times*, September 21, 1998.

2. Since I left Sudan the Intergovernmental Agency for Drought and Desertification had become the Intergovernmental Agency for Development (IGAD).

3. Following his departure from Sudan in early 1996, Carney, still ambassador to Sudan, was based in Nairobi. The State Department permitted him to travel to Khartoum once a month.

4. Human Rights Watch, *World Report, 2001,* "Africa: Emblems of Bad Old Habits." http://www.hrw.org/wr2k1/africa/index.html (November 17, 2002).

5. United Nations Integrated Regional Information Networks, "Sudan: Human Rights Still Problematic," 20 October, 2002. http://www.irinnews.org/report.asp?ReportID=30645 (November 17, 2002).

6. UN General Assembly, 54th Session, 14 October 1999, "Human Rights Questions: Human Rights Situations and Reports of Special Rapporteurs and Representatives: Situation of Human Rights in the Sudan," item 77. http://leden.tref.nl/~ende0098/UNdocuments/a54467.htm (November 20, 2002).

7. United Nations Integrated Regional Information Networks, "Sudan: Special Rapporteur Queries Use of Oil Revenues Statement," 9 November 2001. http://www.irinnews.org/report.asp?ReportID=13800 (December 7, 2002).

8. *Human Security in Sudan: A Report Prepared for the Minister of Foreign Affairs,* Ottawa, January 2000, page 15. http://www.reliefweb.int/library/documents/cansudan2.pdf (November 21, 2002).

9. BBC, "Sudan Branded Over Slave Trade," BBC April 7, 1999. http://news.bbc.co.uk/1/hi/world/africa/313365.stm (November 21, 2002).

10. Center for Strategic and International Studies, *U.S. Policy to End Sudan's War: Report of the CSIS Task Force on U.S.-Sudan Policy* (Washington, D.C.: Center for Strategic and International Studies, February 2000).

11. "Bush Names Envoy to Slavery-Ridden Sudan," United Press International, May 5, 2001. http://www.newsmax.com/archives/articles/2001/5/4/173500.shtml (December 8, 2002).

12. "No Greater Tragedy," Anthony Lewis, *New York Times*, March 24, 2001, A13.

13. "US Envoy Runs into Problem on Sudan Peace Mission," AFP, January 16, 2002. http://leden.tref.nl/~ende0098/articles/020116b.htm (December 2, 2002).

14. "U.S. Peace Envoy on Sudan Says Progress Not Enough," Caroline Drees, Reuters, January 17, 2002. http://leden.tref.nl/~ende0098/articles/020117a.htm (December 2, 2002).

15. "Report of the International Eminent Persons Group," Khartoum, May 22, 2002, p. 9. Released by the African Bureau, Department of State. http://www.state.gov/p/af/rls/rpt/10445.html (December 2, 2002).

16. "Report to the President of the United States on The Outlook for Peace in Sudan: From John C. Danforth, Special Envoy For Peace, April 26, 2002," The White House. http://www.whitehouse.gov/news/releases/2002/05/20020514-11.html (December 3, 2002).

17. Interviews with the author, November 18, 2002.

18. Ibid.

# Index

Abboud, General Ibrahim, 12
Abdulla, Muhammad Ahmad bin
(the Mahdi), 9
Abdullah, Khalifa, 9
Abdulraham, Sheikh Omar. *See*
Conspiracy-terrorism trial
Abuja II. *See* Abuja peace talks
Abuja peace talks, 50, 73, 76
Abu Nidal Organization, 117
Abu Ouf, Ibrahim, 93, 183
Abu Salih, Hussein Suleiman, 67-70,
77, 80, 99, 101, 120, 127-128,
133, 165, 195
Abyei, Southern Kordofan province,
75, 244
Acropole Hotel bombing, 5
Action Contre la Faim, 143
Adly, Khalid, 189, 190
African Americans and Sudan, 82,
154
Afwerki, Isaias, 186
meets with Bashir, 158
*Agrément* process, 211. *See also*
Irwah, Fatih
AICF. *See* Action Contre la Faim
AICN, 143, 144
Aid donor countries, 58, 59, 190, 192
Air deliveries and airdrops of food.
*See* Humanitarian Relief
program, airdrops and air
deliveries of
Air raids on civilians, 119, 122, 123,
130-131, 146, 189, 233, 239, 241,
243. *See also* Southern Sudan,
civil war

Akon, Bahr al Ghazal province, 143,
145
Albright, Madeline, 221
meets with Garang, 225-226, 237
visits Khartoum (as U.S.
ambassador to the U.N.), 132-
133
Ali, Siddiq. *See* Conspiracy-terrorism
trial
Alier, Abel, 76-77, 141-142
Al Qaeda, 114-115, 117, 240
Ame. *See* Triple-A camps
American Anti-Slavery Group, 235
American community in Khartoum,
88, 93-94
American embassy Khartoum
ambassador's residence, 22
American staff removed (1996),
220
returns, 220
anti-American demonstrations at,
87, 90, 94-95
criticized by Sudanese media, 46,
184-185
employees' medical hazards, 129-
130
evacuations of dependents and
staff, 15, 56, 87-90, 179
harassed by security police, 80
Marine security guard detachment,
98
morale of American employees, 56,
95, 108-109
press statements by, 46-47, 90-91,
120

security precautions, 5, 60, 95
staffing problems of, 98, 128-129
Sudanese employees of, 87, 88, 94, 135
and terrorists in Khartoum, 4-5, 113-114, 117
American Foreign Service, ix-x, 4
American School, 56, 88, 93
Amnesty International, 134, 231
Anglo-Egyptian condominium, 9
Antonov aircraft, 144, 175, 178
Antugua camp, Equatoria province, 177
April 21 agreement, 224
Arakis oil concession, 230
Aswa. See Triple-A camps
Atabani, Dr. Ghazi Salah Eddin, 45, 192
   accuses U.S. of hostility, 167, 196, 211
   background/description of, 26-27
   at IGADD peace talks, 162
   on internal settlement of the war, 183, 196
   on Juba executions, 26-27, 29
   relationship with Turabi, 104, 226
   on sharia, 162
   and Sudan's importance, 170
   and travel restrictions, 24
   on U.S. government, 88, 154
   warns about Irwah rejection, 212, 214
Atepi. See Triple-A camps
Atwood, Brian, 148
Ayod, Upper Nile province, 65, 72, 78
Azzam, Abdullah, 114-115

Baas, Mark, 122, 213
Bahr Olo, Equatoria province, 125, 175
Bakulo, Edward, 176, 177
Baqqara Arab raiders, 81
Al-Bashir, Omar Hassan Ahmed 13, 20-21, 56, 151, 195, 204, 210, 222, 232
   accuses U.S. of supporting SPLA, 132

   accuses Red Cross of supporting SPLA, 49
   background/description of, 20
   clashes with Turabi, 226-228, 246
   criticizes U.S. policy, 100, 167, 197
   on democracy in Sudan, 48-49
   denies Sudan guilty of wrongdoing, 45, 48, 70, 85, 132, 223
   denounces Israel, 197-198
   denounces U.S. sanctions, 225, 246
   dislike of Operation Lifeline Sudan, 70
   and execution of Andrew Tombe, 27, 29
   on human rights, 48-49, 70, 223
   and IGAAD, 131
   on INGOs, 49
   on Irwah appointment, 212, 213
   meets with Sadiq al-Mahdi, 231
   and National Islamic Front, 103
   and Osama bin Laden, 16, 115
   reacts to U.S. warning, 91-92
   and regional leaders, 158, 210
   relationship with Petterson, 92, 131
   on relations with the U.S., 47, 167
   role in the government, 103, 226
   on secularism and self-determination, 162
   seizes power, 11

Baum, Gerhart, 232, 235
Becker, Carole 27-28, 30
Benedict, Gloria, 56, 109, 130, 180
Benedict, Larry, 27, 30, 57, 69, 86, 152, 180
   and embassy morale, 56-57, 108
   trip to Juba, 46
Berido, Omar, 88-89, 91, 123, 124, 208
Bin Laden, Osama, 15, 114-118
Biro, Gaspar, 70, 133-134, 233
Bor, Upper Nile province, 71
Bor Dinka, 74, 100, 177
Borton, Nan, 148
Brentwood, New Hampshire, 219
Brewer, William, 34

Brook, Charles, 28, 30-31, 46, 106
Buckee, Jim 234
Bush, George H. W., 45
Bush (George H. W.) administration, 13, 83, 169
Bush, George W., 16, 239, 245, 246
Bush (George W.) administration, 16, 239, 246, 247

Canadian government
    report on Talisman
Carlos the Jackal, 113-114, 160-161
Carlucci, Frank C. III, 44
Carney, Timothy, 213, 214, 222
Carter, Jimmy, 203-205, 209, 217
Carter, Rosalyn, 203-205, 217
Carter Center, 203-204, 208, 229
Catholic Relief Services (CRS), 176, 189
Center for Strategic and
    International Studies
    Task Force on U.S.-Sudan Policy, 236-237, 238
Chevron, 230
China, 172, 222
China National Petroleum
    Company, 230, 233
Christianity, 8, 9
Christian Solidarity International, 234, 235
Christopher, Warren
    designates Sudan state sponsor of terrorism, 86, 169
Chukudum, Equatoria province, 155
Civil war. See Southern Sudan, civil war
Clinton administration, 15, 110, 122, 169, 229, 247
    warns Sudanese government, 92
Clinton, Bill, 45, 69-70, 80
    appoints special representative, 148, 237
Cohen, Herman, 13, 55-56
Cold War, 12, 83
Concern, 38, 39, 59, 74
Congress, U.S.
    Black Caucus of, 82

congressional delegations of, 55
and Sudan, 80-81, 82, 198, 215, 221
House Foreign Affairs Committee, 100, 131
Conspiracy-terrorism trial, 199-200
CRS. See Catholic Relief Services
Cruise missile attack, 237
CSI. See Christian Solidarity International
CSIS. See Center for Strategic and International Studies
Cush, 8

Danforth, John, 244-245
    appointed special envoy 16, 240
Da'wa Islamia, 106, 140
Declaration of principles, 158. See also Intergovernmental Agency for Drought and Desertification(IGADD), peace initiative/peace talks
Deng, Francis, 238
Dinka, 65, 125, 143. See also Bor Dinka
Displaced persons, 14, 20, 37-39, 64, 74-75, 99, 106, 123, 125, 143, 145, 156, 189. See also Khartoum, displaced-persons camps; Transition Zone
Disputed areas (Abyei, Nuba Mountains, Upper Blue Nile), 244, 248
Dongola, Northern province, 184
Dust storms. See Haboob
Dymally, Melvin, 151

Egypt, 12, 167, 170
    accuses Sudan, 217
    ambivalence about Bashir government, 67
    disinformation campaign of, 52
    initial view of Bashir government, 13
    and the Nile, 67
    relations with Sudan, 14, 173, 228-229
    and Sudan in ancient times, 8-9

Eid, Guy, 4, 34
Elections, 201, 227, 231
Eminent Persons Group, 242
Eritrea, 158-159, 224
  and IGADD peace talks, 120, 148,
    162, 195
  relations with Sudan, 158, 173,
    186, 195, 229
  and SPLA, 159, 223
Eritrean Islamic Jihad, 186
Esposito, John, 35
Ethiopia, 14, 120, 173, 224
  and IGADD peace talks, 120, 146,
    148, 162
  relations with Sudan, 158, 173,
    186, 217, 229
  and SPLA, 159, 223
European Community, 58, 69, 172
Execution of USAID employees, 25-
    33, 47, 54-55, 169

Ford administration, 12, 34
Foreign policy formulation. See
    United States government,
    policy toward Sudan
Foreign Service Officers (FSOs), x, xi,
    3, 206
France, 172
Franco, Leonardo, 233, 235
Friends of IGADD, 163, 209
FSOs. See Foreign Service Officers

Gama'at Islamiya, 117
Garang, John, 63, 65-66, 78, 108, 156,
    208
  and Abuja peace talks, 73, 76
  and Albright, Madeline, 225-226,
    237
  background/description of, 72-73
  and IGADD peace talks, 155
  and Machar, Riek, 100, 232
  military operations of, 50, 196
  on a united Sudan, 65, 155
  in Washington, DC, 76, 100
Germany, 172, 222
El Gezira, 200-201
Ghost houses, 134

Goal, 74
Gordon, Charles George ("Chinese"),
    9
Great Britain, 9, 58, 172, 241, 242
Greater Nile Petroleum Company,
    230, 233-234
Guinea worm, 126, 204, 217

Haboob, 19, 22, 153, 215-216
Haggar, Anis G., 220-221, 226
Al-Haj, Ali, 147, 153
  and IGADD peace talks, 161
Haleib Triangle, 173
Hamas, 117
Hamid, Fiona, 129-130
Harvey, Trevor, 143, 145, 177
Herman, Richard, 177
Hizbollah, 99, 117
Houdek, Robert, 56, 122
Humanitarian relief program, 58, 65,
    142-146, 189-191
  airdrops and air deliveries of, 122,
    143, 146, 190, 206-207
  barge, rail and train shipments of,
    156, 190, 191
  and donor countries, 58, 59
  obstruction of, 14, 20, 58-59, 72,
    99-100, 109, 140-141, 156, 243-
    244
  See also Operation Lifeline Sudan
Human rights, 120, 140, 168, 170
  assessments of. See UN special
    rapporteur on human rights for
    Sudan
  violations of. See Sudanese
    government, human rights
    abuses of; SPLA, human rights
    abuses of

Ibrahim, Mahdi, 152, 263(n1)
ICRC. See International Committee
    of the Red Cross
IGAD. See Intergovernmental
    Agency for Development
IGADD. See International Agency
    for Drought and Desertification
Imam, Alison, 129, 130

IMF. *See* International Monetary
Fund
INGOs. *See* International non-
governmental organizations
Intergovernmental Agency for
Development (IGAD), 222, 224,
236, 242, 243, 244, 246
Intergovernmental Agency for
Drought and Desertification
(IGADD)
peace initiative/peace talks, 120-
122, 131, 146, 147, 158-159, 162,
182, 195, 196, 209, 224, 236, 242-
244
International Committee of the Red
Cross (ICRC), 49, 106, 189, 191,
192
International Monetary Fund (IMF),
151, 211
International non-governmental
organizations (INGOs), 39–41,
49, 70, 99, 106-107
operational difficulties of, 58–59,
75, 190
*See also specific organizations*
Iran, 51-52, 184
Iraq, 14, 51
Iraqi terrorists, 59
Irwah, Fatih, 31, 208, 210
ambassador to the U.N., 214,
255(n1)
designated ambassador to U.S., 211
U.S. denies *agrément* for, 212-215
Islam, 9, 91
Islamic fundamentalism. *See*
Political Islam
Islamists, 53, 90 103, 104, 128, 170,
182
Islamization, 10-11, 40, 170
Ismail, Mustafa Osman, 30, 104, 140,
246
Israel, 170, 173, 197-198

Jacobs, Charles, 235
Jaeger, Christoph, 191, 192
Janvid, Per, 189, 190
Johnson, Harry, 55, 100

special representative for Sudan,
237, 240
Johnson, Hilde Frafjord, 242
Jonglai canal, 106
Juba, Equatoria province, 25, 30-32,
46, 223
food shortage in, 189
1947 conference at, 10

Kajo Keji, Equatoria province, 141,
143, 1856
Kansteiner, Walter H. III, 238, 239
Kapoeta, Equatoria province, 142,
178, 192
Karai, battle of, 9
Karima ruins, 184
Kenana sugar plantation, 185
Kenya
and IGADD peace talks, 120, 147,
148, 162
relations of with Sudan, 229
Kerubino Kwanyan Bol, 192, 207,
232
Khalifa, Abdul Aziz, 223
Khalifa, Mohamed el-Amin, 47, 161,
167
Khartoum
descriptions of, ix, xiii, 4, 22-23,
164, 183
displaced-persons camps, 14, 19-
20, 41-42, 107, 138, 189
forcible removals from, 14, 107,
168, 181
origin, 22
power outages, 209
weather, 3, 45
Khatmiyya, 180
Khuddeir, shooting incident at, 181,
184-185, 191
Kiir, Salva, 77-78, 79, 222
Kissinger, Henry, 34
Kobel, Armin, 191, 192
Kongor, Upper Nile province, 65, 72-
73, 74, 78
Kontos, C. William, 220-225,
236
Kontos-Petterson report, 224-225

Kunder, James, 30-31, 46, 72-74, 138
Kuwait, 14, 51

Labone camp, Equatoria province, 143, 175-176, 189
Lafon, Upper Nile province, 156
Lake, Anthony, 108
Lako, Chaplain, 33, 46
Libya, 50-51, 81
List of state sponsors of terrorism, 86, 89, 160, 169
Logale, Hillary, 141-142
Lokichokio, Kenya, 70, 73, 142, 143, 145
Lord's Resistance Army, 176, 229
Loyak, Camillo Odong N., 68, 69

McGovern, George, 149
Machakos, Kenya. See IGAD peace talks
Machar, Riek, 63, 65-66, 76, 78, 108, 125, 207, 208
  and Garang, 65, 100, 232
  and IGADD peace talks, 156
  on independence for southern Sudan, 65
  joins Sudanese government, 224
al-Mahdi, Gubti, 116
al-Mahdi, Sadiq, 67
  background/description, 103
  escapes from Sudan, 223; returns, 231
  imprisoned, 211, 216
  meets with Bashir, 231
  and National Democratic Alliance, 223, 231
  as prime minister, 11, 12-13
Mahdist uprising of 1881–1885, 4, 9
Mahdiyya, 180
Malakal, Upper Nile province, 39-40, 50, 106
Malaria, 40, 143, 178, 184
Malaysia, 173, 222
Malnutrition/starvation, 38, 39, 74, 119, 126, 143, 144, 145-146, 156-157, 189, 190
Malwal, Martin, 141-142

Mansavage, Gary, 46, 72-74
Manyang, Kuol, 144
Maridi, Equatoria province, 124, 125, 126, 175, 176, 177
Martyrs' Association, 133-134, 202
Mayen Abun, Bahr al Ghazal province, 192, 207
Medécins sans Frontières-Belgium (MSF-Belgium), 177
Medécins sans Frontières-France (MSF-France), 143, 146
Meiram, Kordofan province, 39, 75
Merowe, Northern province, 184
Mesfin, Seyoum, 158,
Millington, Jeffrey, 243
Al-Mirghani, Mohammed Osman, 231
Moi, Daniel Arop, 131, 210, 222, 224
Monghale camp, Equatoria province, 143
Moore, George Curtis, 4, 34
Moorhead, Alan, 22
Moose, George, 76, 86, 89, 110-111, 210
Moose, Richard, 89, 97-98, 110-111, 128, 206
Morris, Dominic, 33, 46
Morrison, J. Steven, 238
MSF-Belgium. See Medécins sans Frontières-Belgium
MSF-France. See Medécins sans Frontières-France
Mubarak, Hosni
  attempted assassination of, 217, 228, 237, 240
Mujahidin, 126, 197
Mundri, Equatoria province, 126, 145
Murahileen. See Baqqara Arab raiders
Murphy, Kim, 71
Museveni, Yoweri, 72, 229

Nafi, Nafi Ali, 26, 31, 197
Nasir, Upper Nile province, 189, 190, 191
Nasser, Gamal Abdel, 12
National Congress, 226, 231

National Democratic Alliance (NDA), 223, 231, 239
National Islamic Front (NIF), 11, 21, 54, 60, 92, 103, 138, 226
dominance in Sudanese government, 103
National Security Council (NSC), 152, 221
Natsios, Andrew, 138, 239
NDA. See National Democratic Alliance
Netherlands, 48, 172
News media. See Sudan, news media attacks on U.S.
NGOs. See Non-governmental organizations
Nichols, Paulette, 143
NIF. See National Islamic Front
Nile River, ix, 23, 94, 160, 183
Nimule, Equatoria province, 74, 99, 124, 130, 141, 143, 189
relief workers evacuated from, 190, 192
shelled by Sudanese army, 192
Nixon administration, 34
Noel, Cleo, 4, 34
Non-governmental organizations (NGOs), 70, 157
Sudanese, 39-40
See also specific organizations; INGOs
Norway, 241
Norwegian People's Aid (NPA), 75, 176
NPA. See Norwegian People's Aid
NSC. See National Security Council
Nuba Mountains, 244
cease-fire in, 241, 243
Nubia, 8
Nuer, 65
Numeiry, Gaafar Muhammad, 11, 12, 34, 105, 137
Nyuon, William, 125, 156

OAU. See Organization of African Unity

El Obeid, Kordofan province
riots in, 105
Obel camp, Upper Nile province, 106
O'Brien, Philip, 64, 77, 123, 143, 196, 208
OFDA. See Office of Foreign Disaster Assistance
Office of Foreign Disaster Assistance (OFDA), 30, 71, 148
Oil and Natural Gas Corporation Ltd., 234
Oil production, 230
foreign countries involved in, 231
and the war, 233
OLS. See Operation Lifeline Sudan
Onyenka, Zachary, 182
Operation Lifeline Sudan (OLS), 64, 70, 109, 143, 146, 192, 244
Organization of African Unity, 35

Pageri, Equatoria province, 125
Palestinian Islamic Jihad, 117
Panthou, Bahr al Ghazal province, 206
Parajok, Equatoria province, 124, 125, 189
Parmalee, Jennifer, 120-121
Payne, Donald, 82
PDF. See People's Defense Force
Peace talks. See Abuja peace talks; Intergovernmental
Agency for Drought and Desertification (IGADD), peace initiative/peace talks
People's Defense Force (PDF), 130, 178, 253(n6)
Petterson, Brian, 5, 27, 67, 75
after Sudan, 220
arrival in Khartoum, 19
departure from Sudan, 219
evacuation from Sudan, 89
in Mexico, 185
return to Sudan, 216
Petterson, Donald
and Abu Salih, 67-69, 79, 80, 99, 120, 127, 128, 165, 195

access to Bashir, 92, 131
on ambassadorial authority, 187-
    188
and American community, 88
arrival in Khartoum, 19
assignment to Sudan, 3-6
attacked by Sudanese media, 29,
    75, 101-102, 108, 127, 166, 184,
    202, 216
attends USAID conferences in
    Nairobi, 122, 148
and Bashir, 20, 47-49, 59, 69-70,
    131-132, 210
and Berido, 88-89, 91, 123, 124
confers with Egyptians, 67
on congressional delegations, 55
correspondence with Bashir, 27, 53
delivers warning to Bashir and
    Turabi, 91-92
departure from Sudan, 219
as donor group chairman, 58, 99
and evacuation/staff reductions,
    87-89, 93-94, 97, 129, 135, 178-
    179
and execution of USAID
    employees, 25-33, 47, 54-55
feelings about job, 60-61, 205
and Garang, 66, 72-73, 155-156
and Ghazi, 26-27, 31, 33, 45, 196,
    205, 212, 214
on human rights violations, 47-48,
    68-69 133-134
attends IGADD peace talks, 146-
    147, 158-159
on IGADD peace talks, 121, 149,
    162-163, 182, 195, 209
on INGOs, 49
interaction with Sudanese officials,
    52, 80, 92-93, 99, 140, 181, 206
and Irwah, 208, 212-215
and Kontos, 220-225
lodges protests, 123, 148
and Machar, 65-66, 78, 156, 208
marriage and family of, 5
and Martyrs' Association, 133, 202
on military offensive impact, 121
and Moi, 210

and Nafi, 26, 197
negotiates cease-fire
    for Starvation Triangle, 77-79
in New Hampshire, 219-220
policy recommendations of, 110,
    163, 171, 211
praises relief workers, 157
presents credentials, 20, 21
press conferences of, 66, 74, 126
and Pronk, 209
on relief program needs, 65, 146,
    190
on religion and government, xi
returns to Sudan (1997), 222-224
and Sahloul, 29, 53-55, 57-58, 59
and Sadiq al-Mahdi, 102
and Sammaniyya Sufi sect, 179-
    180
on security precautions and safety
    of Americans, 5-6, 59-60, 94-95,
    99, 199-200
and southern Sudanese in
    Khartoum, 76, 130, 141-142
on special representative for
    Sudan, 110-111, 149-150
on State Department personnel
    system, 164
submits resignation, 46, 209
and Taha, 182, 202
and terrorism/terrorists, 85-86
travels in southern Sudan, 64-65,
    72-74, 78, 124-127, 142-146, 155-
    157, 175-178, 206-208, 217
travels in transition zone, 23, 37-
    40, 75-76, 106
trip to Dongola and Merowe, 183-
    184
trip to Juba, 30-31
trip to Port Sudan, 200-201
and Turabi, 34-35, 59, 114, 122-
    123, 138, 160-161, 186, 202
typical workday of, 179
and UN agencies in Khartoum, 30,
    37, 58, 106, 187-193
on U.S. policy toward
    Sudan, 167-168, 215, 224-225,
    247

on U.S.-Sudanese relations, 45-46, 52-53, 83
visits Khartoum camps, 41, 107
on weaknesses of UN system, 187-188
and Wells, 152-154, 161
and Zanzibar revolution, 43-44
Petterson, Julie, 4, 27, 67, 75
after Sudan 219-220
anger about evacuation, 88, 98, 111
arrival in Khartoum, 19
departure from Sudan, 219
evacuation from Sudan, 89-90
marriage and family of, 5
in Mexico, 185
return to Sudan, 216
teacher at American School, 56
Picard, Frederick, 44
Pickering, Thomas, 221
Political Islam, xi, 6, 35, 51, 249(n1)
Popular National Congress, 222, 231
Port Sudan, Eastern province, 200-201
Powell, Colin, 239
Pronk, Jan, 209

al-Qaddafi, Muammar, 50-51

Rafsanjani, Ali Akbar Hashemi, 51
RCC. See Revolutionary Command Council
Refugees. See Southern Sudan, refugees from
Relief and Rehabilitation Commission (RRC), 192
Relief workers, 74-75, 143, 145, 157-158, 176, 178, 190, 206-207. See also Humanitarian relief program; INGOs; NGOs
Renk, Upper Nile province, 37-38
Restrictions on diplomatic travel, 24
Revolutionary Command Council (RCC), 102-103
Rice, Susan, 237
Richburg, Keith, 63

River blindness, 205, 217
RRC. See Relief and Rehabilitation Commission
Russia, 172

SAF. See Sudan Alliance Forces
Sahloul, Ali Ahmed, 29, 53-55, 57, 59
Saleh, Mohammed al-Zubeir, 226
Sammaniyya, 179-180
Saudi Arabia, 14, 51, 170
Secularism, 158, 162
Security police, 22, 24, 32, 38, 41, 42, 105, 201
and American embassy, 80
Security precautions. See American embassy, security precautions
Self-determination. See Southern Sudan, self-determination for
Selin, Ivan, 97
September 11, 2002, impact on U.S. policy, 240
Shams al-Din, Colonel Ibrahim, 103
Sharia, 121, 138, 162
definition of, 121, 194(n2)
Shiddu, Abdel Aziz, 33
Shinn, David, 164, 214
Short, Clare, 242
Slavery in Sudan, 9, 15, 81, 234-235, 242
Sobat River, 189
Solarz, Steven, 149
Southern Sudan
drought/famine, 119, 123
people of, 10
refugees from, 37
self-determination for, 121, 142, 243
serious food shortages in, 71, 74, 145-146, 189, 190, 233
war in, 10-11, 50, 63, 119, 123, 130-131, 141, 143-145, 185, 192, 223, 232-233, 243
death toll of, 37, 120, 252(n1)
impact on the North of, 37
Soviet Union, 12

Special envoy/representative for
    Sudan, 16, 80, 81, 82, 130, 148-
    150. *See also* Wells, Melissa;
    Danforth, John
Special rapporteur. *See* UN special
    rapporteur for Sudan
SPLA/M. *See* Sudan People's
    Liberation Army/Movement
Starvation Triangle, 65, 76, 77. *See
    also* Ayod; Kongor; Waat
State Department, U.S., 55, 72-72,
    77, 79, 86, 242
  Bureau of African Affairs, 3, 83
  Bureau for Diplomatic Security, 98
  condemns Khuddeir shooting
    incident, 181, 184, 191
  criticizes imprisonment of Sadiq
    al-Mahdi, 211
  denounces air raids, 123, 132, 241
  on executions of USAID
    employees, 28
  officials attend symposium on
    Sudan, 100
  orders evacuation/staff reduction
    of embassy, 87
  and policy toward Sudan, 109
  protests treatment of ambassador,
    106
  on Sadiq's arrest, 216
  statement on Wells's mission, 154
  Sudanese government's view of,
    151-152
Streams, Peter, 28, 120
Struck, Doug, 71
Suakin, Eastern province, 201
Sudan, xii(map)
  ancient history of, 8
  became independent, 7
  civil war. *See* Southern Sudan, war
    in
  economic problems of, 11, 37, 50,
    105, 222
  and Egypt, 8, 9, 14. *See also*
    Sudanese government, and Egypt
  ethnic groups, languages,
    population, religions of, 7
  foreign relations of. *See* Sudanese

    government, international
    relations of
  governments of, 11
  news media attacks on U.S., 46,
    54, 86, 100, 108, 166, 184, 199,
    216
  reputation of people, 92
  western media coverage of, 71
Sudan Alliance Forces (SAF), 223
Sudanese Communist Party, 12
Sudanese government
  accusations of regarding U.S.
    government, 76, 82, 100, 170,
    198
  alleges OLS aiding SPLA, 192
  and African Americans, 82, 154
  on air raids, 123-124, 241
  American critics of, 239
  on American officials' travel to
    Juba, 29
  anti-U.S. propaganda campaign of,
    87, 89, 99
  and April 21 agreement, 224
  demonstrations against, 105, 209,
    227
  denies accusations of wrongdoing,
    14-15, 45, 81, 135
  dislike of INGOs, 39, 40-41,
    58, 99
  and executions in Juba, 28-33, 169
  human rights abuses of, 13-14, 68-
    69, 133-135, 147, 168, 196, 201,
    202, 223, 231-232
  and IGADD peace initiative, 121,
    146-147, 162, 195, 243, 244
  imprisons Sadiq al-Mahdi, 211
  and internal settlement of the war,
    183
  on international aid to transition
    zone, 39, 75, 107
  international relations of, 172-173.
    *See* also specific countries; U.S.-
    Sudanese relations
  Islamic orientation of, 13
  obstructs relief operations, 14, 20,
    58-59, 99-100, 109, 243-244
  ceases doing so, 244

organizes anti-U.S.
  demonstrations, 87-89, 90, 108
on Petterson travel to southern
  Sudan, 66, 75, 80
purges army, 103, 106
removes people from Khartoum,
  14, 107, 138, 168
on sharia, 121
signs agreement with
  anti-Garang rebel factions, 224
signs Machakos protocol, 243
and slavery, 81, 235
on southern self-determination,
  121, 158, 161
squanders agricultural potential,
  200
on U.S. special representative, 130,
  151
supports terrorists, 14, 85-86, 132,
  133, 165, 169
unpopularity of, 50, 105
upbraids Secretary Albright, 133,
  226
view of State Department and
  White House, 151-152, 154
and Western pressures, 52
Sudanese Ministry of Foreign Affairs,
  29
and formal meetings with
  American embassy, 57-58, 101
Sudan People's Liberation
  Army/Movement (SPLA/M), 23,
  34, 49, 141, 142
blows up oil pipeline, 230
human rights abuses of, 72-73, 159,
  198, 231, 232-233
and IGADD peace talks, 121, 122,
  147, 159, 222, 224, 243, 244, 246
internecine fighting of, 63-64, 70,
  74, 76, 192
misuses relief supplies, 58, 66, 140
obstructs relief program, 64, 72-73,
  109, 140, 190, 192
rejects April 21 agreement, 224
and self-determination, 142
signs Machakos protocol, 243
SPLA-Mainstream, 63, 64, 72, 74,

76, 77, 79, 125, 192
SPLA-United, 63, 64, 73, 74, 76,
  78, 125
  See also Garang, John; Machar,
  Riek; Southern Sudan, war in
Sudd, 106, 126
Sufis, 180
Sumbeiywo, Lazaro, K., 242
Surur, Eliaba, 141-142, 147-148
Sutton, Angela and John, 159-160

Taha, Ali Osman, 158
  becomes foreign minister, 182
  becomes vice president, 226
  comments on Irwah imboglio, 24
  on internal settlement of war,
  183
  relationship with Turabi, 104, 226
  on U.S.-Sudanese relations, 167,
  202
Talisman Energy, 230, 234
Tally, Baudouin, 28, 31-33, 46, 47
Taposa, 178
Tarnoff, Peter, 110,-111
Terrorism/terrorists, ix, 4, 5, 14, 59-
  60, 85-86, 113-118, 165
  attacks on American embassies,
  49, 96
  See also bin Laden, Osama; Carlos
  the Jackal; specific terrorist
  organizations
Thiet, Bahr al Ghazal province, 78,
  156, 207-208
Tombe, Andrew, 26-29, 31-33, 46, 47
Tombe, Father David, 68, 69
Torit, Equatoria province, 73-74, 142,
  147, 192, 243-244
Torture, 48, 68, 134, 140
Transition zone 23, 37, 75, 99, 106,
  107. See also Abyei; Malakal;
  Meiram; Renk
Triple-A camps, 99-100, 120, 123,
  176, 189
Al-Turabi, Dr. Hasan, 11, 20, 59, 131,
  216, 231, 240
  accuses U.S. of anti-Islam bias,
  123, 139, 161, 167, 186

anti-Semitism of, 139, 140
assaulted in Canada, 138
background of, 137
and bin Laden, 115
on Carlos the Jackal, 114, 160
on CIA, 114, 161, 186
description of, 34
disciples of, 104
on execution of USAID employees, 34
on human rights violations, 34-35, 202
imprisoned by Bashir, 228
on Iran, 51
on Libya, 51
and National Congress, 226, 227
and National Islamic Front, 11, 21, 137-138
opinions about the U.S., 34-35, 71, 139-140, 161
on Organization of African Unity, 35
physical and mental condition of, 138-139
and Popular National Congress, 227
reviles Hosni Mubarak, 217
rumors about, 104
seeks to displace Bashir, 226-228
and *sharia*, 138
speaker of the National Assembly, 222
status in Sudanese government, 71, 103-104, 186
on Sudan's importance, 161, 170
on terrorism, 85, 140, 198
on United Nations, 35
on warning from U.S. government, 91, 161
and Western journalists, 71

Uganda, 224
and Bashir government, 173, 186, 229
and IGADD peace talks, 120, 148, 162
and SPLA, 173, 223

Ulang, Upper Nile province, 65, 78, 191
Umma Party, 231
UN. *See* United Nations
*Understanding Islam*, 180
UNICEF. *See* United Nations International Children's Emergency Fund
United Nations (UN), 99
agencies in Sudan, 187-193
appoints special rapporteur for Sudan, 169
dedicated workers of, 188
and donor governments, 187-188
ignores some human rights violations, 191-196
and Khartoum displaced people's camps, 14, 107
operations in Sudan. *See* OLS; Relief workers; UNICEF; WFP
relief workers of killed, 74
sanctions against Sudan, 240
and Sudanese government, 14, 107, 188
and transition zone, 107
weaknesses of UN system, 187-188
United Nations General Assembly, 231
resolution condemning Sudan, 54, 169
United Nations Human Rights Commission, 70, 169, 173, 231, 235
United Nations International Children's Emergency Fund (UNICEF), 106, 122, 203-204, 235
UN special rapporteur on human rights for Sudan, 169, 189. *See also* Baum, Gerhart; Biro, Gaspar; Franco, Leonardo
United States government
aid to Sudan, 12, 71-72, 148
condemns air raids and military offensive, 122, 123, 132, 241
criticizes imprisonment of Sadiq al-Mahdi, 211

cruise missile attack by, 115, 237

denies *agrément* for Fatih Irwah, 212

human rights report of, 169

imposes new sanctions against Sudan, 225

intervention in Sudan, reasons against, 108

and Islam, 91

orders American officials depart Sudan (1996), 220

policy toward Sudan, 12, 82-83, 109-110, 168-169, 215, 237

relations with Sudan. *See* U.S.-Sudanese relations

on SPLA, 198

on Sudan's support of terrorism, 14, 85-86, 132, 133, 165, 169

supports IGADD peace talks, 120, 195

warns Bashir and Turabi, 91-92, 99

United States Agency for International Development (USAID), 20, 37, 40, 122, 144, 148, 177

compound and employees in Juba, 25-26, 46-47

United States Information Agency (USIA), 45

United States Institute of Peace, 100, 236

University of Khartoum, anti-government demonstration, 105

USAID. *See* United States Agency for International Development

USIA. *See* United States Information Agency

U.S. policy toward Sudan. *See* United States government, policy toward Sudan

U.S. Senate resolution on Sudan, 80-81

U.S.-Sudanese relations, 12-17, 21, 52, 54, 60, 108, 122-123, 140, 151, 171, 220, 225, 226, 236, 237, 238-239, 240, 246-247

Vandenbroucke, Lucien, 57, 152, 180, 182

Waat, Upper Nile province, 65-74, 78

Wagner, Gordon, 145, 175, 177

Wau, Upper Bahr al Ghazal province, 153, 191, 196

Wells, Melissa, 154, 158

appointed U.S. special representative, 148-150

at IGADD peace talks, 159

policy recommendations of, 163

trips to Sudan, 152, 154, 161

Western journalists, 63, 71

Western pressures on Sudan, 52, 108, 172

WFP. *See* World Food Program

White House, 108, 109, 111, 130, 149, 152, 154-155, 213

Wisner, Frank, 108

Wolf, Frank, 55, 81, 234, 238

World Food Program, 40, 144, 189, 190, 192, 233, 241

World Trade Center bombing, 86

World Vision, 156-157

Yambio, Equatoria province, 125

Younis, Mahmoud, 216-217

Yuai, Upper Nile province, 72, 78

Zanzibar, 43-44

Zenawi, Meles, 158

Zones of tranquility, 122, 241-242